# Russian Theatre in the Age of Modernism

*Edited by*

## ROBERT RUSSELL
*Senior Lecturer in Russian*
*University of Sheffield*

*and*

## ANDREW BARRATT
*Senior Lecturer in Russian*
*University of Otago*

St. Martin's Press    New York

First published in the United States of America in 1990

Printed in Great Britain

ISBN 0-312-04503-4


Library of Congress Cataloging-in-Publication Data
Russian theatre in the age of modernism / edited by Robert Russell and
    Andrew Barratt.
        p.    cm.
    ISBN 0-312-04503-4
    1. Theater—Soviet Union—History—20th century.    I. Russell,
Robert, 1946–    .  II. Barratt, Andrew.
PN2724.R867    1990
792'.0947'09041—dc20                                    89-70291
                                                            CIP

# Contents

vi                          *Contents*

# Preface

Few periods in the history of modern culture have witnessed a greater upsurge of energy and ferment than the first three decades of this century in Russia. These were the years in which political and social instability combined with a characteristically Russian tendency for maximalism to produce exciting new developments in all areas of human endeavour. In the arts, this was Russia's age of modernism, an age whose major representatives – such as Chekhov, Diaghilev, Stravinsky, Chagall and Kandinsky – have long been known throughout the world. But despite the eminence of such individual figures, the full range of the Russian experience of modernism, its uniqueness, and its significance both as a national and international phenomenon are perhaps only now beginning to be fully appreciated. This is especially true of the Russian theatre and it is the purpose of the present volume to bring some of the major achievements of these years to the attention of a wider audience.

The essays collected here do not pretend to offer a comprehensive account of theatrical life in early twentieth-century Russia. Each is a self-contained study which may be read independently of the whole. Taken together, however, they provide a picture not only of the sheer diversity of the dramatic enterprise during these turbulent years but also of the central issues confronting the student who would wish to understand them better.

For most people the modern Russian theatre is synonymous with the name of Konstantin Stanislavsky and the Moscow Art Theatre. Inevitably, these are names which feature prominently on the pages that follow. In most instances, however, the focus is placed not so much upon the Art Theatre's long-acknowledged role in the professionalisation of the Russian theatre and the development of dramatic naturalism as upon its role as a catalyst for the many anti-naturalistic experiments which followed in its wake. Nick Worrall's article, with which the collection opens, is the exception to this rule. Drawing upon a detailed examination of Stanislavsky's working notebooks, Worrall reconstructs one of the Art Theatre's most famous productions, the staging in 1901 of Chekhov's *Three Sisters*. The importance of this production, which even today has the status of a 'canonical' reading, can scarcely be overestimated, and Worrall's commentary draws attention to many of the interesting questions of interpretation which it raises.

The rise of the Russian cabaret in the years following the abortive revolution of 1905 was one of the most characteristic features of artistic life, reflecting both the sense of 'crisis' voiced in so many contemporary articles on the arts and an intense theatrical self-consciousness which is the essence of the modernist spirit. The next two articles deal with the contribution to the Russian cabaretic movement of two of its most influential figures. Laurence Senelick looks at the career of Boris Geyer, a man whose endeavours were devoted entirely to the so-called 'miniature' theatre. Placing Geyer's work first of all against the tradition of nineteenth-century satirical writing, Senelick proceeds to discuss his often difficult collaboration with Nikolay Yevreinov at the celebrated 'Crooked Mirror' theatre. Senelick is particularly alert to the pessimistic, misanthropic vision which finds expression in Geyer's most important work, and sees in his theatrical experiments a prefiguration of techniques later employed by Pirandello, O'Neill and Brecht.

If it has been Geyer's fate to have been upstaged by a more flamboyant collaborator, the same is true also of another Boris – Boris Pronin – who has lived very much in the shadow of his erstwhile colleague, the legendary Vsevolod Meyerhold. Michael Green seeks to restore the balance in a sketch of Pronin's theatrical life. Tracing his development from his painful first attempts to establish a cabaret to the highly successful 'Stray Dog' (perhaps the most famous of all Russian cellars) Green sheds valuable light on Pronin's breach with Meyerhold. He concludes by considering the place of the 'Stray Dog' in the life and work of three major poets, Blok, Akhmatova and Mayakovsky.

Although the contribution of the Russian Symbolists to the theory and practice of theatre does not come in for detailed consideration in any of the essays represented here, the Symbolist heritage provides the focus for Andrew Barratt's re-examination of Leonid Andreyev's well-known play *He Who Gets Slapped*. Arguing against the tendency to read the drama as a straightforward piece of neo-Romanticism, in which the central figure of He is cast in the role of rejected prophet, Barratt suggests that Andreyev's presentation of He is thoroughly ambivalent and that the play as a whole may be viewed as a brilliantly effective critique of the Symbolist hero.

Three other dramatists to follow in the train of Symbolism were also important poets – Mikhail Kuzmin, Nikolay Gumilev and Marina Tsvetayeva. Simon Karlinsky identifies the dramatic works of these three writers as representative of a post-Symbolist neo-Romanticism. Drawing on the corpus of their plays, he provides a workable typology of the Russian neo-Romantic drama, tracing its connections both with the national theatrical tradition and with European trends.

Nikolay Yevreinov is one of the most prolific and controversial writers associated with the Russian modernist theatre. His career was also one of the longest, spanning both the pre-revolutionary and post-revolutionary periods, and continuing into the years of emigration in Europe. Spencer Golub presents a comprehensive survey of Yevreinov's work in the theatre, which he describes as a 'drama in two acts'. Drawing extensively on archive materials, Golub adds significantly to our understanding of Yevreinov's less-well-known later works, showing how, to use his own words, these plays 'filter and magnify' the themes and techniques in his earlier dramatic productions.

Our last five articles deal specifically with the theatre of early Soviet Russia, a period no less turbulent and exciting in its own way than the first seventeen years of the century. One of the central questions of the era – and perhaps of Soviet literature as a whole – was the desire by Russia's new leaders to make the theatre into a vehicle for the propagandisation of socialist Utopianism. This is the subject of Robert Russell's essay, 'The First Soviet Plays'. Surveying the attempts by contemporary dramatists to harness their work to the demands of the military and political struggle, Russell examines both the primitive *agitki* and the larger-scale productions by writers associated with the Proletkult movement.

If drama and theatre were to be effective as propaganda, then the impact of productions on the audience, and indeed the very nature of the audience itself, had to become a subject of scientific study. In his essay Lars Kleberg discusses the different approaches to audience research in the Soviet theatre of the 1920s and shows how Russian theatre specialists, motivated by their heightened awareness of the propaganda potential of theatrical productions, were decades ahead of their Western counterparts in this field.

Harold B. Segel takes up another neglected area of early Soviet theatre, namely the strong presence of an Expressionist tradition which had its roots in contemporary Germany. Segel traces the connections between the work of Russian and German dramatists, showing how Expressionist concerns and techniques informed plays by such pre-revolutionary dramatists as Blok, Andreyev and Yevreinov, but became a dominant feature only in the 1920s. Analysing plays by Olesha, Mayakovsky and lesser-known writers like Sergey Tret'yakov and Aleksey Fayko, Segel demonstrates the presence of a quintessentially Russian Expressionism which has subsequently been ignored by generations of Soviet theatrical historians anxious to deny the place of 'bourgeois modernism' in the foundation of the new socialist culture.

J. A. E. Curtis takes up another part of the early Soviet experience later suppressed by the proponents of Socialist Realism in her discussion of theatrical satire. The decade of the 1920s in Russia was one of the great ages of satire and its dramatic products (one has only to think of plays by Bulgakov, Mayakovsky and Erdman) rank among the finest yet written in Soviet Russia. A central question of the era, as Curtis shows, was one which continues to exercise the minds of those who control artistic life in the Soviet Union: to what extent is the practice of satire compatible with the goals of a society dedicated to the building of communism? Stressing its connections with the pre-revolutionary tradition of cabaret and music-hall, Curtis traces the story of Soviet theatrical satire from its beginnings in the Theatre of Revolutionary Satire through the debates of the NEP (New Economic Policy) years to its effective abolition at the end of the decade.

The restoration of a past obscured and distorted in the Stalinist and post-Stalinist eras has become a major feature of the politics of *glasnost'* presently associated with the name of Mikhail Gorbachev. In the final essay, Lesley Milne addresses the problems attaching to such a venture by outlining the task of Soviet scholars currently preparing the publication of the dramatic works of Mikhail Bulgakov. Reviewing the sorry tale of Bulgakov's abortive career as a playwright, Milne shows how the exigencies of politics left a mark on the texts of many of the plays themselves. In some cases – *The Days of the Turbins* and *Flight* are perhaps the outstanding examples – the job of establishing a proper text is a particularly complex and difficult matter, yet one which is essential if Bulgakov's status as one of the most important dramatists of his time is to be fully appreciated.

Except in direct citations from Russian sources, Russian names have been transliterated using the standard simplified form. Where a generally accepted English form of a Russian name exists (for example, Meyerhold, Gogol, Eisenstein) this has been used throughout except for direct citations. It should be noted in particular that no indication of the soft sign is given in well-known names, whereas in the case of less well-known figures it is marked. In direct citations the system of transliteration is the 'Matthews' system recommended by the *Slavonic and East European Review*. The name Kommissarzhevskaya/Komissarzhevskaya exists in both forms (she herself used the former, but following the spelling changes of 1918 the latter has become common). No attempt has been made to impose one standard spelling throughout this volume. Similarly, where there is no universally recognised English version of a Russian play title the editors have retained the translations of the individual contributors.

# Notes on the Contributors

**Andrew Barratt** is Senior Lecturer in Russian, University of Otago, New Zealand.

**J. A. E. Curtis** is British Academy Research Fellow, Robinson College, University of Cambridge.

**Spencer Golub** is Associate Professor of Theatre, Brown University, Providence, R.I.

**Michael Green** is Director of the Program in Russian, University of California, Irvine.

**Simon Karlinsky** is Professor of Slavic Literatures, University of California, Berkeley.

**Lars Kleberg** is a research fellow at the Swedish Council for Research in the Humanities and Social Sciences, and Associate Professor of Slavic Literatures at Stockholm University.

**Lesley Milne** is Lecturer in Russian, University of Nottingham.

**Robert Russell** is Senior Lecturer in Russian, University of Sheffield.

**Harold B. Segel** is Professor of Slavic Literatures, Columbia University, New York.

**Laurence Senelick** is Fletcher Professor of Drama, Tufts University, Massachusetts.

**Nick Worrall** teaches in the Faculty of Humanities, Middlesex Polytechnic, London.

# 1

# Stanislavsky's Production of Chekhov's *Three Sisters*

## NICK WORRALL

### INTRODUCTION

It is interesting to speculate as to why, in the Soviet Union, there was no major revival of any Chekhov play between Konstantin Stanislavsky's first productions (staged between 1898 and 1904) and Vladimir Nemirovich-Danchenko's production of *Three Sisters* ('Tri sestry') staged in 1940 – at a time when the Moscow Art Theatre was being officially promulgated as a model of 'socialist–realist' and 'anti-formalist' theatrical practice. Why was it that, during roughly the same period, several productions of Chekhov's major plays were staged throughout Western Europe as well as in the United States of America? The answer would appear to lie in the historical significance of the Russian Revolution which, in philosophical terms, was founded on the notion of a non-tragic universe where human beings could intervene meaningfully in determining their own fate. In a Soviet world, the problems of three provincial sisters who, between them, possessed the price of a ticket, could well have been resolved by a trip to the nearest railway station. The predicament of Chekhov's heroines could no longer be sustained within those existentialist terms which can now be seen, in retrospect, to have anticipated specific forms of European 'absurdist' drama where waiting for 'Godot' can be construed as a simple imaginative extension of waiting for 'Moscow'.

Since 1917, it could be argued, non-socialist countries have had a vested interest in the ideologies of pessimism to precisely the extent that socialist countries (and especially revolutionary Russia) have invested most of their ideological capital in an optimistic view of the world. Seen from one side of this ideological divide, Chekhov's drama of twilight Russia was sociologically explicable

1

and contingent on a *fin-de-siècle* mood with its limiting attachment to the feelings and attitudes of a dying class. But is a play such as *Three Sisters* essentially a pessimistic play? Western theatrical interpretations have tended to suggest that this is the case and have, generally, identified sympathetically with the plight of the characters in both existential and class terms. In the Soviet Union, similar forms of sympathetic identification have taken place within the framework of an obligatory, officially enshrined humanism. Western literary interpretations have not needed to distort the dramatic text to find justification for conflating apostrophes to an enlightened future (Vershinin in *Three Sisters*) or premonitions of revolution (Trofimov in *The Cherry Orchard*, 'Vishnevyy sad') with tea-drinking or a preoccupation at critical points with lost galoshes.

In this context, Stanislavsky's production of *Three Sisters* emerges as a phenomenon of peculiar interest. It was staged by someone who, since his death in 1938, has been canonised within both the major power blocks as probably the greatest director and man of the theatre this century has produced. Equally important is the fact that his production of *Three Sisters* can be described as an ideological fusion of opposites – form and content, positive and negative, optimism and pessimism, meaning and non-meaning and, even, 'East' and 'West'. If an optimistic interpretation can be described as one which expresses a positive belief in the meaning of life irrespective of evidence to the contrary then, equally, a pessimistic interpretation can be described as one posited on a belief in the final and absolute fact of death – a standpoint which would seem to be contradicted by the fact of life itself.

History and ideology will continue to quarrel over the body of Chekhov's plays. Only a genuine theatre production can bring it to life. Irrespective of their optimistic or pessimistic perspectives, many productions of Chekhov during the course of the past eighty years or so, and in particular of *Three Sisters*, would appear to have been little more than 'death warmed up'. What appears to have distinguished Stanislavsky's production was the sense of vivid life which animated the realisation of the play in performance, to the extent that its positive and negative referents appear to have been in a constant, and creative, state of tension. The resolution of the irresolvable question of human meaning was dramatised in the space where these tensions are capable of assuming their most poignant and intensely involving forms – on a stage peopled by live actors.

Stanislavsky's production of *Three Sisters* was his and the Moscow Art Popular-Accessible Theatre's[1] third production of a Chekhov play. His first, working as usual in close collaboration with Nemirovich-Danchenko, had been of *The Seagull* ('Chayka') in 1898 (in which Stanislavsky acted the role of Trigorin), the success of which had saved the theatre financially in its first season. His second Chekhov production, in 1899, of *Uncle Vanya* ('Dyadya Vanya') was staged almost by default. The dramatist had first offered the play to the Moscow Maly Theatre, then rescinded the offer when that theatre demanded changes, and handed it instead to the Art Theatre, whose production of *The Seagull* had left Chekhov dissatisfied in certain crucial respects.[2] *Three Sisters* was then written in the wake of the successful production of *Uncle Vanya*, which Chekhov had seen when the company visited Yalta in April 1900 and in which Stanislavsky's performance as Astrov had clearly improved, in the author's eyes, on his earlier portrayal of Trigorin.

*Three Sisters* was also the first play which Chekhov wrote specifically with the actors of the Art Theatre in mind. His schoolfriend from Taganrog days, A. L. Vishnevsky, was now a member of the company: 'I've prepared a role for you of a school inspector, husband of one of the sisters', Chekhov wrote to him, 'You will be dressed in a uniform frock coat with a medal round your neck.'[3] Chekhov had also fallen in love with the theatre's leading actress, Olga Knipper, whom he was to marry three months after the première of *Three Sisters*, and conceived the role of Masha with Knipper in mind. 'What a part I've written for you in *Three Sisters!*', he wrote to her on 28 September.[4] For the first time Chekhov also took a keen interest in rehearsals, which he attended during the autumn of 1900, and again the following season when the theatre reopened on 19 September. He saw a complete performance of the play on the evening of the 21st.

*Three Sisters* was about nine months in the writing. On 8 August 1900 Stanislavsky met Chekhov in the town of Alupka when the latter announced 'in deepest secret' that he was writing a play about military life with four young female roles and as many as twelve male which he hoped to complete by 1 September.[5] Stanislavsky wrote excitedly to Nemirovich-Danchenko the following day informing him. The latter had, in fact, known of the existence of the work since the previous year when Chekhov told him that he had a subject for a play, *Three Sisters*, but that he would not be getting down to writing it for a while.[6] A great deal must have already been written by the following August when Stanislavsky had his conversation with the playwright. Chekhov tended to compose quickly, spending only two or three days on a single act, but then leaving a substantial interval before commencing another rapid burst of work.[7]

On 23 October 1900 Chekhov arrived in Moscow, on his way to France, with a completed although still unrevised manuscript. He stayed at the Dresden Hotel and visited the Art Theatre, in company with Gorky, almost every day between 25 October and 1 November. The play was cast and the parts distributed to the actors prior to a reading which was held on 29 October in the foyer of the Hermitage Theatre on Carriage Row.[8] It was immediately apparent that the play which Chekhov had written 'in a permanent good mood' and which he considered 'a vaudeville'[9] puzzled and perplexed members of the company. When questioned, however, Chekhov seemed reluctant to offer answers or to justify himself. When asked about the significance of the musical exchanges between Vershinin and Masha in Act 3 he simply replied, 'It's nothing special. A joke.'[10] However, he admitted to the actress Vera Komissarzhevskaya that the play was 'complicated, like a novel' and that the mood, according to others, was 'devastating'.[11]

He began revising the play while still in Moscow as well as attending some of the first rehearsals at which he was, for the most part, a passive observer although he took an active interest in the staging of alarm noises in Act 3. Chekhov then left for France, having revised the first two acts which he left with his sister, Masha, in Moscow. It was at this point that Stanislavsky began work on the production score, planning the first two acts with his usual speed. Having received the text on 9 December, he handed the score of Act 2 to the theatre on the 16th (the plan for Act 1 had been handed over earlier). On the same day, Chekhov sent the third act from Nice, retaining Act 4 for a couple of days in order to effect some substantial changes.[12] The model which Stanislavsky followed was virtually identical with the one which he used for his production score of *The Seagull*[13] with the author's text pasted on one side of the promptbook and with numbers entered in the text corresponding to the numbers of his own stage directions on the opposite page. From time to time, his comments are interspersed with detailed sketches indicating stage movement. On most pages, the quantity of directional material is comparable with or, more often, exceeds that of the play itself. A rough run-through of the first two acts was held in mid-December before Nemirovich-Danchenko departed for France to visit a sick relative. Stanislavsky then worked on Act 3 between 19 and 23 December and completed the full score on 8 January 1901, three weeks before the opening.

From the outset rehearsals proved difficult, although Knipper did report to Chekhov on 13 December that the 'tone' of several roles was beginning to emerge, including her own.[14] According to Stanislavsky, early rehearsals of the play brought the company close to despair:

> the play was not lively, it was hollow, it seemed tiresome and long. There was *something* missing. . . . We met daily, we rehearsed to a point of despair, we parted company, and next day we would meet again and reach despair once more. . . .
>
> One evening at one of our agonising rehearsals, the actors stopped in the middle of the play, ceased to act, seeing no sense in their work. They no longer had any trust in the stage director or in each other.[15]

It was at this critical juncture that Stanislavsky's 'creative super-consciousness' was inspired by an accidental sound heard in rehearsal, like the scratching of a mouse.

> It reminded me of home: I felt warm inside, I saw the truth, life, and my intuition set to work. . . . I came to life and knew what it was I had to show the actors. It became cosy on the stage. Chekhov's men revived. They do not bathe in their own sorrow. On the contrary, they seek joy, laughter and cheerfulness. They want to live and not vegetate. I felt the truth in Chekhov's heroes, this encouraged me and I guessed what had to be done.[16]

The change was registered by Vishnevsky during the latter half of December when, in a letter to Chekhov, he enthused about rehearsals and Stanislavsky's contribution to them as well as the advice he was receiving from Nemirovich-Danchenko. Stanislavsky confirmed this impression, declaring that he was very pleased and that 'the play is marvellous and extremely stageworthy'.[17] However, although matters may have improved there were still problems. Stanislavsky was not altogether happy with the acting of Knipper as Masha nor with that of his own understudy as Vershinin, I. Sudbinin, for whom he considered substituting V. Kachalov. He was also dissatisfied with M. Gromov as Soleny, whom he actually replaced (with A. Sanin) only to discover that the latter was not an improvement and so had to revert to his original casting. At the same time, Knipper was expressing dissatisfaction with V. Meyerhold as Tuzenbakh, who was 'too dry'. Meyerhold himself was complaining about unproductive rehearsals during which he was being asked to perform the same action of crossing the stage time and again to the point where he felt he could have cheerfully murdered Stanislavsky. Towards the end of December, a number of the cast went down with minor illnesses. Knipper was unable to attend the dress rehearsal of the first two acts on 23 December, when her part had to be read in for her. Stanislavsky was so involved with direction in the absence of Nemirovich[18] that he did not take over the role of Vershinin until 23 January, just eight days before the opening night.

On the day he completed the production score Stanislavsky wrote to Chekhov describing the mood of each act as he saw them. The first was 'happy' and 'light-hearted', the second possessed a 'Chekhovian mood', while the third was 'extremely nervous' and needed to be played quickly with the tempo only dropping towards the end.[19] At this stage he had not determined the mood of Act 4 but he noted the problem of the play's concluding moments which, in the unrevised version, had Tuzenbakh's corpse being borne across the stage. The Hermitage Theatre had only a very small stage area and bringing a crowd on at that point would probably cause the scenery to rock, quite apart from distracting attention from the three sisters. Could the fourth act not conclude with the sisters' monologues and without the corpse? Chekhov agreed.[20]

On 10 January, Act 3 was rehearsed in the presence of Nemirovich-Danchenko who had returned from abroad. Immediately following this, Knipper reported that Nemirovich had suggested changes in the tempo of Act 3. 'We ran through the third act twice. . . . As staged by Stanislavsky there is a frightful brouhaha with everyone in a nervous state and running about. Nemirovich, by contrast, advises making a clamorous alarm noise off-stage but with a sense of emptiness on stage and unhurried acting and that this will be more powerful.'[21] Chekhov agreed. 'Of course everything must be quiet on stage in the third act so that a sense of people's exhaustion can be felt and the fact that they want to sleep. What's the point of all the noise? It's indicated in the text where the alarm bells are rung off stage.'[22] Nemirovich also disapproved of the way in which Knipper acted the 'confessional' scene in Act 3 (when she declares her love for Vershinin to her sisters). Later he recalled, ironically, that Knipper seemed to him like Nikita in the last act of Tolstoy's *The Power of Darkness*, on her knees before her sisters, her hair falling loose about her face[23] (something which is not, in fact, called for in the production score). Nemirovich suggested that she merely sit while speaking her 'confession' with a smile of excitement. Reporting this to Chekhov, Knipper received the following reply:

> My darling girl, Masha's confession in Act 3 is not in the least confession-like, but only a frank conversation. Deliver it nervously, but not despairingly; don't shout, smile from time to time, but most importantly deliver it so as to convey a sense of the night's fatigue. Also to convey a feeling that you're more intelligent than your sisters, or at least you consider yourself so.[24]

On 22 January Nemirovich-Danchenko wrote praising Stanislavsky's *mise-en-scène* although criticising it as overburdened with detail. He described his own sense of the play as an 'epic' work, where the flow of life is faithfully caught: 'Name-day celebrations, carnival, fire, departure, stove, lamp, grand piano, tea, pie, drunkenness, dusk, night, drawing room, dining room, girls' bedroom, winter, autumn, spring, and so on.'[25] He also suggested making cuts in the monologues of Masha and Irina towards the end of Act 4, which Chekhov apparently heeded.

In addition to seeking advice about the scene of 'confession', Knipper also sought Chekhov's help in deciphering the melodic intimacy of her love duet with Vershinin in Act 3. Chekhov offered the following suggestion:

> Vershinin says 'tram-tram-tram' in the form of a question, and yours is spoken in the form of an answer and this seems to you such an original device that you pronounce your 'tram-tram' with a little laugh. . . . You say 'tram-tram' and give a little laugh, not loudly but just so so.[26]

This was rather different from Nemirovich-Danchenko's original proposal that Vershinin's call be delivered in the style of a bugler[27] and, a week later, Knipper dutifully reported back to Chekhov describing the manner in which the scene was now staged:

> I sit at a writing-table at the front of the stage facing the audience and sketch something with a pencil excitedly. When he calls, she glances up smiling, turns away, i.e. inclines her head and asks – tram tam? After his answer she once again excitedly says 'tra-ta-ta' and finally, decisively, 'tram-tam'. If this is all done with a smile, lightly, it won't seem banal like a straightforward 'rendez-vous'. It's true isn't it that up until this night their relationship has been pure?[28]

There were several dress rehearsals in the week leading up to the opening night on 31 January, the final one being on the 29th after which there was a day-long discussion on the 30th. Chekhov's sister Masha attended the dress rehearsal on 27 January: 'I sat in the theatre and wept, especially during Act 3. Your play is staged and acted wonderfully.'[29] Gorky was later to state that the production seemed to him to be more like music than acting and that it was even better than *Uncle Vanya*.[30] Audiences at the first night, however, were fairly cool as were responses to the first performance generally. The only enthusiastic reaction came at the end of Act 1 when the actors were called out about a dozen times. After Act 3, a few applauded 'in cowardly fashion'[31] and the telegram which was sent to Chekhov announcing the production's tremendous success was something of a fabrication. There were only seven more performances of the play before the season ended on 11 February. Stanislavsky was taken ill at the start of the following season, his place being taken by Kachalov. He resumed the role of Vershinin on 19 October.[32] He considered it took the Russian public three years to appreciate *Three Sisters* and thought the most appreciative reviews were those in the Berlin newspapers during the theatre's first foreign tour in 1906.[33]

The cast of *Three Sisters* on the opening night was as follows: Olga – M. G. Savitskaya; Masha – O. L. Knipper; Irina – M. F. Andreyeva; Andrey – V. V. Luzhsky; Natasha – M. P. Lilina; Kulygin – A. L. Vishnevsky; Vershinin – K. S. Stanislavsky; Tuzenbakh – V. E. Meyerhold; Chebutykin – A. R. Artem; Soleny – M. A. Gromov; Anfisa – M. A. Samarova; Ferapont – V. F. Gribunin; Rodé – I. M. Moskvin; Fedotik – I. A. Tikhomirov. The parts of nanny, housemaid, cook, orderly, yardman and other officers were played by O. P. Alekseyeva, N. S. Butova, A. I. Andreyev, B. M. Snegirev, P. P. Luchinin, V. N. Pavlova and O. E. Shvarts. Despite the significant part played by Nemirovich-Danchenko in rehearsals, especially during January, the only directors' names to appear on the production poster were those of K. S. Stanislavsky and V. V. Luzhsky. The performance began at 7.30 and ended at around midnight.[34]

Following Savitskaya's sad and untimely death in 1911, the part of Olga was taken over first by N. S. Butova and then by M. N. Germanova. N. N. Litovtseva took over the role of Irina from M. F. Andreyeva and was followed in her turn by V. V. Baranovskaya. V. I. Kachalov took over the role of Tuzenbakh from Meyerhold in 1902 when the latter left the theatre. Despite Chekhov's personal liking for Meyerhold and his admiration of his acting talents, he did not consider the change a detrimental one.[35]

The designer, as for all the Art Theatre's productions of Chekhov, was V. A. Simov. The settings were worked out by Stanislavsky and Simov during November and December 1900, the latter retaining in mind an indirect suggestion from Chekhov that the action of the play took place in a provincial town rather like Perm (which is situated near the Urals).[36] However, as Simov later admitted, 'We significantly departed from the author in our depiction of the provincial appearance of things.'[37] They considered that a contradiction between elevated ideals and an enveloping sense of *poshlost'* would be highlighted by their setting the play in an environment less redolent of a general's family (where characters appeared 'behind the columns . . . in the ballroom')[38] but in the much more ordinary and commonplace environment of the home of an army captain. Similarly, in Act 4, instead of the avenue of fir trees and a beautiful view of a river and forest, which Chekhov calls for, all the audience saw was the main entrance to an ordinary, provincial two-storey wooden house with a rustic fence running almost the entire width of the stage and, beyond it, a drab-looking garden with a few birch trees. Chekhov does not appear to have raised any serious objections to these fairly crucial alterations.

'We seek the most subtle sensations and are compelled to utilise the most primitive means', bewailed Simov, cursing the small stage and the beggarly technical resources of the theatre on Carriage Row.[39] Nevertheless, what was achieved by way of setting for each of the acts was extremely effective:

The *Three Sisters* set was not the usual three-sided box. In the foreground was a drawing room with overstuffed furniture in loose-covers – as found in any reasonably well-off household, with a piano on the left [from the audience's point of view, i.e. stage right] and family albums on the low table and a large photograph of 'Mamma' and 'Papa' on a special stand in the corner. . . . The door opened on to the entrance hall with a mirror which visitors invariably glanced into on their way through. Upstage, the drawing room merged into a dining room with a table covered by a red-bordered cloth. And on the left, another dent in the 'box': a window-niche which looked out towards the audience. Irina stood by this window, sprinkling seed into a bird-feeder, as though the fourth wall of a real house had suddenly lifted, while the inhabitants, all unawares, carried on with their daily occupations – setting the table, playing patience, reading, rocking babies to sleep, celebrating name-days and sitting heavy-hearted in the shadows.

The audience recognised the Prozorovs' spacious old house in all its detail: the dining room in early spring and in winter, when the window-niche was curtained off with something warm to cut down the draughts, when the fire roared in the stove, the overhead light was diminished and the familiar armchairs and tables loomed strangely in the half-light; the sisters' room, where old screens stood between iron bedsteads; the garden separated from the street by a gimcrack fence, a drunken lamp-post, a barrel beneath a rain spout, a forgotten spade against the wall, a bell-pull and the insurance company's white plaque by the porch. . . . Stanislavsky . . . made everyone . . . remember – how in spring the double panes are removed . . . and how the panes go back in the autumn; how the birds sing in spring-time . . . and how long the lonely autumn evenings when people prick their ears to the howl of the wind, a distant peal of bells, a slamming door.

Visitors from the Imperial Theatre studying the Art Theatre's sound effects saw Stanislavsky and Luzhsky banging sticks swathed in cloth on a board to imitate a 'troika' team galloping into the distance. Or Stanislavsky in full Vershinin make-up stood off-stage and mimicked the springtime trills of a whole flock of birds.

All this 'mood music' was included in the stage directions; the orchestration of the play embraced not only songs, piano roulades and barrel organs but also . . . tinkling bells . . . a humming top, a squeaking nib, a spoon clinking in a tea-glass. The director himself spent a lot of time trying out the bells, discovering the trills most suitable for various birds.[40]

Those who were ironic about all this 'naturalistic' detail would seem to have found an ally in Chekhov. According to Luzhsky:

> there was to be bird song at curtain rise. Those who took responsibility for the effects were Stanislavsky himself, A. L. Vishnevsky, I. M. Moskvin, V. F. Gribunin, N. G. Aleksandrov, and me, cooing like a dove. Anton Pavlovich listened to this menagerie and, approaching me, said: 'Listen, you coo magnificently, but that's an Egyptian dove!' He was similarly ironic about the portraits of the sisters' parents for which Luzhsky and Savitskaya had posed specially. Of the father's portrait Chekhov commented, 'Look, that's a Japanese general, the like of which we don't have in Russia.'[41]

It was always apparent that Nemirovich-Danchenko, who was in charge of the literary side of the theatre's affairs, had a greater enthusiasm, initially, for the work of Chekhov than did Stanislavsky. The production score for *The Seagull*, for example, gives the impression that a great deal of the invented 'business' on the surface was designed, as much as anything, to compensate for a lack of appreciation of the play's subtleties. How, then, did Stanislavsky understand *Three Sisters* and what was his approach to the play as he saw it when composing the production score? According to Marianna Stroyeva:

> Stanislavsky's idea of the production, its 'ruling idea' was the inner struggle of man with 'the power of banality'. . . . In *Three Sisters*, banal life becomes an active aggressive force. . . . The clash of two hostile forces constitutes the dramatic pivot in the director's promptbook.[42]

After one of the first rehearsals, Meyerhold jotted in his notebook what he took to be the themes of the production:

The longing for life.
The summons to work.

Tragic feeling against a (background) of comedy.
Happiness – is the lot of the future.
Work. Loneliness.[43]

Stanislavsky's production score would seem to support the tenor of both these interpretations, but with a slightly different emphasis. The key to Stanislavsky's view of the play appears to lie in his sense of its conflicts and contrasts – between spring and winter; ideals and banalities; meeting and parting; heat and cold; between the world of Nature and that of human beings; between light and dark and between life and death where arrival is seen as a kind of birth, and departure an intimation of death itself. Instead of 'the longing for life' being seen as the production's 'ruling idea', a preferable alternative might be 'the wish not to have to die'. In this sense, all the set speeches about the future become related to the fact of a personal death which excludes the speaker from that future. The longing to live is constantly being offset by the conscious, or unconscious, recognition that people have to part with one another just as they have to part with life itself. Hence the extraordinary poignancy of a production built, according to the critic Petr Yartsev, less on the movement of external events than 'on the subtle movements of life itself'. The drama was acted out 'in delightful illusions of these movements'.[44] Thus it was that the conjuring up of the feel and texture of life on stage evoked simultaneously a countervailing sense of mortality. Leonid Andreyev recorded: 'I saw life [which] excited me, tormented me, filled me with its suffering and pity – and I was ashamed of my tears. . . . No matter where I looked I caught glimpses of handkerchiefs and downcast heads and, during the intervals, eyes and noses reddened with crying.'[45]

## THE PRODUCTION

Act 1 began on a note of spring-like energy, animated by the bright stage lighting, the open windows in the small bay-room (or window-niche) stage right, bird song and an abundance of flowers. Stanislavsky's properties list for Act 1 calls for two vases of flowers, a basket of flowers, a large basket of flowers (the last brought in by the officers at the end of the act), three bouquets of flowers (of different sizes) as well as four vases for fruit and biscuits, three baskets for bread and cakes, two jars of jam and two boxes of sweets.[46] The atmosphere is celebratory and youthful. Irina is tending to live birds in cages in the bay-room. She feeds them with fresh buds from the trees which are coming into leaf in the garden. She puts fresh water and seed in a cage which is then hung in the open window from the *fortochka*. Some of the seed husks fall on a corrugated iron lintel under the window making a distinctive and evocative sound.

Complementing this happy foreground activity, Olga is busily correcting a pile of children's exercise books while Masha is lounging on a divan covered with a Turkoman rug of bold design reading a book and (a typically Stanislavskian detail) cutting the pages with her hat-pin (91/249). There is the sound of Andrey's violin coming from his room (downstage left) and, importantly, a great deal of physical contact between the players. Olga kisses Irina 'maternally (admiringly)'; Andrey takes a tie from Irina which she has been mending for him and kisses her. There is also a contrasting reminder of the past in the sounds of the clock which solemnly strikes the hour of twelve, reminding everyone of the death of the father. But then, as if in ironic counterpoint to this (while continuing the theme of time passing) a cuckoo clock calls onstage in the dining-room alcove at the rear. Then distantly, from another room are heard the rapid chimes of a tiny clock sounding 'late, as if in a hurry' (91). We are to discover in Act 3, that these last chimes belong to the clock which Chebutykin drops and breaks on hearing the news that the regiment is soon to leave.

There is also an emphasis on festivity in the themes of eating and present-giving which run throughout the first act. Even Protopopov's mundane name-day present of a pie is delivered wrapped up in a coloured tablecloth. Olga pops a biscuit into Irina's mouth; Tuzenbakh takes a sweet, as does Soleny at several points throughout the act. Whilst crossing the room, Irina takes something to eat from one of the four vases for fruit and biscuits which are dotted about. Chebutykin embraces Irina and she feeds him a sweet. Chebutykin is as if energised by the physical contact and performs an *entrechat*. He even kisses Tuzenbakh in spontaneous fashion. Irina is 'as if enlivened'. Chebutykin kisses her hand. Then Tuzenbakh sits at the piano and doodles on the keys while the offstage violin plays scales and exercises (93/250–1).

All of this introductory material takes up some thirty numbered notes in Stanislavsky's score and corresponds to approximately the first three pages of Chekhov's play and is by no means exhaustive. Stanislavsky also draws our attention to the portraits of the parents – one of the general in his youth and one of both of them in old age 'in frames made by Andrey' (89) – the characteristic detail which Stanislavsky has taken up from the moment, later in the act, when the sisters proudly show a slightly bemused Vershinin an empty picture frame which their brother has made. Stanislavsky then enlarges on this suggestion by having the sounds of sawing coming from Andrey's room during Act 2 to imply that this is one of the ways in which he copes with marriage and boredom.

Tuzenbakh's important speech about work (97/253) is delivered whilst revolving himself 'idly' on the piano stool. This is followed by Soleny's voice emerging from behind the tiled stove (stage left) with his line about putting a bullet in Tuzenbakh's head (added by Chekhov to the revised version of the play when he significantly enlarged the role of Soleny). This is then accompanied by Soleny's disembodied arm being extended from behind the stove and taking a sweet, followed by the 'business' with the scent bottle.

When writing the play, Chekhov was clearly impressed by the metaphorical implications of photography, both as a means of halting time and as offering evidence of the fact of people's existence. Hence the poignancy of the moment when the group photograph is taken at the end of Act 1 and the pathos which accompanies Fedotik's cavalier exclamation (in Act 3) that every-thing he possesses has been burned (including, presumably, the photographic evidence of the group's existence). Stanislavsky would appear to have inserted a number of these specifically 'photographic' moments into the score. The final grouping of the sisters at the end of Act 4 is constantly being anticipated, especially in Act 1. As Masha prepares to leave, there is 'a group of three loving sisters at the entrance door' (99/255) and, later, following Vershinin's entry, 'a tender group of three sisters, holding hands' (103/257). Again, following the tearful response to Vershinin's evocation of the past, an 'affectionate close-knit group of three sisters' (105/258) followed by a 'pause for the group of sisters'.

The *leitmotif* of the past is taken up with the mention of the dead parents, when both Vershinin (removing his pince-nez) and Chebutykin go across and examine the portrait. Chebutykin's connection with the dead mother is established by Stanislavsky through the presentation of the samovar as a name-day gift, with its accompanying embarrassment. He notes in the score that 'according to the author' Irina 'is (evidently) Chebutykin's daughter, who lived with her mother' (101). Vershinin then begins his speech with its references to Copernicus and Columbus 'energetically' but halts in mid-flow to light a cigarette. There follows much by-play, with Irina looking for a box of matches, lighting the cigarette, fetching an ash-tray before he continues his speech, which Tuzenbakh accompanies by pacing about the room as if counting the squares in the fading, yellow-painted parquet floor (107/260).

Stanislavsky is constantly at pains to avoid any sense that the sisters could be considered either snobbish or vulgar. So much so that, in order to stress her decency and good manners, he has Masha's comment about Natasha: 'The way she dresses herself is awful!' (109/261) spoken whilst leafing through a photograph album so that the remark, addressed 'at some provincial girl' pictured in the album is not intended to be a comment on Natasha. When the latter makes her entry, Stanislavsky makes it clear that Natasha is to be seen as 'sincere' and genuinely 'confused' (121/268). This suggests that her leaving the table in embarrassment is not a tactic (as it can otherwise seem) designed to put a form of emotional pressure on Andrey which successfully elicits a proposal of marriage. Stanislavsky also notes that she is dressed 'in bad taste' but 'attractively (like a doll)' (121).

Chebutykin helps to lay the table and Stanislavsky stresses that the actor needs to understand the essential elements of the play so as to be able to pause in his activity at the most important points in the dialogue so as not to distract attention and that the pauses need to be made to seem natural (113/263). Fedotik and Rodé enter and Fedotik takes a photograph of the group at the table. He stands downstage of the grand piano (stage right) astride a dining-room chair, resting his camera on the back. Stanislavsky notes that a female servant and an orderly strike unnatural poses so as to look well in the photograph (123/270). At Chebutykin's remarks about Natasha's embarrassment, she runs from the table to the entrance hall (rear stage right) where she is pursued by Andrey. She then runs downstage and enters the small room with the window bay, where they are both caught in an embrace by the incoming officers. In the 1914 photograph, they are seen to be observed by all at the table who crane out from the alcove and look in their direction quite shamelessly while one of the officers stands, very deliberately, his hand resting on the piano, staring directly at them. The actual score reads differently:

> In the window of the bay-room Andrey kisses Natasha. The second officer walks up to the piano where he places his guitar. He is sprightly, with a permanent smile, rather dashing; wipes his nose and smooths his hair on the move. He sees Andrey and says 'Ah!', then walks up to greet him but notices that they are embracing and quickly turns on his heel. At the same time, the third officer has walked over to the piano in order to place his military cap on it. The second officer rapidly leads him away by the arm, turning a frightened face towards the embracing couple. The third officer acquiesces uncomprehendingly. All this has to be done rapidly, without any delay and, above all, simply. Andrey and Natasha do not see the officers. The third officer is a nice old boy, staid, with the rank of captain, sturdy and slow in his movements. In the dining-room they are greeted joyfully.   (127/271)

This Act 1 'finale' follows Stanislavsky's 212th stage direction for the act as a whole.

The score for Act 2 is preceded by a list of properties, lighting and sound effects (68 items in all) which include four or five toys for a seven- to eight-month-old child, placed on a small rug. Among these are a small barrel organ and a Petrushka doll with clapping cymbals. There is also a child's blanket and a basket of children's things on the divan as well as lengths of towelling and a pair of scissors on the piano top (presumably for nappies) with one or two lengths of towelling littering the floor. Sound effects include two metronomes to suggest the ticking of clocks and a harmonium and cello to create the sound of the wind moaning in the stove pipes (129–33).

The atmosphere is in complete contrast to Act 1. The windows of the bay-room have been shut fast for the winter. The furniture inside has been piled together and covered with a cloth. A large military drape now covers the door to the bay and the piano has been moved downstage and blocks the entrance to this area. The stage is in darkness at curtain rise and the spirit of darkness which has entered the house seems to be associated with Natasha herself, signs of whose encroachment are apparent in the proliferation of baby-things. The only light on stage comes from a small guttering lamp and from Andrey's room, from where the muttered tones of his voice can also be heard running over a speech, or lecture, as he paces up and down. From time to time his shadow cuts across the beam of light and the audience can also hear what sound like his tearful sobs. The glass of the bay window is iced over but the light of a distant street lamp can just be seen filtering through. The faint sounds of an accordion penetrate from the street, as do the shouts of drunken passers-by and the strains of a drunken song. There is a sound of wind, and swirling snowflakes are visible. The only other noise on stage is of shuffling slippers worn by Anfisa and Natasha.

Natasha enters with a candle and snuffs the only light on stage, which has been threatening to go out of its own accord. She then extinguishes the candle which Anfisa has brought in and left behind on the piano. She takes her own candle out into the entrance hall, where she wakes the dosing Ferapont, then extinguishes the light in the hall, leaving Ferapont completely in the dark (135–9). Andrey enters and lights a candle. During the following scene with Ferapont (141/274–5) Stanislavsky introduces some comic business with Ferapont's earwrap which he wears, like a footcloth, wound round his head and under his chin. To emphasise the fact that he is hard of hearing, the score has Ferapont unwind and rebind his ears on five separate occasions in the course of a single page of dialogue in response to Andrey's questions.[47] At another point, Andrey exits with the only candle, leaving Ferapont, once more, alone. There is a moment's silence, then the audience hears him yawn in the dark (141).

The score then describes the entry of Masha and Vershinin. They enter the darkened drawing room from the frost outside and there is the usual ritual of handwarming at the small iron stove which can just be seen in the rear entryway. They sit on the small divan downstage left of the large tiled stove, the door of which is situated upstage of the audience and invisible to it. Offstage the nanny sings a monotonous lullaby. The couple move towards each other and their kiss sounds in the dark. Then when the voices of Irina and Tuzenbakh are heard in the hallway, Vershinin moves away and sits on a chair, lights a cigarette (the cue for Tuzenbakh and Irina to notice that they are in the room) and a general conversation begins. However, in production the scene was staged rather differently in a very simple and restrained manner, without any physical contact. The only direct physical embrace between

Vershinin and Masha which the audience was privy to was the final one, in Act 4, at the moment of parting.[48]

Sound effects played a very important part in Act 2. The score indicates that almost the entire act is accompanied by effects of one sort or another – the scratching of a mouse, the sound of a violin playing a plaintive melody, the sound of sawing, the noise of a glass of medicine being dropped by Anfisa, followed by the sounds of the pieces being swept up; the sounds of Andrey pacing in his room, coughing and turning the leaves of a book; the sounds of an accordion and drunken voices in the distance (it is carnival week); the sound of a snowstorm outside and the wind in the stove; the sound of crockery being rattled offstage, the noise of Chebutykin's newspaper, and even the sound of silence – all carefully orchestrated and integrated into the changing moods of the act.

Vershinin picks up the Petrushka and causes its cymbals to clap together. (Stanislavsky wants the audience to see the toy but not realise where the sound is coming from: 151/278–9.) Tuzenbakh picks up the toy barrel-organ and proceeds, idly, to turn its handle. His speech about 'life in a thousand years' time' is accompanied by his turning the handle of the toy which emits 'indeterminate sounds' (153/280). Vershinin's optimistic speech, which follows immediately after, concludes with Stanislavsky's comment: 'In the distance the sound of an accordion and drunken voices as if to remind us, deliberately, that that of which Vershinin speaks will not come to pass very rapidly' (153/280). Masha then extinguishes the two lights on stage and the scene is illuminated for a while by moonlight and the glow from the men's cigarettes. Of Stanislavsky/Vershinin's 'philosophical' speeches, Knipper recalled:

> He spoke these tirades about a happy life, these dreams of how to start life anew, quite consciously, not with the inflections of a man who loved to philosophise. One felt that what he said came from inside him, giving purpose to his life, giving him a chance to rise above the drab environment and all the trials that he so patiently suffered.[49]

One of the classic Chekhovian scenes is the moment of stasis in Act 2 when, against the background of a general discussion of the meaning of life, Chebutykin reads out incongruous snippets from a newspaper, Irina plays a solitary game of patience and Tuzenbakh unexpectedly announces that he is resigning his commission. The sequence appears to have been staged by Stanislavsky with uncharacteristic insensitivity. Tuzenbakh's speech, which puts a case for the absence of meaning in natural phenomena, is spoken whilst constantly, and distractingly, on the move. Then, surprisingly, Masha's urgent speech on the need for meaning which concludes 'or else . . . nothing matters . . . everything's just wild grass', is accompanied throughout by comic stage business between Fedotik and Rodé:

> Suddenly they enter [later than indicated by Chekhov] and strike a pose like gypsies strumming the strings of their guitars while taking up the first notes of a dance-song quite loudly. Irina quickly tells them to 'shush' (they'll wake the baby). They clutch their heads comically then hide behind the table with only their heads visible. Irina and Chebutykin laugh. Fedotik crawls under one side of the table and out the other, then they both sit at the dining-room window in the corner and strum and sing quietly. Vershinin, Tuzenbakh and Masha have glanced in their direction to see what they're up to, have also said 'shush' and laughed. (155–7)

Quiet then ensues and Tuzenbakh exits into Andrey's room on the line 'it's useless arguing with you'. There is a prolonged pause accompanied by the rustling of Chebutykin's newspaper and the soft sounds of a polka being played on two guitars. The voices of Tuzenbakh and Andrey can be heard from the adjoining room. Another pause. Fedotik crosses to the hall and lights a candle. Irina hurries after him (abandoning the game of patience which Chekhov's direction says she is just laying out). Fedotik takes a package out of his greatcoat pocket (his present of a pen-knife and coloured pencils). At this point, Tuzenbakh leaves Andrey's room speaking his lines about having handed in his resignation and heads for the dining room. There follow sounds of the snowstorm and noise in the stovepipes (157/281–2).

This scene is one of those key atmospheric moments in a Chekhov play, where so many different kinds of mood and feeling run together and where an inconsequential line such as Chebutykin's 'Balzac's marriage took place at Berdichev' can be made to seem like a desperate groping for certainty in a world where everything appears contingent and tenuous. If interpreted in this spirit, then Tuzenbakh's line about 'throwing in his hand' or 'the die' being 'cast' becomes both a casual and a fatal act, a kind of self-inflicted death sentence which Soleny will execute in Act 4. This, it has to be said, is the only point in Stanislavsky's score where the interpretation appears not to be fully alive to the sensitivity and subtlety of the dramatic text.

A former conductor of the Moscow Art Theatre orchestra, B. Izrailevsky, stressed the importance of music in Stanislavsky's production of *Three Sisters*, especially in Act 2:

> Tuzenbakh . . . plays the piano, improvises. Rodé starts to strum the guitar. Imperceptibly, there arises the duet 'Nochi bezumnyye' ['Nights of Madness'] sung by Irina. All others present at the party fall silent and listen. An unforgettably intimate atmosphere is created. The singing stops. All are under the spell of the romance. But yet again the guitar rings out, 'Akh, vy seni, moi seni . . .' ['My porch of maple wood . . .'] and all animatedly take up this delightful Russian song. A general dance begins.[50]

This was developed into a party number. Where Chekhov has Masha dancing on her own, Stanislavsky has Rodé dance with Masha, Fedotik with Irina, while Andrey tries to persuade Chebutykin to get up and join in. Natasha's breaking-up of the festivities is then very effectively done as, to begin with, the music stops but the couples carry on dancing, then wonder why the music has stopped before they, too, notice Natasha and realise that it is her presence which has brought the proceedings to a halt (173/288–9).

The arrival of the carnival maskers is signalled by three tugs on a jangling bell outside. At this point, Stanislavsky conceives the idea of staging a scene with the maskers. A crowd of them suddenly appears in the hallway frightening Anfisa and the housemaid. They all wear grotesque masks and some have bells on their costumes. One is dressed as Mephistopheles, another as a Capuchin monk (177/290). Following their disappointed departure, Protopopov's arrival is announced. His position in the town is relayed to the audience by the housemaid who 'enters hurriedly' and 'speaks secretively'. Stanislavsky explains that 'Protopopov cuts a figure in the town and the fact that he has called on Natasha is an honour in the housemaid's opinion' (181/292).

At the act curtain, Irina slumps across the piano and groans as if in pain as she speaks the lines 'To Moscow! To Moscow!'. A metronome sounds, like the tick of a clock – the 315th stage direction in the promptbook for Act 2 (187/293).

Act 3 is set in an attic room. Signs of genteel poverty are apparent in the peeling wallpaper and in the general clutter of the room which serves as a bedroom for Irina and Olga, with two sections divided off at the rear by curtains. Stanislavsky's and Simov's intention in designing the setting for this act was to convey a total illusion of a 'fourth wall'. To this end, nine separate items of furniture were placed directly across the proscenium opening – a trunk, the couch from Act 1 covered with the same rug, a small five-sided 'Turkish' table, a pouffé, a writing-table, a chair, another writing-table, a chair and another trunk.

Two sets of church bells, at different pitches, sound the fire-alarm offstage. Stanislavsky prescribes a great deal of activity (most of which was toned down by Nemirovich-Danchenko). The housemaid rushes to look out of the window, pulls back the curtain, and the audience sees the red glow from the fire. Kulygin and the nanny run in and out. The stage is dark apart from a green-shaded lamp hanging in the sleeping area of the room and a single candle on one of the tables. A strip of light from the rear corridor can be seen through one of the doors. Among the thirty properties are ordinary everyday items such as soap, towels and toothbrushes, but also two cages with live birds in them. The sounds of the striking clocks are now in reverse – the loud one distant, as is the cuckoo clock, but the sound of the little clock striking last, 'as if hurrying', now reverberates in the room. A fire engine passes outside and the audience hears its warning bells in two or three different tones, the clatter of wheels and horses' hooves, the rattle of empty water barrels (187–91). Stanislavsky specifically requests that a rapid tempo and a nervous feeling predominate and that there be few pauses as well as much crossing and re-crossing of the stage. He is also careful about not wishing to bore the audience with repetitions of some of the effects, such as the fire effect each time the curtain is held back. He notes: 'Remind the housemaid, Natasha and the others that whoever pulls back the curtain pulls it to more firmly each time' (199). At one point, Natasha happens to catch sight of herself in the mirror, stops, stands in profile and smooths herself in front: 'They say I've got stouter.' Stanislavsky notes: 'I'll tell you a secret. She's in an interesting condition' (199/296). Her remarks about Anfisa's redundancy, addressed to Olga, are not unpleasant but spoken 'in the tone of a mentor, with aplomb but good-naturedly' (201/296).

With Chebutykin's entry, Stanislavsky does not follow Chekhov's stage direction 'Olga and Natasha leave the room without him noticing' (207/298), but has Natasha leave on her own. Olga goes behind her curtain to lie down. This has the, possibly intentional, effect of excusing the bad manners of Kulygin's decision to conceal himself and overhear Chebutykin's monologue about which he chaffs the doctor later ('In vino veritas') as he is now not the only potential eavesdropper. Kulygin conceals himself behind an archway, from where he keeps peeping out while Chebutykin conducts a drunken conversation with someone he imagines is in the room with him, addressing him directly as he enters. He then 'secretly' combs his beard with Irina's comb in front of the mirror (a typically Stanislavskian touch) then, following the revelation of his guilty feelings about the death of a patient, begins to cry and 'sits with his hands covered in soap' looking at them 'suspiciously' (207–9/298–9).

When Vershinin makes his entry he is smoking a cigarette and gallantly stands in the doorway so as not to pollute the girls' bedroom. He sports a cigarette-holder and, from time to time, comes into the room to flick ash into a receptacle (209/299). This contrasts with Soleny who, when he enters later, proceeds to blow smoke everywhere (prompting Irina's request to him to leave). The line 'It's gone three' (209/299) is altered to 'It'll soon be four o'clock.' Tuzenbakh picks up the small china clock from Olga's table, examines it, then puts it down in front of Chebutykin who is folding a towel 'as if it was a mathematical operation' (209/299). Chebutykin then sits with his back to the audience. In the promptbook Stanislavsky tries to work out in advance how to achieve the effect of dropping the clock. Should Chebutykin drop something else which makes the necessary sound or should the task be left to someone in the prompter's box? The clocks strike four. Chebutykin picks up the china clock 'as if he wants to stop its striking' (213/300), shakes it, then drops it. Irina proceeds to pick up the fragments which Vershinin and Kulygin attempt to piece together again with some glue which Irina brings them. Kulygin soon tires and is overcome by sleep (213).

Stanislavsky's explanation of the sub-text to the love duet between Masha and Vershinin needs to be seen in the light of the earlier descriptions by Knipper and Chekhov of how the scene was, or how it should be, played. 'Act it as if Masha is asking him "Do you love me?"', suggests Stanislavsky. 'Vershinin answers: "Yes, very much." Masha: "Today I will belong to you." Vershinin: "What joy, what bliss"' (215/301–2). This sequence is interrupted by Fedotik's delirious announcement that he has lost everything in the fire. Stanislavsky places a series of five plus (+) marks in the text to indicate at which points, during the course of a very short speech, Fedotik is helpless with laughter (217/302). Irina attempts to disperse Soleny's smoke with the help of a scent spray. The smell of the scent 'wafts over the audience' (219/304). The springs of Olga's bed creak as she turns over. The clocks strike five. When later they strike six, Stanislavsky makes the wry observation: 'The tiny broken clock no longer answers' (229/306–7).

Masha, awaiting her assignation with Vershinin, lies on her back on the couch with her eyes open, thinking, whistling to herself. When Kulygin interrupts her reverie and kisses each of her fingers, she conjugates the Latin verb 'to love' not 'angrily', as Chekhov's stage direction suggests, but with a sort of serious emphasis on the peculiarity of the word. She then distances herself from her husband quietly, not in the least abruptly or rudely.[51]

Following Irina's hysterical outburst, the sisters tenderly minister to her. Olga strokes her head like a child and speaks to her in caressing, maternal tones. Masha moves to her, sits at her feet and strokes her legs while Olga wipes away her tears. There follows another tender, intimate 'photographic' moment with Masha on her knees at the bedhead holding Irina by one hand and Olga with the other. There is then a pause with the direction 'an affectionate group of three sisters', followed by a five-second pause before Andrey's entry (231/307–8). Stanislavsky specifically makes the point that Masha's tending to Irina is out of character (233), something with which Chekhov agreed when suggesting to Knipper that the scene be played differently. Acting on the advice of both Chekhov and Nemirovich, Masha/Knipper did not, finally, take any part in the calming of Irina's crying and spoke her 'confession' sitting, her arms cradling her knees, only occasionally covering her face with her hand.[52]

Act 3 concludes with its 278th note: 'A five-second pause. Alarm sounds – either the large bell or that of passing firemen. Possibly Natasha could cross the stage again with a candle' (239/310).

Chekhov's directions at the beginning of Act 4 state that the action, which involves the departure of the military, takes place at mid-day (exactly the same hour at which the play opens with its memories of the permanent departure from this life, the previous year, of the girls' father). It was in this act that the fusion of departure and death appears to have taken a firm hold on Stanislavsky's imagination. This feeling is intensely apparent in the score at points where Tuzenbakh, apparently suppressing an inner premonition, is described as frequently 'swallowing saliva' (267) before he departs to be killed in the duel. The acted intensity of the farewell between Vershinin and Masha was like a death scene in which Masha (clad in black since the beginning of the play) is once more being torn away from her father (the former battery commander) in his resurrected guise as Vershinin. Stanislavsky's score indicates, among the properties, a 'box for packing the portrait of the general' (241), which can be imagined being carried carefully from the house like a coffin. A spade (also in the property list) stands against the house wall throughout the act assuming a significance, in this context, which connects it with death and burial. Stanislavsky also calls for yellow leaves to fall periodically throughout the act. There are several directions which indicate a preoccupation with time. Characters are constantly consulting their watches (on far more occasions than Chekhov indicates) or else they cuddle their watches to their ears to ensure they are still working (249 and 255). At other points, Chebutykin shows his watch to the baby and dangles it in the pram (259 and 261).

The properties list for Act 4 includes a child's pram with a squeaky wheel and a dark-blue canopy. Stanislavsky sketches two variants – the first with even-sized wheels, the second with large wheels at the back and a small wheel in front. He has then crossed out the second variant. Other properties include a small trunk for Chebutykin tied up with rope, and a very large trunk which is so heavy that it needs to be dragged from the house on a length of towelling. Among the sound effects called for are the echo of Rodé's voice and the sound of wild geese in flight. For the latter Stanislavsky suggests using the sound effect previously employed in the production of Hauptmann's *Lonely Lives*.[53]

The act opens with the sound of bells from a nearby church marking a mass held for the departing troops. A reflector, placed in the wings, casts light (like the sun's rays) on the steps leading to the house (upstage right) with its typical upper storey like a balcony with two large windows made up of small panes of glass. In front of the picket fence, which extends from a wooden veranda stage left of the entrance, are a couple of piles of abandoned bricks, a bench and an old rickety kerosene street lamp.[54]

The opening pages of the score contain a great deal of stage business and the mood is far from solemn. Fedotik, resting his camera on the fence, takes a photograph of a small group on the entrance steps. Rodé then disrupts the group pose, much to Fedotik's annoyance, before proceeding to run around kissing goodbye to the trees, saluting them and sitting on each of the benches in the garden in turn. An old woman crosses the forestage carrying a jug of milk by way of explanation that the space in front of the Prozorov house is also a public right of way. Later a hawker passes through selling fresh fruit (247–61).

Masha is on edge, constantly leaving the stage through the gate to the street (stage right) and returning, permanently on the look-out for Vershinin. When Soleny enters, he is described as being at ease, almost majestic, smoking a cigarette from a holder (265/319). The baron, by contrast, is extremely nervous and Irina's behaviour indicates, according to Stanislavsky, that 'she knows everything' (265). In fact, Chekhov's letter to Tikhomirov (Fedotik) states that 'Irina doesn't know that Tuzenkakh is going to a duel, but guesses that something untoward happened the previous evening which could have important and even unfortunate consequences. And when a woman intuits something, she always says, "I knew it, I knew it".'[55]

At one point in the score, Stanislavsky debates whether or not Protopopov himself should make an appearance. Amidst the laughter which can be heard coming from the house, his bass voice rings out prominently. Then Stanislavsky fantasises an episode which might have come from Gogol. A ball could roll out of the house and down the steps, pursued by a fat man with a cigar in his mouth who has difficulty in bending down to pick it up. Once it has been retrieved, 'he vanishes for ever with the ball' (271). When the street musicians appear, whose music for harp and violin has been heard getting gradually nearer (playing a waltz tune 'Ozhidaniye' ('Expectation')), they are not the 'man and a girl' whom Chekhov prescribes but 'a boy playing a violin, with his mother' (273). The song which they then sing extends the theme of death and parting: 'Nadenu chernoye plat'e' ('I'll wear a dress of black').[56]

Vershinin appears and is described as 'very nervous and distraught'. 'This is very important', declares Stanislavsky, 'so as to excuse his behaviour' (275/324–5). Olga eats an orange bought from the fruit vendor. Someone can be heard sweeping the street beyond the fence. Vershinin is constantly consulting his watch. When he and Masha meet, 'Masha sobs on Vershinin's chest; he can scarcely refrain from crying' (279/325–6). Throughout this scene Stanislavsky is at pains to stress that, for Vershinin, this has been no casual love affair. For example, he is aware of the danger of Vershinin seeming merely callous when he asks Olga to remove Masha (281/326). 'This is a very dangerous moment as it could appear as if he is anxious to be rid of her, that she bores him.' He therefore stresses that Vershinin must speak 'in heartfelt fashion', 'softly' and 'as if moved' (281).

This scene was, without doubt, the most powerful and moving in the production. 'I can't think without inner convulsions of the scene in which I part from Vershinin', recalled Knipper. 'I did not feel my body as I went from my dressing-room to this parting on the stage, as though some strange force was bearing me there.'[57]

Rushing up to Vershinin, she would suddenly stop short and her arms would drop loosely at her sides. The brief scene that followed – Masha gazing into Vershinin's face as if to imprint it on her mind for ever, her single word of farewell, their last embrace and Masha's scarcely human, gasping sobs – this brief scene, as played by Knipper and Stanislavsky, was never forgotten by those who saw it.[58]

According to Petr Yartsev, 'the thirst for life and the hatred of life, a power of almost demonic proportions is felt in the tiny phrase "Goodbye!" as spoken by Knipper'.[59] According to N. Efros, the beauty of the scene between Vershinin and Masha put him in mind of Maeterlinck's words: 'Les larmes des hommes sont devenues silencieuses, invisibles et presque spirituelles' as well as of the phrase used by an Italian critic to describe the effect of a performance by Duse – 'una vita vissuta'.[60] Masha's repetition of the lines from Pushkin at this point seemed to Efros to indicate the presence of a malignant determining Fate which extended on some mysterious thread. There was also a sense in which this evoked a feeling of sympathy, of spiritual solidarity, with Masha so that the lines of verse which revolved tormentingly in her mind, did so in the mind of the audience as well.[61]

Just as Stanislavsky was anxious to stress Vershinin's sincerity during this act, so is he anxious to present Kulygin not as a Chekhovian 'man in a case' (*chelovek v futlyare*) and a pedantic bore, but as a thoroughly decent, sincere human being who forgives his wife everything. He brings her a glass of water and valerian drops. He is 'on the verge of tears' and 'carefully embraces' Masha (283/326–7).

The sounds of a military band (playing K. Frant's 'Skobolev March')[62] draw nearer until they almost drown the stage. Everyone, including the yardman, the cook, the housemaid, the nanny and a small boy either emerge from the house, appear on the veranda or else hurry across the stage towards the street as the band passes. Gradually, the music fades away and the sisters are left, once more, in a 'photographic' grouping to speak their final lines with Stanislavsky's instruction to 'speak cheerfully, as far as possible' (287). They freeze. Irina and Olga look upwards, their eyes full of tears. Masha has calmed down and leans affectionately against Olga (287/329).

Stanislavsky's revised finale, after persuading Chekhov to dispense with the passage of Tuzenbakh's corpse across the stage, runs as follows:

> OLYA: If only we knew!
> The sound of the garden gate – slowly, sadly, the cook, Anfisa, the boy return. . . . Ferapont comes out of the house in a cap with a file of signed papers. Everyone is sad and there's a feeling that the town has become deserted. Chebutykin sings 'tararabumdiya' whilst leafing through the newspaper. Andrey pushes the squeaky pram. The gate knocks with the comings and goings. The distant march music is scarcely audible. The despondent, monstrous sound of the yardman's broom is heard from the street.
> OLYA: If only we knew!
> Kulygin comes on stage from the house cheerfully carrying a ladies' cape as the curtain falls.    (289/330)[63]

Chekhov himself was well pleased with the production which, when he saw it in September 1901, he said was staged better than the play was written.[64] However, some of the initial critical reactions were fairly damning. Typical of one kind of response was the critic who could not see what all the fuss was about. Why should the striving for Moscow, for these three sisters, have been such an unrealisable dream? After all 'they have both means and a pension'.[65] Suvorin's *Novoye Vremya* described the company as 'the Meiningens of Carriage Row' and accused them of going in for 'crude naturalism'.[66] This accusation was echoed by someone who became a long-standing opponent of the Art Theatre, the critic A. Kugel'. The theatre, in his opinion, had exchanged poetry for properties.[67] Other critics accused Chekhov of being ignorant of Russian provincial life. Even in far-flung places such as Samara and Kishinev, wrote one critic, where Pushkin had found little apart from crows, there were now various societies and Sunday schools, a local press, theatrical groups, choirs and drawing circles. Here, members of the intelligentsia concerned themselves with the provision of local libraries. 'Where', he asked, 'was all this in the play by this likeable writer?'[68]

Knipper wrote reassuring Chekhov that, despite all the cursing in the press, the play was a success with audiences and Vishnevsky assured him that, even if the Kugels and the Suvorins damned them, this was only to be expected as they were known to be swine and ne'er-do-wells in any case. The public itself damned *them*, witness the fact that all seats for the Petersburg tour that spring had been sold out well in advance.[69] The theatre took encouragement from those who, at least, recognised the truth of the production. An army officer in the February number of *Russkiy invalid* acknowledged the authentic depiction of military life,[70] as did another army officer who wrote to Stanislavsky:

> I am a layman as far as evaluating theatre art is concerned, but on the average person such as your ordinary army officer, your acting produces an impression of absolute pleasure. In each of the players I recognised someone among my former fellow service-men in the regiment. Your depiction of the life of a circle of officers in the provinces is so close to the truth that the illusion is total and, in the auditorium, you begin to feel at one with the actors – as if all the officers were known to you.[71]

But more sophisticated, as well as appreciative, responses came from critics who were also fellow artists such as Gorky and, in particular, Leonid Andreyev, part of whose article in *Kur'yer* was quoted earlier. His review continued:

A person normally goes to the theatre for the sake of distraction but, in this case, he is turned over like a worn-out mattress and beaten with a stick until all the dust of petty personal cares, banality and incomprehension fly out of him. . . . When I left the theatre at the end they could have given me someone else's galoshes or placed a woman's hat and cloak on me with total impunity and I would hardly have noticed. And the first words which my companion and I exchanged when we found ourselves under a starry sky were: 'How sorry one feels for the sisters! How sad! And they so desperately want to live! . . .' The longing for life – that is the powerful mood which permeates the play from beginning to end and whose heroines sing a hymn to this same life with tears. . . . It is the howl of a robbed and dying man who calls for justice and revenge. Dying . . . they realise that they are sacrificial victims and beg that their sacrifices will make sense to succeeding generations so that some answers will be given as to why they suffered. . . . Go, feel sorry for the sisters, weep with them their bitter fate and catch their invocatory cry on the wing: 'To Moscow! To Moscow!' Towards the light! Towards life – freedom and happiness![72]

## Notes

1. The name adopted by the theatre at its inception. By 1902, as a result of having to increase seat prices, the theatre had reluctantly dropped the 'Popular-Accessible' (*obshchedostupnyy*) element from its title.
2. Chekhov wrote to Gorky on 9 May 1899 following a performance staged without decor in Moscow, 'I can't judge the play with equanimity because the seagull herself acted so vilely, bursting into tears all the time, and Trigorin (the belle-lettrist) walked about the stage and talked like a paralytic; he has "no will of his own" and the performer understood this in a way that made me sick to watch' (E. Surkov (ed.), *Chekhov i teatr* (Moscow, 1961) p. 101). However, writing a week later to P. F. Iordanov, he described the same production as 'wonderful' (letter of 15 May 1899, in *Chekhov i teatr*, p. 103). Stanislavsky's own memory of the occasion was that Chekhov 'was delighted with the performance as a whole', although he admits that the author did offer some mild criticism of his (Stanislavsky's) performance as Trigorin. See Elizabeth Reynolds Hapgood (ed. and trs.), *Stanislavski's Legacy* (London, 1968) p. 93.
3. Letter of 5 August 1900, *Chekhov i teatr*, p. 113.
4. Letter of 28 September 1900, ibid., p. 116.

5. I. Vinogradskaya, *Zhizn' i tvorchestvo K. S. Stanislavskogo – letopis'*, 4 vols, vol. 1: *1863–1905* (Moscow, 1971) p. 306.
6. Letter of 24 November 1899, *Chekhov i teatr*, p. 108.
7. N. Efros, *'Tri sestry': P'esa A. P. Chekhova v postanovke Moskovskogo Khudozhestvennogo Teatra* (Petrograd, 1919) p. 8.
8. The theatre building hired from the entrepreneur Yakov Shchukin in 1898 where the company acted until the beginning of 1902. They moved to new, permanent premises on Kamergersky Lane later that year.
9. Efros, p. 8.
10. Ibid.
11. 'nastroyeniye, govoryat, ubiystvennoye' (letter of 13 November 1900, *Chekhov i teatr*, p. 117).
12. I. N. Solov'eva (ed.), *Rezhisserskiye ekzemplyary K. S. Stanislavskogo, 1898–1930*, 6 vols, vol. 3: *1901–4, P'esy A. P. Chekhova 'Tri sestry', 'Vishnevyy sad'* (Moscow, 1983) p. 20.
13. *'The Seagull' Produced by Stanislavsky*, Production Score for the Moscow Art Theatre, edited and with an Introduction by Professor S. D. Balukhaty, translated by David Magarshack (London, 1952). This is one of only two of Stanislavsky's production scores available to date in English translation, the other being of *Othello* (1930).
14. Letter of 13 December 1900, *Chekhov i teatr*, p. 338.
15. Konstantin Stanislavsky, *My Life in Art* (Moscow, n.d.) pp. 278–80. This book is published in English.
16. Ibid., p. 280.
17. Vinogradskaya, p. 323.
18. His assistant director was V. V. Luzhsky, who also acted the part of the sisters' brother, Andrey.
19. Letter of 9 January 1901, *Chekhov i teatr*, p. 283.
20. At this stage there were still three monologues instead of just the one spoken by Olga. Stanislavsky's feelings about the finale were communicated in greater detail to Chekhov by Knipper in a letter of 13 January 1901. He replied to Stanislavsky's letter on 15 January.
21. Letter to Chekhov dated 11 January 1901, *Chekhov i teatr*, p. 339.
22. Letter of 17 January 1901, ibid., p. 120.
23. *Rezhisserskiye ekzemplyary K. S. Stanislavskogo*, vol. 3, p. 48.
24. Letter of 21 January 1901, *Chekhov i teatr*, pp. 120–1.
25. Letter to Chekhov dated 22 January 1901, ibid., p. 323.
26. Letter to Knipper of 20 January 1901, ibid., p. 120.
27. Knipper's letter to Chekhov dated 13 January 1901, ibid., p. 339.
28. Letter to Chekhov of 26 January 1901, ibid., pp. 340–1. The scene is not so elaborately sketched in the promptbook.
29. *Rezhisserskiye ekzemplyary K. S. Stanislavskogo*, vol. 3, p. 330.
30. Letter to Chekhov of 19 December 1902, *Chekhov i teatr*, p. 362.
31. Efros, p. 16.
32. Stanislavsky continued to act the role of Vershinin until 1928, although less frequently after the Revolution. He acted in an extract from the play staged for a jubilee performance on the occasion of the thirtieth anniversary in 1928, when he suffered a heart attack which led to his permanent retirement as an actor, although not as a director.

33. Efros, pp. 47–8.
34. Most of the extant photographs of moments of action in the 1901 production (as opposed to stills of individual characters photographed in a studio) were taken in 1914, and so, with a few exceptions (Stanislavsky, Knipper, Vishnevsky), the cast depicted in these photographs is not the original one.
35. Letter to L. Sulerzhitsky of 5 November 1902, *Chekhov i teatr*, p. 137.
36. Chekhov had said as much in a letter to Gorky of 16 October 1900: 'The action takes place in a provincial town, like Perm, in a military, artillery milieu' (*Chekhov i teatr*, pp. 116–17).
37. Yu. I. Nekhoroshev, *Dekorator Khudozhestvennogo Teatra Viktor Andreyevich Simov* (Moscow, 1984) p. 71.
38. Anton Chekhov, *Plays*, translated by Elizaveta Fen (Harmondsworth, Middx, 1954) p. 249.
39. *Rezhisserskiye ekzemplyary K. S. Stanislavskogo*, vol. 3, p. 7.
40. Elena Polyakova, *Stanislavsky* (Moscow, 1982) pp. 122–3. This book is published in English.
41. V. V. Luzhskiy, 'Iz vospominaniy', *Chekhov i teatr*, p. 353.
42. M. Stroyeva, *Chekhov i Khudozhestvennyy Teatr* (Moscow, 1955) pp. 113–15. An abridged translation of the article on *Three Sisters* which later became a chapter in Stroyeva's book appears as 'The Three Sisters in the Production of the Moscow Art Theater', in Robert Louis Jackson (ed.), *Chekhov: A Collection of Critical Essays* (Englewood Cliffs, NJ, 1967) pp. 121–35; also as 'The Three Sisters at the MAT', in Erika Munk (ed.), *Stanislavski in America: An Anthology from the Tulane Drama Review* (New York, 1966) pp. 45–59.
43. *Rezhisserskiye ekzemplyary K. S. Stanislavskogo*, vol. 3, p. 23.
44. Petr Yartsev, 'Tri sestry', *Teatr i iskusstvo*, no. 8 (1901), cited in Stroyeva, p. 149.
45. 'James Lynch' (Leonid Andreyev), 'Tri sestry', *Kur'yer*, no. 291 (21 October 1901), cited in Nekhoroshev, pp. 75–6.
46. *Rezhisserskiye ekzemplyary K. S. Stanislavskogo*, vol. 3, p. 89. Henceforth, where two numbers appear in the text separated by a stroke (/), the first refers to the relevant page of the production score in *Rezhisserskiye ekzemplyary*, the second to the corresponding page of the dramatic text in Chekhov, *Plays*, tr. Fen. Numbers on their own simply refer to the relevant page in the production score.
47. Earliest photographs of Ferapont show him wearing a rough, plain-coloured cloth around his head. By 1914 this has been exchanged for what looks like a woman's polka-dot silk scarf, with its added sense of incongruity.
48. Ye. Polyakova, *Stanislavskiy – akter* (Moscow, 1972) p. 165.
49. Olga Knipper-Chekhova, 'Man and Actor', in S. Melik-Zakharov and S. Bogatyrev (eds), *K. Stanislavsky, 1863–1963* (Moscow, 1963) p. 89. This book is published in English. There appears to have been little sympathy for Vershinin's wife in this production or for the sense that the 'love-sick' major might be something of a philanderer and his wife's repeated suicide attempts pleas for attention.
50. B. Izrailevskiy, *Muzyka v spektaklyakh MKhAT*, *Zapisi dirizhera* (Moscow, 1965) p. 66.

51. *Rezhisserskie ekzemplyary K. S. Stanislavskogo*, vol. 3, p. 48.
52. Ibid., p. 49.
53. Staged by the Art Theatre in 1899, directors Stanislavsky and Nemirovich-Danchenko, designer Simov.
54. The famous photograph of the finale to Act 4 shows the sisters grouped beneath this street lamp. In fact, the lamp features in nearly all the photographs of Act 4 and can, invariably, be seen to be lit. As the action takes place soon after mid-day and not towards dusk, the lamp must have served simply to localise and intensify light for the photographer and the photographs need not, therefore, be totally accurate guides to where the actors were actually placed on stage. However, it seems clear from the production score that at the end the three sisters are positioned on stage precisely where they appear in the photograph.
55. Letter of 14 January 1901, *Chekhov i teatr*, p. 119.
56. Izrailevskiy, pp. 66–7.
57. *K. Stanislavsky, 1863–1963*, pp. 89–90.
58. Harvey Pitcher, *Chekhov's Leading Lady* (London, 1979) p. 193.
59. Cited in Stroyeva, p. 145.
60. Efros, pp. 62–3.
61. Ibid., pp. 63–4.
62. Izrailevskiy, pp. 66–7.
63. Kulygin's entry in Stanislavsky's score is placed later than in Chekhov's text. Chekhov's direction runs: 'The music grows fainter and fainter. Kulygin, smiling happily, brings out the hat and cape [which Masha has asked for earlier]. Andrey enters; he is pushing the pram with Bobik sitting in it.' Chebutykin then 'sings gently to himself' Tararaboomdiay etc. and reads the newspaper. His next line, 'What does it matter? Nothing matters!' ('*Vse ravno! Vse ravno!*') was added by Chekhov to the revised version of the play but is missing from the text which Stanislavsky used.
64. Letter to S. V. Sredin of 24 September 1901, *Chekhov i teatr*, p. 124.
65. Efros, p. 18.
66. Stroyeva, p. 149.
67. Ibid.
68. L. Ye. Obolenskiy, writing in the liberal newspaper *Rossiya*, 19 March 1901, cited in *Rezhisserskiye ekzemplyary K. S. Stanislavskogo*, vol. 3, p. 39.
69. Stroyeva, pp. 142–3.
70. Efros, p. 38.
71. Letter from A. Krasnov to Stanislavsky of 2 March 1901, cited in Polyakova, pp. 395–6.
72. Nekhoroshev, pp. 75–6.

# 2

# Boris Geyer and Cabaretic Playwriting

## LAURENCE SENELICK

*'Does this sort of thing appeal to you?' she asked the young Russian, nodding towards the gay scrimmage of masqueraders and rather prepared to hear an amused negative.*

*'But yes, of course,' he answered; 'costume balls, fancy fairs, café chantant, casino, anything that is not real life appeals to us Russians. Real life with us is the sort of thing Maxim Gorki deals in. It interests us immensely, but we like to get away from it sometimes.'*

'Saki', *The Unbearable Bassington* (1913), Ch. 15

I

In the theatre, time is the most elastic of dimensions. Or, as Dr Johnson put it when defending Shakespeare for not following the dramatic unities, 'Time is, of all modes of existence, most obsequious to the imagination.'[1] Not only are we, the spectators, capable of imagining a prolonged passage of time taking place in a few moments, but the actual temporal length of the performance fluctuates in our perception, depending on the intensity of our interest or boredom.

The critical confusion of these two notions of dramatic time – the time represented as passing within a play's action, and the duration actually spent in the theatre – has persisted ever since Europe rediscovered Aristotle's *Poetics*. Aristotle had suggested that a proper tragedy ought not to extend beyond the confines of a single day, 'only as long as memory could embrace'; commentators then puzzled over whether he meant that the plot or the performance was to be limited by twenty-four hours. Meanwhile, playwrights themselves began to develop rules of thumb concerning the length of pieces, and by the end of the seventeenth century, that great age of dramatic legislation, the established hierarchy of genres indicated what was believed to be the correct span of a play. Act divisions, which hitherto had been mere formal adoptions from Latin models, now became strict denominators of a genre's prestige. The length of an act itself might be determined by such pragmatic considerations as how long it took the candles illuminating the *salle* to burn down before needing replacement, but the length of a play was tailored to theoretical measurements. Five acts were set down as the correct length for a tragedy or a verse comedy (anything longer was thought shapeless and barbaric), three acts for a prose comedy, and a single act for such lesser modes as farces, interludes and musical pantomimes. These not-entirely-arbitrary conventions derived from the sense that 'more is more': that the gravity and weight of a tragic theme required an elaborated structure whereas a comic anecdote could and should be told in brief space.

The equation of size with significance has persisted in the theatre well into our own times. The nineteenth century had a penchant for the grandiose: it espoused as congenial Wagner's concept of *Gesamtkunstwerk*. Once the epic scope and titanic ambitions of his music-dramas won entitlement to stretch beyond the normal bounds of audience attention-spans, even bedroom farces burgeoned into three and four acts. Meanwhile, the one-act play was relegated to curtain-raisers and afterpieces, the appetisers and desserts of the dramatic banquet. Chiefly comic, such playlets might be wrought into exquisite cameos and intaglios by Labiche, Planché and Chekhov; but their temporal slightness bespoke their insignificance. The lyrical one-act 'dramatic étude' or *proverbe* perfected by poetic talents such as Pushkin, Turgenev and Alfred de Musset were seldom staged in their lifetimes.

By the end of the century, although ornate genre painting, grand opera and the three-decker novel persisted, a high-spirited revolt against grandiosity was fermenting in most of the arts: painters rebelled against the vast canvases of the academies, composers turned to chamber music, poets to such minor forms as the villanelle and the sonatina, prose writers to the perfecting of the anecdote and the *conte*. In the theatre, the ennoblement of the one-act play was a product of the naturalistic school. The playwrights featured at André Antoine's Théâtre Libre in Paris claimed they were presenting 'slices of life', best exposed in short, striking format; these *comédies rosses* (literally, red-headed comedies, but implying malice and nastiness) or *quarts d'heure* (though they lasted well beyond fifteen minutes) were meant to hit the spectator in the gut and leave him reeling. A short jab was more effective than a prolonged bout. No wonder the naturalists' most enduring offshoot was the Grand Guignol, which could pack a melodrama of acid-burns, gouged eyes and lunacy into an hysterical forty-five minutes, the brevity contributing to stomach-churning effect.[2]

Antoine's playwrights did not make a theoretical tenet of length; this was left to the young August Strindberg, who, in the early 1880s, was eager to be thought a naturalist. In his now-famous preface to *Miss Julie* ('Fröken Julie', 1888), he justified the elimination of act-divisions in a play lasting one-and-a-half hours, declaring that

> our decreasing capacity for illusion might be disturbed by intermissions, during which the theatregoer would have time to engage in reflection and thereby escape the author-mesmerizer's suggestive influence. . . . My hope is that we may some day have audiences so educated that they will sit through a whole evening's performance of a play consisting only in one act.[3]

Strindberg's characteristic fear that an intermission would break the spell cast by the playwright was shortly and implicitly to become an operative principle for symbolist dramatists, whose vogue succeeded that of the naturalists. In the plays of Maeterlinck and his epigones, dramatic conflict was replaced by atmospherics of tension and suggestion, which could best be sustained over a short haul. *L'Intruse* in one act, for instance, is much more successful in realising its aesthetic programme than is *Pelléas et Mélisande* in five.

The increasing taste for reduced forms was also indulged by the emergent *cabaret artistique*. These haunts had begun as gathering places for poets and humorists who would read their latest productions to one another; success and publicity brought a wider popularity, and by the 1890s a more diverse public was flocking to such cabarets as the Chat Noir in Montmartre. To amuse this heterogeneous crowd of bohemians, middle-class pleasure-seekers and tourists, more elaborate entertainments, including the shadow play and the literary parody, were fashioned. The cabaret offered the low-brow attractions of diversified, rapidly alternating acts, eating, drinking, smoking and good fellowship, along with the more elevated allure of rubbing elbows with avant-gardism, if only in a diluted form. In Paris, the cabaret's founding geniuses were men of letters who wrought the *chanson* into a terse and sardonic art-form; in Berlin and Munich, the promulgators often included actors and directors, so that the offerings tended to run to one-act plays, exploiting an in-crowd's knowledge of the latest trend in staging or playwriting. The one-act thus became a vehicle for comic attacks on innovation and convention in the arts and occasionally in social life (censorship prevented the pre-war cabaret from being political in any explicit way, although its sympathies were libertarian, not to say anarchic). The terse and gaudy cabaret one-act needed to evolve innovative forms to convey its satiric message with as much impact as possible.

## II

Cabaret in Russia followed the German, rather than the French, model by originating in a theatrical milieu, and, from its inception, the term *cabaret* was seldom used. To Russian ears, it bore a connotation of European, sexually-tinged frivolity, more black-guard than avant-garde. After the Revolution, the constructivist director Nikolay Foregger would condemn *cabaret* as 'a filthy, petty art, the imperialo-capitalist, decadent and bourgeois product of a fading Europe, shoddy craftwork which sins against Faith, Hope, Charity and their common mother, Wisdom',[4] a statement which, pared of its Bolshevik jargon, might characterise the cultivated Russian's attitude in Tsarist times as well. The Germans denominated lesser types of artistic activity in the performing arts as *Kleinkunst* or minor art. The diminutive seems to be echoed in the accepted Russian terms *teatr miniatyur* ('theatre of miniatures') and *teatr malykh form* ('theatre of small forms') which evoke the legitimate stage rather than the tavern, and imply a succession of carefully-burnished gems.[5]

With the most important and influential Russian cabaret, *Krivoye Zerkalo* or 'Crooked Mirror' (more precisely, 'Distorting Mirror'), founded in St Petersburg in 1908 as a theatrical club, *nomen est omen*. Art and particularly the theatre were to be refracted by a funhouse glass; throughout its long career, it never altered its emphasis on parody.[6] Other miniature theatres, such as *Letuchaya*

*Mysh'*, or 'Bat', in Moscow, relied on a witty master of ceremonies, solo numbers, song and dance, recitations enlivened by the occasional skit or decorative tableau. The Mirror differed from its counterparts by specialising in the one-act play.

For some years the nominal proprietor was Zinaida Kholmskaya, a buxom actress from the Maly Theatre who made a speciality of *grandes dames* and battle-axes; a sort of cognisant Margaret Dumont, she played even the greatest absurdities in deadly earnest, thereby enhancing their comic quotient. But the brains behind the Crooked Mirror was her husband Aleksandr Rafailovich Kugel', a critic and editor of *Teatr i iskusstvo* ('Theatre and Art'), whose tastes and prejudices predominated. Kugel', although obsessed with theatre, distrusted artistic extremes and found both naturalism and symbolism inimical to the basic nature of theatre; he also deplored the growing primacy of the director in the theatrical process. Because of his connections in the literary world, Kugel''s roster of writers included outstanding humorists, *feuilletonists* and dramatists, but, as Kholmskaya recalled, the first contributions were 'written in an old, stereotyped form of the standard vaudevilles, farces and revues, whereas I envisaged a theatre of new forms'.[7] The Mirror's first real success came with Mikhail Volkonsky and Vladimir Erenberg's nonsensical *Vampuka or The Bride of Africa* ('Vampuka ili Afrikanskaya nevesta'), which was not so much a spoof of *Aïda* or *L'Africaine* as an exposé of grand operatic clichés and overblown 'Verdism'. Kugel' disdained parody that was too specific and topical; his later boast was to be that the Crooked Mirror had discovered a new dramatic form, a theatrical 'theory of relativity', expanding and exploiting the one-act's potential by playing variations on a single theme. It was the Mirror's unique and influential contribution to the theatre of its time, and both Kholmskaya and Kugel' attributed it and most of the innovations to Boris Geyer,[8] whose career, unlike those of the Mirror's more illustrious participants, Leonid Andreyev, Fedor Sologub and Nikolay Yevreinov, was played out entirely within the confines of the miniature.

Boris Fedorovich Geyer, sprung from a family of Russified Germans, was a lesser journalist associated with the liberal humour magazine *Novyy Satirikon*; at the time he joined the Crooked Mirror, attracted by the chance to strike out in new directions, he was virtually unknown in the theatre world. He was soon made a member of its exclusive literary council, whose other members were Kugel' and Lev Urvantsov.[9] A photograph in the archives of the Bakhrushin Museum in Moscow shows a short, bald, moustachioed man in pince-nez, with a pretty wife, enjoying himself at a champagne luncheon; it is a graphic depiction of his happy-go-lucky, bohemian way of life and what Kugel' called his 'Mozartian' insouciance.

Geyer's earliest efforts for the Crooked Mirror, *In the Gloaming of the Dawn* ('V sumerkakh rassveta', written 1907), *Snout and Love* ('Morda i lyubov'') and *The Idea and Katerina Ivanovna* ('Mysl' i Katerina Ivanovna') were parodies, primarily of his colleague Andreyev and of the Moscow Art Theatre's misguided stabs at staging symbolist drama. He also contributed to other theatres: the St Petersburg Society for Art and Literature put on his *Mystery of the Sun* ('Tayna solntsa'). This one-act 'legend' is uncharacteristic of him both in its setting – the court of a Pharaoh in 300 B.C. – and its message – the power of true love to overcome adversity and a plague of darkness. The Geyerian touch comes only at the very end, when, as *amor vincit omnes*, the aged Pharaoh sighs, 'In a single moment I have endured an eternity. I have discovered what had been hidden from me. . . . [*Sadly*] The sun is shining. . . . But darkness still reigns in my soul.'[10]

For Geyer's basic world-view is a profound pessimism, expressed with cynical flippancy. This is baldly manifested in a one-act *sharzh* (caricature) which may never have been performed, but was published by *Teatr i iskusstvo* in 1912. (By that time miniature theatres had become so popular that theatre magazines carried dozens of advertisements for collections of one-act plays intended for small stages.) *Chameleons* ('Khameleony') paints an unrelieved portrait of meanness and hypocrisy. In the parlour of a government dignitary, he, his family, petitioners, clerks and private secretary act obsequious or insolent, apologetic or overbearing, ingratiating or despotic, depending on the given circumstances and the social status of the persons involved. Owing to a misunderstanding over a love-letter sent by the dignitary to his mistress, the secretary manages to engineer a marriage with his superior's daughter, although she knows he is an ambitious climber and he knows she is a heartless flirt. By the final curtain, all the characters are well aware of the deceptions pulled, but they work together to maintain the masks they have donned. The play's last line is the dignitary's, 'Isn't life wonderful when everyone has an open conscience'.[11]

At first glance, this one-act seems to be well situated in the tradition of Russian comedy. The last scene of Ostrovsky's *Too*

*Clever by Half* ('Na vsyakogo mudretsa dovol'no prostoty') in which dupes conspire to uphold the man who duped them; the curtain-speech in Saltykov-Shchedrin's *Pazukhin's Death* ('Smert' Pazukhina') with its concluding line, 'Vice is punished, and virtue – where the hell is virtue anyway?'; the crueller moments of Sukhovo-Kobylin's trilogy – all come to mind. These savage satires, after neglect and suppression by the censorship, were finally being revealed to audiences: the Ostrovsky and the Shchedrin enjoyed successful revivals by the Moscow Art Theatre (1910, 1914), and Sukhovo-Kobylin's *Tarelkin's Death* had been staged by the same Petersburg Society of Art and Literature in 1900. Geyer could also draw from a long line of Russian literary hypocrites, including Shchedrin's Yudushka Golovev and Dostoyevsky's Foma Opiskin.

But these earlier plays are essentially old-fashioned *comédies de caractère*; the characters' duplicity is a static given, to be exfoliated in the course of the intrigue. Geyer's methods, however, derive from the debate over the problem of dramatic 'characterisation' initiated by the naturalistic school. The French psychologist Ribot had defined personality as a constantly shifting coalition of conscious states, and the wide acceptance of this description caused many to despair of expressing the complexity of personality in drama. Edmond de Goncourt looked to the novel for salvation: 'What is the value of our characters without psychological development, and in the theatre there is none and can be none!'[12] Rather than abandon the drama, Strindberg hypothesised the *agon* of 'characterless characters', individuals constantly shifting personae in the ceaseless battle for supremacy in human relations; he underpinned this notion with pseudo-biological claims. Gerhart Hauptmann postulated an ongoing internal contention among the multiple selves into whom the ego is subdivided; this view of human self-consciousness was primarily psychological.

Geyer inherits these ideas of the multifariousness of the personality; his cast of 'chameleons' shift their shapes at every encounter to accommodate the shape-changing of their interlocutors. But, as heir to the tradition of Russian stage satire as well, he insists on the social context. Rather than heredity or environment, sex wars or biological urges, rank, station and ambition are what impel the rapid transformations of character, and at the bottom of every seemingly generous or unselfish action there is inevitably an egoistic motive. So the *reductio ad absurdum* of Geyer's parodies always strips human aspiration down to its basest, most despicable mainsprings. Kugel' was later to attribute the Crooked Mirror's 'negation and scepticism' to the profound depression that washed over the Russian intelligentsia during the reaction following the abortive revolution and reforms of 1905–8.[13] But Geyer's cynicism seems deeper-dyed than that of most of Kugel''s crew. In an earthier manner, his skits perpetuate the disillusionment of Aleksandr Blok's lyrical one-acts *The Little Showbooth* ('Balaganchik', 1906) and *Incognita* ('Neznakomka', 1906–7).

Blok's *Showbooth* had debunked the mystical trends in contemporary theatre. Typically, in Geyer's first Crooked Mirror play to cause comment, *The Evolution of the Theatre* ('Evolyutsiya teatra', première: 20 January 1910), the principal target of his satire was also the modernist debate over 'the crisis in the theatre'. The title proclaims an attack on Sergey Rafalovich's essay, 'The Evolution of the Theatre', which two years earlier had appeared as the initial piece in a volume of manifestos by Meyerhold, Sologub, Bryusov, Bely and other symbolist ideologues, *'Teatr' kniga o novom teatre* ("'Theatre'' a book about the modern theatre'). Rafalovich's contribution comprised a potted history of the theatre, in which, like the book's other contributors, he spoke of the degeneration from its Greek religious origins and the need for a new synthesis of dance and song to invigorate it. In his view a crucial turning-point had been reached: the old theatre was dead, and the theatre of the future would have to be international, religious or mystical, with no distinction between the passive spectator and the active performer. The only Russians he cited in his survey were Meyerhold and the actress-manageress Vera Kommissar-zhevskaya, whose experiments in two-dimensional staging and hieratic acting he judged to be imperfect but admirable in motive.[14]

Geyer reduced this fashionable attitude to absurdity by bringing it down to cases. A lecturer – a common device at the Crooked Mirror to cover scene changes and to substitute for the *compère* or master of ceremonies, standard at other cabarets – explains the series of scenes to follow as object lessons in 'where the theatre is headed, how far it has progressed over the ages, how we have made the transition from coarse, primitive and unintelligible forms to the depiction of the most subtle psychic experiences, the most refined symbols, total intelligibility and profound thought'.[15] There ensue four versions of a banal triangular relationship presented as it might have been handled by Gogol, Ostrovsky, Chekhov and

Andreyev (the last was particularly topical since the evening's bill began with a play by Andreyev).

This kaleidoscopic approach was not original. The earliest use of such 'variations on a theme' seems to have been concocted by Max Reinhardt and associates as the initial offering when his Berlin cabaret *Schall und Rauch* ('Noise and Smoke') opened in 1901. Reinhardt presented a tabloid version of Schiller's *Don Carlos* in these varieties: *Don Carlos or The Infante of Spain or The Unnatural Son*, improvised and mangled *auf der Schmiere* (that is, by provincial barnstormers); *Karle* ('Charlie'), a thieves' kitchen comedy in the style of Gerhart Hauptmann; and *Carléas und Élisande*, a 'Gobelinesque' by 'Ysidore Mysterlinck'. This last was introduced by a certain 'Samuèle Rindérer, Mysterlinck specialist and biographer, president of the Mysterlinck Society', whose lecture disintegrates into Maeterlinckian repetition and incoherence. That same year, at the Berlin cabaret *Die Böse Buben* ('The Bad Boys'), Rudolf Bernauer revealed the winning entries in an ostensible competition to renovate the last scene of Ibsen's *Doll's House*: Frank Wedekind, again Maeterlinck (possibly the most parodied dramatist of the *fin de siècle*), and the bombastic, chauvinistic Josef Lauff, said to be the Kaiser's favourite playwright.[16]

But if Geyer was not the originator of the form, he was a deft manipulator of it. The Gogol parody was perhaps the least pointed, for it stuck to popular conceptions of Gogol's style without ever capturing his true alogic and fantasy. On the other hand, the spoof Ostrovsky and Chekhov were triumphs because they carefully observed and imitated the pet devices of those playwrights.[17] *Petrov*, the Chekhovian pastiche, was a keen but affectionate intercutting of lines, situations and attitudes from the four major plays, spliced to create an hilarious exposure of lyrical vagary.

> LIDIYA PETROVNA.   All last night the old lindens were rustling in the garden . . . the old lindens . . . That have seen so many tears and sorrows . . . When we moved here, it seemed to me that we had been buried in a grave . . . a grave . . . Moscow . . . Oh, if only I might see Moscow once again . . . [*Sits, burying her head in her hands.*] *Moskva . . . Moskve . . . Moskvoy . . .*[18]

Reducing the three sisters' recurrent plaint to grammatical declensions is a masterful use of bathos.

The Andreyev episode was as much a lampoon of the Art

Theatre's production of *Anathema* as it was of Andreyev himself, with 'Someone in Grey' from *The Life of Man* added for good measure. This progression from the highly-coloured farce of Gogol to the obscure wool-gathering of Andreyev made hash of the modernists' claims that a mystical theatre would naturally evolve into the perfection of the drama. Etiolation was not to be read as consummation.[19]

Part of Geyer's audacity was in taking on cultural icons: the Art Theatre production of *Anathema* had gained prestige by being banned, and Chekhov, a mere six years after his death, had already assumed a halo of sanctity. Contemporaries were shocked that Geyer should poke fun at a recently deceased writer whose jubilee had just been celebrated; one reviewer, while admitting that that skit enjoyed great success with the 'numerous public', deplored its 'coarse, malicious' mockery of Chekhov 'who is least deserving of mockery. He wrote sincerely and if his heroes (Ivanov, Three Sisters, Uncle Vanya, Gayev) are humdrum, they are still a sign of the times'.[20] We hear an early devotee of the cult of St Anton that would become endemic in the West.

Geyer's next endeavour was equally hilarious, but much less timely: *A Cossack's Love* ('L'Amour d'un cosac' or 'Lyubov' kazaka', première: 26 April 1910), 'a sensational French drama of the life of Russian farmers', made fun of French authors' claims to be conversant with Russian life. Ever since Alexandre Dumas wrote of riding in troikas drawn by bears and sitting in the shade of the notorious spreading cranberry-bush, French expertise about Russia was a subject for ridicule. The play opened with Pietro Kudilishny, a rich Russian landowner, dressed in a Persian dressing-gown, sitting before an immense samovar, drinking *tchay*, *tchas* and vodka, and adding to every statement *'Taiya, taiya'* (the *taye* that tongue-tied Akim keeps uttering in Tolstoy's *Power of Darkness*). His daughter Aksenka (pronounced by the cast with the accent on the last syllable) was played as an artificial French *ingénue*. As for the Cossack himself, Prokofio Nikitishnovo, he wielded a cat-o'-nine-tails, wore an enormous fur-hat and crossed himself after every statement. The characters greeted one another by clinking coloured Easter eggs and exclaiming, 'A wheaten-crust pea-pie in your mouth', which the French playwright explains to his manager is 'the famous Russian bon-jour'.[21] (In the same Tolstoy play, *'V rot tebe sitnogo piroga s gorokhom'* is a frequent imprecation cast by the workman Mitrich at evil-doers.)

The direct target for this satire may have been Antoine's production of *La Puissance des ténèbres* at the Théâtre Libre in 1888, but there was certainly no urgent relevance to it. Critics with a political bias were already complaining that the Crooked Mirror catered too much to a theatrical in-crowd, while it stood aloof from grimy reality. The leftist humorist Vatslav Vorovsky, reviewing the theatre's tour to Odessa in 1909, had noted that the theatre's repertory clearly bespoke a 'shrinking from, a "non-acceptance" of the hustle and bustle of everyday life [which] suggests it is in danger of degenerating into an in-joke society for *littérateurs* and performers'.[22] But the many Soviet historians who dutifully trot out that quotation fail to cite Vorovsky's further observation that the Russian general public was not mature enough for subtle satire (many provincial spectators took *Vampuka* to be a genuine effort at grand opera), and that, in all likelihood, for the sake of the box-office the Crooked Mirror would have to follow the trend of European cabarets and turn into a mere *café-chantant*. This was in fact the case with some of the Mirror's competitors: the Liteyny teatr, which had begun as grand guignol, switched to operetta and recitations by 1910, and by 1912 the Troitsky teatr, best known for the clever sets of Ya. S. Shkol'nik, was showing silent films between the acts.

That the Crooked Mirror, after two successful seasons, avoided these fates is due to three factors. The first was Kugel''s artistic puritanism, the second was the Mirror's special audience in the capitals. From the 1870s, a new theatre public had developed, which was educated, well-read, politically progressive, economically comfortable, and interested in artistic trends; private stages and amateur dramatic societies had proliferated in the wake of the 1882 cancellation of the imperial monopoly on theatres in the capitals. The limited size and intimacy of the cabaret had snob appeal for those who wanted to be 'insiders' in the glamorous yet alien world of actors and journalists, and who prided themselves on being *au courant* with the latest backstage gossip and cultural book-chat. It was the same left-leaning, right-thinking audience of students and professionals that attended, in Moscow, the Art Theatre, its competitor Nezlobin's, and its offshoot, the Independent (*Svobodny*), and, in Petersburg, Vera Kommissarzhevskaya's theatre on Officer Street, the Theatre in the Passage, and the Liberated (*Vol'ny*) Theatre, all of them respectably 'advanced' in their programmes. This relatively homogeneous community, whose members shared tastes and background, could be expected to catch hints and allusions to the latest thing in the art world. It was also demanding, with a voracious appetite for novelty.

The third factor in the Mirror's survival was the annexation in October 1910 of Nikolay Yevreinov as artistic director and member of its literary council, which answered critics like Vorovsky in an unexpected manner. With an idiosyncratic aesthetic agenda of his own, Yevreinov kept the Mirror's comic, apolitical dragnet spread over all forms of theatrical extremism and vulgarity as before, but his strong opinions about the 'intimisation of theatre' and its interrelationship with life promoted the repertoire's wider application to human behaviour and social institutions. His philosophic outlook, along with his sophistication as a director (he fed the troupe with actors from his own defunct 'Merry Theatre for Middle-aged Children') turned the Crooked Mirror from a night-club into a distinctively experimental theatre, thus enabling Geyer to venture more boldly into 'new forms'.[23]

It was with his next contribution that Geyer's pessimism surfaced without disguise, possibly in response to Yevreinov's wish to reflect real life in the Mirror's distorting lens. *The Components of Life* ('Elementy zhizni', première: 12 December 1910, in the fourth programme supervised by Yevreinov) was a *Bildungsstück*, in which a young man, a latter-day Candide, sets out on his journey of discovery. Perhaps with a mocking side-glance at Vorovsky's accusation that the Crooked Mirror had 'shrunk from' life, the youth explains to an aged sage: 'I am stepping into life. . . . I will learn its components. . . . I will not shrink from grief nor joy, hard labour nor idle recreation, nor youthful, beautiful, open and triumphant love.'[24] In short order, he runs up against surrogates of these abstract qualities. Joy turns out to be a synonym for *Schadenfreude*, a writer's glee at the failure of his friend's play. Leisure dwindles into a drunken brawl in a low tavern. Love is an encounter with a prostitute, hatred – petty rage directed against a tailor who forgot to sew on a button. At the end, the youth returns to the old man who points the moral: 'Remember this great truth, elaborated over the centuries: spit on everything and look out for your health!' One reviewer noted it was as if Andreyev's *Life of Man* with its message of indomitable human dignity in the face of ineluctable mortality had been turned inside out before being refracted in the Crooked Mirror.[25]

Not for the first time Geyer was congratulated on compressing a vast and original idea into a very compact space, even though there were complaints of the 'anecdotal' nature of some of the episodes. 'Anecdote' was a term of abuse among those critics who wished the theatre of miniatures to soar above the common *shutka* or one-act farce, and the literary quality of the Mirror's plays was carefully scrutinised.

Geyer's next effort was less innovative. *Cinema or The Innocent Victim of Mad Passion and an Old Man's Bloodthirsty Love* ('Kinemato-graf ili nevinnaya zhertva bezumnoy strasti i krovavaya lyubov' starika', première: 8 February 1911) was a straightforward satire of a 'powerfully dramatic drama 11764 metres long in coloured colours with natural nature and dialogues'. The novelty here lay in the staging: the actors performed in jerky, angular movements, abetted by an intermittent lighting fifty years before strobe effects became normal for this kind of parody. A title-reader stood to one side, melancholically ending each explication with the call to the projectionist, 'Mishka, keep cranking!' Of course, it ended in a chase, which proved to be so popular that Yevreinov revived it later as the final episode in his *Government Inspector*.[26]

### III

When the Crooked Mirror's next season opened, it was clear that Geyer was responding to Yevreinov's new proponency of the monodrama. Yevreinov's celebrated 'Introduction to Monodrama' was published as a pamphlet in 1908 and read as a public lecture three times by March 1909. A great deal of heavy weather has been made of this concept, partly because Yevreinov kept up an elaborate fan-dance of erudite citation, convoluted syntax and wide-ranging allusion to shroud an essentially simple idea. The audience is to identify and empathise with only one character on stage, the *deystvuyushcheye litso* or active participant. Everything in a play is to be staged from that character's point of view, and all scenic means are to be bent to portray his state of mine at any given moment. If the presentation is successful, the spectator will undergo a co-experience (*soperezhivaniye*) with the protagonist, and the divisive split between stage and auditorium will be obliterated. This last point approximated Yevreinov to the symbolist notion of a communal desideratum for the theatre.[27]

The first monodrama on the stage of the Crooked Mirror was

not by Yevreinov, as it turned out, but by Geyer.[28] Yevreinov had written what he touted as the first true example of monodrama in 1910: *A Show of Love* ('Predstavleniye lyubvi', with *predstavleniye* here meaning 'declaration', 'performance' and 'representation'), the elegaic reminiscence of a lost love by an aged man (a subject Samuel Beckett would later handle more economically in *Krapp's Last Tape*, thanks to the technical innovation of the tape recorder). Despite Yevreinov's assertion that the play occasioned the theory, *A Show of Love* tries so hard to illustrate his thesis that it succeeds as drama only when it introduces the pathetic fallacy as a novel stage technique. As Yevreinov's protagonist idealises the past, the lights go up at his sweetheart's arrival, the stage darkens at the entrance of his rival, and dims when he despairs; the appearances of characters similarly alter in extreme form depending on the mood of the remembrancer.

*A Show of Love* was never produced in Russia, but Geyer probably read it on its publication in the almanac *Studiya impressionistov*. His own *Aqua Vitae* ('Voda zhizni', première: 18 September 1911), which comes across as a subversion of Yevreinov's *Show*, presented not the world-view of a single protagonist but, rather more ambitiously, the changing perspective of a room full of people. It led Kugel' to wonder if 'polydrama' might not be a better name for such a play. The scene is a cheap basement-level restaurant, whose barman sets out the play's programme in his instructions to a new waiter:

BARMAN.     This ain't no cruddy little inn where we're working, this is a restaurant. Know what I mean?
AFANASY.     Right you are, sir. A restaurant, in short, of the first class sort, sir.
BARMAN.     Yes and they better behave nice and quiet here. And I ain't talking about breaking crockery, you also gotta keep an eye on the customers' morials. [. . .] If it's a guy you don't know, you gotta make sure he don't go past a certain point. Let him get tanked up to that point and then ease off . . . But I mean without making no trouble. [. . .] Now in figuring out how drunk each guy is, there's a system. At first they'll talk about their family, the kids and their relatives, so you can give 'em whatever they order. Next they start talking about the office and complain about their bosses – no problem, go ahead. Next they start arguing about politics and swapping dirty

jokes, that's when you start easing off. Give 'em what they ask for, but don't rush. Know what I mean?

AFANASY.   I get the point.

BARMAN.   Now, when they start in talking about God and philosophy and all that – that's when you stop. One more shot and that's it. And if you follow my rules, you'll never have no trouble.[29]

From this point on, the play is divided into 'four carafes'; as each carafe is drunk, the customers – among them some civil servants, a bank clerk, two German sausage-makers and a couple of unaccompanied girls – pass through the stages of inebriation catalogued by the barman. This in itself is unexceptional; what distinguishes the play are the 'monodramatic' scenic devices used to enhance the effect. As the first carafe is drunk up, the tacky restaurant remains as it is, and one irritated customer even insists that the rackety gramophone be switched off. With the second carafe, as the characters grumble about work and pick fights over minor issues, the lighting grows brighter, the tables fill up with people and the two civil servants and their companions are better-looking and better-dressed than before. (A curtain is let down between scenes to acomplish this.) The third carafe produces a more heated atmosphere with patriotic talk of war (including a parody of lines from the first act of Gogol's *Government Inspector*) with a transition to ribaldry and heavy flirtation. To show the restaurant as it now appears to the characters, the lighting grows even brighter, so that the scenery sparkles and seems to quiver in the glare. All the customers and even the waiters (who have doubled in quantity) have assumed an improved appearance; and when the gramophone is switched on again, a backstage orchestra amplifies its music. Finally, with the consumption of the fourth carafe, there is a total transformation; as the characters grow depressed and speculate about the soul, the lights gradually fade into a dismal gloom, the gramophone plays a funeral march, tears rain down. As the customers depart into real life, the cold grey light of early dawn washes over them.

The originality of this play was so great that, typically, some of the reviewers thought it an unpleasant and naturalistic slice-of-life, saved only by Yevreinov's ingenious staging.[30] But Yevreinov simply implemented what was already in Geyer's stage-directions, and the credit for the conception must go to the playwright.

Whether or not he intended it as a parody of monodrama, as some suggested, is moot; but it was granted that if the spectators did not 'co-experience' the action, they certainly 'co-beheld' it.

About this time Yevreinov was deeply embroiled in disputes over the Spanish Golden Age season at the Starinny teatr, which may explain why Geyer's next play *The Baroness's Handkerchief* ('Nosovoy platok Baronessy', première: 20 October 1911) seems a throwback. Its laughing-stock was high society drama as performed by country hams, accompanied by a vulgar military band.[31] It provided a plum for the actors, but this sort of spoof had deep roots in the vaudeville, in such early lampoons of provincial amateurs as A. A. Shakhovskoy's *Not-quite-gentlemanly Carryings-on* ('Polubarskiye zatei', 1818) and of professional thespians as Dmitry Lensky's *Lev Gurych Sinichkin* (1839).

After this retrogression, Geyer's move towards monodrama was confirmed by a play which even at the time was deemed to be his masterpiece, and which, with *The Evolution of the Drama*, was his only work to remain in the repertoire of the Crooked Mirror up to its demise in 1931. Writing about *Memories* ('Vospominaniya', première: 11 November 1911), Kugel' even went so far as to say, 'The artistic perfection of a truly stageworthy monodrama undoubtedly belongs to Geyer. Here was the organic confluence of form and matter.'[32]

For his 'illustrated novella' (*povest'*) Geyer once again chose a squalid milieu, akin to the ambience of Dostoyevsky's *A Nasty Story* ('Skvernyy anekdot') and Chekhov's *Wedding* ('Svad'ba'). Neonila, the overripe, ill-favoured daughter of the widow Krynkina, has managed to trap Spichkin, an insignificant telegraph clerk, into a marriage proposal, and at a tawdry dinner party the betrothal is announced. The other guests include Lakeyev, a drunken rhymester, Tabachinsky, a gloomy dry-as-dust who sees death and destruction in everything, and a couple of tow-haired, illiterate girls. The party ends with the ejection of the drunken guest who had started to importune the bride. The plot is humdrum and banal, but it serves as a necessary prelude to what follows.

The next day, the guests, having drunk themselves sober, recall, each in his own way, the previous night's events. The fiancé, in reality a downtrodden nonentity, sees himself as a proud and handsome champion, condescending but indulgent to his inferiors, a man of action in a crisis. He recollects the bride as charming and attractive, the old biddy of a mother as a noble matron, the guests as distinguished. The drunken poetaster remembers the party as a carouse with all the women as bacchantes hiking up their skirts, and himself as honoured guest, a talented artist toasted by his admiring friends. The gloomy guest enshrouds the event in a murky light: memorial tapers instead of lamps, a coffin instead of a table, conversation dwelling on deaths, mutilations and disasters, himself the only lively soul there. At the end he throws the drunken troublemaker from the top of the stairs, killing him.

Up to this point the critics were delighted. Although they had misgivings about the 'anecdotal' nature of Tabachinsky's scenario, they had nothing but praise for the accurate psychology of the groom's self-delusion and the subtlety of the drunk's merry nostalgia. But the greatest praise was lavished on the final episode: fifteen years later, the mother, fallen into dotage, attempts to remember the party; she considers the couple's happiness due entirely to her efforts. But owing to her senility, the result is a series of fragmentary, distorted vignettes emerging from darkness and absorbed back into it. This was a highly ingenious attempt to pictorialise a state of mental debility.

As usual, there were complaints that Geyer's writing was hasty and unpolished and that the device of a narrator between the episodes to cover scene changes was tiresome, but these cavils did not efface the distinction of his achievement. In forty-five minutes, he had packed a number of momentous ideas (enough for four hours, Kugel' had estimated on reading the manuscript) and found a viable dramatic format for them. The panorama of monodramatic perspectives went beyond Yevreinov's desire for audience co-experiencing to make a bigger aesthetic point: since all art is a variant of reality, to reappraise reality through a multiplicity of views – what we today might call the *Rashomon* principle – offers fresh possibilities to artistic creativity. The capturing of the past through the distortions of diverse consciousnesses was absolutely new to the stage. Without too much overstatement one might suggest that what Joyce and Proust were attempting on broad canvases, Geyer was exploring in miniature.[33]

Geyer's conception of human memory was, however, more Schopenhauerian in its pessimism than Proustian. All of the recollections, informed by vanity and egotism, are essentially mendacious and self-serving; whether or not there is an objective reality (the preliminary episode was entitled 'Reality' in the programme), the subjective interpretations invariably manipulate 'truth' or 'facts' to their own advantage. By the time we reach the dim scraps of recollection dredged up by the senile old lady, memory has become a symbol for death. Memory has served as life's connective tissue and, as it disintegrates with the passage of each of life's moments, the human fabric crumbles. That memory should be a self-worshipping lie and yet indispensable to the maintenance of human life is a profoundly misanthropic concept. Yet Geyer's means of conveying it richly entertained a cabaret audience.

*Popular Fiction* ('Van'kina literatura', roughly, *Literature for the Million*; première: 23 January 1912) applied the principle of subjective realities to the Russian equivalent of the Mills and Boon Romance. The stage was divided into two compartments, on the left a comfortable boudoir, on the right a sordid apartment. On the left, a loving couple reads the latest instalment of a new novel whose characters are noble, well-spoken, elegant and self-sacrificing; the wife keeps interjecting how wonderful the author of such a work must be. On the right, the author is seen to be a contemptible penny-a-liner, trying to grind out his weekly quota while plagued by a shrewish wife, a flirtatious milliner, an alcoholic friend and a janitor who tries to evict him for non-payment of rent. Each passage read aloud from the novel is ironically counterpointed by the sleazy reality which underlies it. Geyer's sarcasm proceeds beyond the butt of cheap fiction and its devotees to encompass family life in general.

COOK [*crude, dirty, enters with the roast*].　Boss, that guy's here about that little matter. He says, when you gonna pay the rent? You owe a awful lot, he says, so the landlord's nervous.

WIFE.　Oh, my God . . . Hm. I don't see why he can't wait. Well, tell him we'll pay tomorrow.

COOK [*goes out*].　Tomorrow, tomorrow. Nobody'll believe you, you derelick. [*Exits.*]

WRITER.　And give him something to eat so he'll leave me in peace for a while. Damn the bastard. [*He writes:*]

HE [*reads*].　'The door opened softly and on the threshold stood the pretty coquette of a parlour-maid, bowing respectfully. – "Master", she said, "the Nutrition Committee for the Poor Children has sent someone to see you . . ." "Very good", Roksanov interrupted her. "I am very busy. Tell your mistress to give them thirty roubles and make my excuses. I am working on an urgent report." The trim figure was heard to disappear behind the thick portières and Roksanov plunged back into his papers.'[34]

*Napoleon and Love* ('Napoleon i lyubov'', première: 13 September 1912), a rather simplistic exercise in contrast between great and small occasioned by the centenary of the French invasion,[35] preceded Geyer's next important experiment, *The Dream* ('Son', première: 13 October 1912). It should be noted that in this particular bill at the Crooked Mirror, Geyer's play immediately preceded Yevreinov's important monodrama *Backstage at the Psyche* ('V kulisakh dushi'), which came almost a year after Geyer's experiments in the genre. To some degree, the two complemented one another, since Yevreinov's play takes place within a man's body, presenting a tussle among aspects of his consciousness, and Geyer's takes place within a man's mind, while he is unconscious in sleep. Whereas Yevreinov divided his hero's consciousness into rational, emotional and eternal selves, Geyer more traditionally presented an undivided psyche; but both playwrights were seeking a way to dramatise subjectivity and subconscious action from within.

*Dream*'s basic motive was Gogolian (after all, *Son* is *Nos* backwards): a minor bureaucrat feels aggrieved when his proposal is turned down by a wealthy spinster. But the handling was Geyerian. In a subsequent dream, the events the pen-pusher has undergone are recreated oneirically: 'confused, with unexpected transformations, excursions into the realm of childhood'.[36] Strindberg had, of course, already ventured into this field with *A Dream Play* ('Ett Drömspel', 1901–2, first produced 1907), setting forth his purpose in its preface:

> to reproduce the detached and disunited – although apparently logical – form of dreams. . . . On a flimsy foundation of actual happenings, imagination spins and weaves its new patterns: an intermingling of remembrances, experiences, whims, fancies, ideas, fantastic absurdities and improvisations, and original inventions of the mind.[37]

But Strindberg's play, which was barely, if at all, known in Russia, is heavily symbolic, relying on personal imagery and Vedantic religion for its rich poetic texture. Most 'dream plays' of the time, from Hauptmann's *Hanneles Himmelfahrt* (1893) to J. M. Barrie's *A*

*Kiss for Cinderella* (1916), presented the dream as a perfectly coherent if idealised vision of reality. Geyer's playlet, tailored to the exigencies of a satiric cabaret, is more extreme, garish and, consequently, proto-surrealist in its presentation of the mind's workings during sleep.

In a reversal of the situation in *Memories*, the beautiful bride appears as a superannuated gargoyle; the cards the dreamer has been cheating at grow enormous and unwieldy for his hands (shades of Lewis Carroll!); the administrator of his department has become a literal monster, terrifying the wits out of the dreamer; an uncanny Chinaman drifts by holding an ostrich plume; and at a climactic moment, the dreamer loses his trousers. Reviewers, accustomed to seeing visions staged behind gauze, appraised the staging to be too realistic for the subject, and thereby missed the monodramatic point that the audience was to grant the dream the same credence as the dreamer did. Geyer called his piece 'a realistic phantasmagoria' and intended the abrupt transitions and unwonted transformations to look as naturalistic as anything in a play by Naydenov.

Although this manipulation of what Freud called 'dream-work' includes such Freudian items as condensation, displacement, sensory intensity and absurdity, and culminates in the embarrassment of nakedness, it is unlikely that Geyer was familiar with *The Interpretation of Dreams*, first published in 1900, particularly since he does not adhere to Freud's principal tenet of the dream as wish-fulfilment. More probably, like Strindberg before him, Geyer subscribed to Eduard von Hartmann, whose cult of pessimism was widely embraced in the late nineteenth century. In his *Philosophy of the Unconscious* (1869), Hartmann had stated of the dream, 'with it all the troubles of waking life pass over into the sleeping state'.[38] Since in Hartmann's view, happiness is unattainable here and now or in the immediate hereafter, a dream is bound to be an unrelieved nightmare, unless mitigated by scientific and artistic enjoyment, the same thing which reconciles a cultured person to life in general. But, as Geyer's heroes are vulgar boors, this amelioration is impossible; only the Mirror audiences, which received the play enthusiastically, partook of aesthetic pleasure.

Geyer's next sketch, *The Legend of the Holy Black Swan* ('Legenda o svyashchennom chernom lebede', première: 15 November 1912), written in collaboration with the composer Erenberg, cast a superci-

lious glance at that artistic process itself. As prologue, the devil
steps on to the forestage and explains that legends are often based
on sordid reality. The next two scenes illustrate the discrepancy:
the first tells the tale of a sculptor Licinius, whose friends kill the
swan in order to fulfil the prediction of a vestal virgin and prevent
the completion of a statue he is carving; all the principals commit
suicide. This is followed by the case that inspired the legend: some
drunkards kill a black hen and devour it. This new exercise in
reduction was judged to be clever but longwinded, its most
interesting feature the human statue who held a pose for thirty
minutes.[39] It appeared on the same bill as Fedor Sologub's *The
Same Old Affair* ('Vsegdashniye Shashni'), a cabaretic reworking of
his play *Van'ka the Steward and the Page Jehan* ('Van'ka Klyuchnik i
Pazh Zhean'), which used the 'variations on a theme' format to
contrast an interclass sexual triangle in Russian folklore, a mediaeval French ballad and the intensely vulgar modern Russia of Ivan
Ivanovich: the staleness of the story was overcome by Sologub's
ingenuity in recreating the idioms of each period. Any impression
made by *The Swan* was effaced by Sologub's play and, two weeks
later, by Yevreinov and Kugel''s *Government Inspector* ('Revizor'),
their attack on fashionable modes of directing. By staging scenes
from Gogol's comedy as directed by Stanislavsky, Gordon Craig,
Max Reinhardt and Max Linder, Yevreinov claimed he had invented
a new style of parody, independent of the written word: the parody
of directorial styles. Its success was so great that a play of Geyer's
under rehearsal, *Reflections of Solar Rays* ('Solnechnyye zaychiki'),
was cancelled to allow Yevreinov's comedy a longer run. The irony
here is that the basic structure of *Government Inspector* came from
*The Evolution of the Theatre* and Yevreinov would use it again for
*The Laughter Kitchen* ('Kukhnya smekha', 1913), a simple anecdote
retold according to four national senses of humour.

From this point on, Geyer's contributions to the Crooked Mirror
seem diminished in novelty, which may reflect the strain of regular
production for a satiric theatre. *When Knights Were Bold* ('Kogda
rytsari byli otvazhny', première: 23 October 1913), another collaboration with Erenberg, was a pantomime version of romantic melodrama. *Tat'yana Larina* (première: 14 December 1913) was a reversion
to a tried-and-true formula: how the silent film would adapt
*Yevgeny Onegin*; the new stage gimmick was to make up the
actors with black-and-white hands and faces.[40] *A German Idyll*
('Nemetskaya idilliya', première: 1 October 1914) was a wartime

propaganda piece, flaying the spiritual vacuity and vulgarity of the
Teutonic man-in-the-street by depicting the life of a degenerate
baronial family. It was praised as a 'stylish comedy',[41] which
provided rich opportunities for an ensemble of comic actors, but
marked no advance in Geyer's inventiveness.

His last two plays, however, attempted to return to the kind of
'split-screen' effect he had used before with such success. The title
of 'the psychological experiment', *What They Say, What They Think*
('Chto govoryat, chto dumayut', première: 16 December 1914),
reveals its intention. The structure was bipartite: in Part One, a
General's family is shown awaiting the arrival of a millionaire,
from whom they hope to elicit a large contribution for charity. In
Part Two, the same scene is played over, this time with the
characters speaking aloud the thoughts which had underlain their
earlier statements. Geyer made this particularly difficult for the
actors by insisting that the characters use the same gestures and
facial expressions as in Part One, even as they are belied by the
true thoughts. Needless to say, once the veil is drawn, the
characters reveal themselves to be crass, vile and self-seeking. The
charity is simply a swindle staged by the impoverished General to
get money to pay his debts; the *mir* delegate from a starving
peasant village is a hired ex-convict; the millionaire, who pays not
with cash but with shares in a company, has every intention of
unloading the company the next day. Here is a sample of the
technique:

SECRETARY [*grips his foot*].
O-o-ee . . .

It's that shoe . . . It pinches,
how it pinches . . . a regular
torture.

DAUGHTER.   What's the matter?

What's eating you? Aren't you
well?

SECRETARY.   Absolutely nothing
. . .

It had to start up. If I say my
boot is pinching, it'll spoil the
mood . . . O . . . o . . . I'll try to
slip it off a bit.

DAUGHTER.   But you're wincing?
Are you unwell?
Do tell me right away.

Something's bothering him.
What an idiot. I'll have to perk
him up . . . What's wrong with
you?

SECRETARY.   M–m–m . . . All
right . . . m . . . m . . . well,
you see, I once fought a duel,
and was shot in the foot, right

O–o . . . Should I make up a lie?
Right, something appropriate
though. A duel . . . A duel,
Nadezhda Pavlovna . . .

there . . .

**DAUGHTER.** You fought a duel? That's a lie, a stupid, impertinent lie. The man's an incredible dimwit.

**BUTLER.** [*entering*] Here's your powder, your excellency. [*as if announcing someone*] I had to break my back looking for it. You'd tossed the powder under the bed . . .

**DAUGHTER.** Merci. Put it down here. [*very sweetly*]. You blockhead, you idiot . . . Don't give it to me in front of him . . . Oh, why do you have to . . .

**BUTLER.** Yes ma'am. [*Butler puts down powder and exits.*]

**SECRETARY.** You really need powder? With your smooth, pale, pensive face? . . . O–o–o . . . [*lyrically*]. You're going to powder yourself? You think your kisser is going to be any smoother? What a goose. But that's not important. The main thing is the dowry. Her old man's bound to have lots tucked away. I'll propose right now . . . Nadezhda Pavlovna . . . O–o . . . My foot, my foot . . . And my pet corn too . . . Well, can I get away with it?

**DAUGHTER.** You should be ashamed . . . Stop dragging it out. Say what you have to quick . . . It's incredible what men are like . . .

[. . .]

**VAGRANT.** Who was that?
**BUTLER.** The young mistress, His Excellency's daughter.
**VAGRANT.** Izat so? . . . The girl's a reg'lar lump o' sugar . . . So where's the gen'ral hisself? What a slut . . . Never in all my born days have I seen one like that . . . So this is the humble home . . . An' it's easy to see, pal, that you been keepin' your belly nice an' healthy on the boss's grub.

**BUTLER.** Coming right away. You can talk to him. [*benevolently*]. I wish he'd get here, I can't leave you here, because more than likely you'd swipe something off the table . . .

**VAGRANT.** I got to. Folks is practically starvin'. The report If this guy was human, he'd offer me a drink. But it's just we drew up'd bring tears to your eyes.    yap, yap, and no sense to it.

[. . .]

| | |
|---|---|
| GENERAL [enters, grey-haired, in a double-breasted uniform jacket]. Aha . . . you're here already! . . . Well? Got the petition? | [inspects him]. A poor specimen. He's as like a peasant as I'm like the Pope of Rome. The treacherous face of a Judas. Look at me, you . . . |
| VAGRANT. Right here, your wuship, 'cause I'm a peasant, from the village of Dog's Seat, Onuch district, where we ain't got the strength to go on much longer. | Glad to give it a try, your highness. The way I'm the centre of attention'd make a cat laugh. |
| GENERAL.  What's your name? | [sternly]. If you drop a clanger, the whole scheme's shot to hell . . . Come on, lie, the way you were told, lie. |
| VAGRANT.  How's that again? | |
| GENERAL.  What do they call you? | |
| VAGRANT.  Uncle Kovylyay's what I'm called. Uncle Kovylyay's what you can hear 'em shoutin' all round the village. The mir sent me, I mean, as delegate, on account of the food situation, I mean . . . | I'm Uncle Kovylyay . . . That's right anyways. And the place is called . . . oh hell, I forgot, the village just slipped right out of my head. Dog Shi . . . no, that's not it. Bottom . . . backside . . . seat . . . Dog's Seat, your highness. |
| GENERAL.  All right, all right . . . Remember, when you're called in – keep your mouth shut . . . If you're asked a question answer it . . . Understand? | Bad, very bad, not worth three roubles. This old rascal's been up on charges in his life . . . Should have dumped him a long time ago.[42] |

When set out this way, the contrast is both brutal and funny. But by dividing word and thought into two consecutive episodes Geyer vitiated his effects, and it would not be until 1928 when Eugene O'Neill followed speech directly with spoken thought in *Strange Interlude* (and Groucho Marx lampooned the device in *Animal Crackers*) that a proper mode was found to portray this discrepancy. O'Neill, heir to three decades of literary experimentation, was trying to create interior soliloquies that would be the dramatic equivalent of the novel's stream of consciousness. Geyer had fewer models to follow. In any case, his critics were not disturbed by the clumsiness of his structuring, but instead opined that the subject was too banal, and a broader scope might have been adopted.[43] Kugel' was later to complain that Geyer had misrepresented human psychology, since our minds hold not one, but a multiplicity of thoughts, of which the tongue translates only a few; which was not so much to denigrate Geyer's achievement as to indicate the complexities Kugel' thought his cabaret capable of dramatising.[44]

*Æolian Harps* ('Eolovye arfy', première: 16 November 1915) has a disputed authorship. As Spencer Golub, relying on Yevreinov's recollections, sums up the situation:

> The authorship of *Æolian Harps* was originally credited to Gejer alone. However, Evreinov protested to the directorate of the Crooked Mirror Theatre that Gejer had not only appropriated the form devised by Evreinov – monodrama – but the subject as well. It seems that Evreinov had earlier proposed a parody of theatre critics. Eventually, the dispute was resolved and Gejer and Evreinov were listed as co-authors of the play.[45]

Yevreinov, chafing at Geyer's primacy in the field of comic monodrama, was always hypersensitive to what he considered the kidnapping of his brain-children; but contemporaries regarded *Æolian Harps* as Geyer's play, embellished by Yevreinov's stagecraft and improvements during rehearsals.

Since the comedy was an attack on reviewers, most reviewers made an effort to be well-disposed towards it, although *Rech'* snarled that it was too reminiscent of earlier Crooked Mirror plays such as *Vampuka* and *Government Inspector*. Actually, the structure was most reminiscent of *Memories*: three newspaper critics attend a saccharine psychological drama saturated with love. An impresario then stages their reviews of that performance. The first, a well-intentioned critic, views the play as a magnificent symphony; infatuated with a walk-on actress who, as the maid, says only 'Dinner is served', he attributes all the play's success to her 'violin-like' reading. (The title *Æolian Harps* alluded to Surguchev's sub-Chekhovian play *Autumnal Violins* ['Osenniye skripki'] which had just made a hit at the Moscow Art Theatre.) With her exit, he loses interest and the stage goes dark. The second critic, hostile to the play, conjures up a series of disasters: the leading man loses his dentures, the door in the flat falls off its hinges, the prompter's voice overtops the actors. The third, who arrives late and drunk, confuses the play with the convivial scene he has just left: the stage is covered in white muslin to represent his muzzy state of mind, the dialogue is garbled, champagne corks pop and an inebriated voice calls for the bill.[46] However familiar the technique, Geyer and Yevreinov had certainly improved on Bernard Shaw, who, in *Fanny's First Play* (1911), needed three acts before filling his epilogue with recognisable caricatures of London critics, trying to find something nice to say about the play they had just been shown. (Shaw may be considered a Crooked Mirror playwright, since his *Doctor's Dilemma* was performed there in Yevreinov's adaptation.) More radically, in *Æolian Harps*, the polydramatic principle is reversed so that the spectator, rather than seeing the stage action through the eyes of the protagonist, sees it through the eyes of another spectator, a rather Pirandellian device.

Whether Yevreinov's resentment against Geyer might have stunted the latter's work at the Crooked Mirror cannot be deter-mined, since Geyer died of typhoid dysentery at a mineral-springs resort in August 1916. He was only forty, and, in the opinion of his colleagues, at the height of his powers. The following February a special bill of his plays was presented in his memory at the Crooked Mirror.[47] In a list he composed late in life to enumerate the theatre's parodic specialities, Yevreinov included only three of Geyer's plays – *The Evolution of the Theatre* (which had been staged before Yevreinov had become artistic director), the relatively trivial *Baroness's Handkerchief*, and *A Victim of Love's Passion, or The Adventures of a Hapless Working-girl* ('Zhertva lyubovnoy strasti ili Priklyucheniya neschastnoy rabotnitsy', the post-revolutionary retitling of *Cinema*).[48] Significantly, none of Geyer's mono- or polydramatic achievements was listed.

IV

Yevreinov was later to claim that the goal of the Crooked Mirror was 'to use *negative* treatments of a theme to create a *positive* work of art'.[49] If Geyer's cynicism was unrelenting, the pre-revolutionary Yevreinov could still be classified as an ironic optimist, accentuating the positive even when his characters face death. What the two playwrights shared, perhaps unwittingly, was the taste for Henri Bergson which coloured so much philosophic, political and aesthetic thought from 1900 to the outbreak of the First World War. In those decades Bergson's fundamental ideas were the common currency of every educated European, much as Freud's became a few decades later. Bergson goes unmentioned amid the name-dropping in Yevreinov's 'Introduction to Monodrama', but it would appear that the mono- and polydramatic experiments made at the Crooked Mirror were daring steps towards solving the problem of putting Bergson's notion of *l'expérience vécue* on stage.

The concept of *l'expérience vécue*, the flow of immediate subjective experience ungraspable by thought, was anti-abstract, an attempt to break the bonds of scientific determinism and religious predestination that fettered human freedom. Such an idea would obviously have an appeal to the innate scepticism of the Crooked Mirror's leaders, who opposed both the positivism of the Moscow Art Theatre and the mysticism of the Symbolist school. Bergson insisted on the mutability of perception, not only among individuals but within the individual consciousness. Constantly moving within time,

> the same reasons may dictate to different persons, or to the same person at different moments, acts profoundly different, although equally reasonable. The truth is that they are not quite the same reasons, since they are not those of the same person, nor of the same moment. That is why we cannot deal with them in the abstract, from outside, as in geometry, nor solve for another the problems by which he is faced in life.[50]

Any artist who hoped to recreate *l'expérience vécue* had to discover how to represent directly its dynamism, velocity and fluidity. This last quality particularly required an illusion of spontaneity. As William James clarified Bergson, 'What really exists is not things made but things in the making.' (An unexpected echo sounds in the title of Sologub's novel *Tvorimaya legenda* (first part published in 1908), not, as the English translations have it, *The Created Legend*, but *A Legend in the Making*.) 'The dramatic flux of personal life', wrote James, is made up of 'the unstructured, but introspectable, confusion of thoughts, sensations, and images';[51] he called the flux 'dramatic', but traditional dramatic techniques could not capture it. In cancelling out the notion that one could section a 'slice' out of life for stage consumption, the Bergsonian idea breaks ground for a new theatrical method. Two generations later Brecht would make similar demands. Brecht's insistence that dramatic action be presented not as foregone conclusions to be passively accepted by the audience, but as rational options chosen for a number of evident causes, sanctions such action's fragmentation and contingency. His Epic Theatre, with its disjunct tableaux, was one way of doing it, which has provided a model for less political dramatists.

Pre-Brechtian innovators who sought to dramatise *l'expérience vécue* had perforce to reject standard act and scene structures without a model. Yet the relativistic, fractional method they employed did bear some resemblance to the Impressionist painters' disintegration of volume into atoms of light and colour and the Expressionist painters' shattering of objective reality into idiosyncratic, deformed visions. The analogy between painting and the dramaturgy of the Crooked Mirror did not go unnoticed at the time. Valerian Chudovsky, a member of the World of Art circle, reporting to the circle's journal *Apollon* in 1912, specifically related the Mirror to contemporary aesthetic trends. After romanticism, after naturalism, after symbolism, wrote Chudovsky, the art world is dominated by the 'school of no schools' (*shkola bezshkol'nosti*), the movement of individualism and anarchic subjectivity. If, in the graphic arts, each individual is permitted an idiosyncratic vision, then in the theatre, the concept of monodrama comes to the same thing, the subjectivity of apprehension. Taken separately, the Crooked Mirror's sketches may seem trivial, but in aggregate they appear as significant inquiries in that direction. Their farcical nature is appropriate, since, in Chudovsky's view, 'all extreme subjectivism is comic' and farce is one of the few wholly admissible ways of structuring life.[52]

Chudovsky warned against over-exaggerating this significance and carefully relegated the work of the Crooked Mirror to the category of *Kleinkunst*. But in our time the hierarchies of art have fallen into desuetude and we do not have to apologise for admiring so-called minor forms. The cabaret play, as Geyer practised it, may be ranked with the most interesting experiments of the modernist stage, their brevity not a drawback but a handicap overcome. His best works, in their unpretentious way, focus the converging rays of popular philosophies – Bergson's theory of life's flux, Hartmann's pessimistic view of human aspiration and dream sublimation, Nancy school concepts of the multifarious personality – and rediffuse them as derisive comedy. In Geyer's hands, the Crooked Mirror refracted modern concerns of subjectivity and the subliminal self, and then shattered them into a myriad of shards, each one reflecting a separate reality.

## AFTERWORD ON CABARET BILLING

Geyer's prestige at the Crooked Mirror cannot easily be determined from his place on the bill. The standard Mirror programme was made up, on an average, of four sketches; their number never fell below three or rose above six. Unlike American vaudeville where the choice position was 'next to closing', there was apparently no especially desirable slot. Although Yevreinov was fond of placing his own contributions in the last two slots, the positioning of plays seems to have been dictated by exigencies of set and costume changes or by the desire to end with something musical. Thus, the six-item programme of 10 December 1910 opened with *The Components of Life*, which required several changes of scenery, and ended with two dance pieces, both performed in simple settings. Of Geyer's 'polydramas', *Aqua Vitae* played second on a bill of five, which culminated with the immensely popular two-act *Rychalov's Guest Appearance* ('Gastrol' Rychalova'); *Memories* was number three on a bill of five, finishing with Yevreinov's *School for Stars* ('Shkola etualey'); *Popular Fiction* opened a bill of three closing with Yevreinov's production of Reinhardt's pantomime *Sumurun*; *The Dream* was second on a bill of four, directly preceding Yevreinov's *Backstage at the Psyche*; *What They Say, What They Think* opened a bill of three; and *Æolian Harps* was the only play by Geyer ever to close a bill, following three other pieces, among them a pantomime by Yevreinov.

## Notes

I should like to thank Spencer Golub of Brown University and Anthony G. Pearson of the University of Glasgow who, over the years, have shared their knowledge of Yevreinov and their perceptions of miniature theatre with me.

1. Samuel Johnson, 'Preface to Shakespeare 1765', in W. K. Wimsatt Jr (ed.), *Samuel Johnson on Shakespeare* (New York, 1960) p. 39.
2. See D. Gerould, 'Oscar Méténier and *Comédie rosse*', *Drama Review*, vol. XXVIII, no. 1 (Spring 1984) pp. 15–19.

3. Preface to *Miss Julie*, in Arvid Paulson (ed. and trs.), *Seven Plays of August Strindberg* (New York, 1960) pp. 70–1. In a lesser-known essay of 1889, 'On Modern Drama and Modern Theatre', Strindberg proclaimed the short play the ideal of modern drama. See the translation by Børge Gedsø Madsen in T. Cole (ed.), *Playwrights on Playwriting* (New York, 1961) esp. pp. 18–21.

4. *Ermitazh*, VI (1922) p. 6; Foregger was for a while a Crooked Mirror director himself. All translations, unless otherwise indicated, are my own.

5. On Russian terminology for forms of *Kleinkunst* see Béatrice Picon-Vallin, 'L'Atelier de Foregger et le courant comique dans le théâtre soviétique', in C. Amiard-Chevrel (ed.), *Du Cirque au théâtre* (Lausanne, 1983) p. 135. For a comprehensive, though not always accurate account, of pre-revolutionary Russian cabaret, see Yu. Dmitriev, 'Teatry miniatyur', in *Russkaya khudozhestvennaya kul'tura kontsa XIX–nachala XX veka (1908–1917): Kniga tret'ya: Zrelishchnyye iskusstva, muzyka* (Moscow, 1977) pp. 191–207. In English, see Anthony Pearson, 'The Cabaret Comes to Russia: "Theatre of Small Forms" as Cultural Catalyst', *Theatre Quarterly*, vol. IX (Winter 1980) 31–44; Harold Segel, 'Russian Cabaret in a European Context: Preliminary Considerations', in Lars Kleberg and Nils Åke Nilsson (eds), *Theater and Literature in Russia, 1900–1930* (Stockholm, 1984) pp. 83–100; and Segel's *Turn-of-the-Century Cabaret* (New York, 1987) pp. 255–320.

6. Kholmskaya later claimed that the name derived from the mirror in Andersen's fairy-tale *The Snow Queen*; but the homonymous collection of verse parodies by A. A. Izmaylov published by Kugel' in 1908 is the more likely origin. Ultimately, the source is the epigraph to Gogol's *Government Inspector*: 'Don't blame the mirror if your kisser's crooked.' First-hand accounts of the Crooked Mirror include Kugel''s *List'ya s dereva: Vospominaniya* (Leningrad, 1926) pp. 195–209; Yevreinov's unpublished *V shkole ostroumiya: O teatre 'Krivoye Zerkalo'*, in the Central State Archive of Literature and Art of the USSR; Kholmskaya's 'Krivoye Zerkalo', *Rabochiy i teatr*, vol. IX (September 1937) pp. 52–6; and A. Deych, 'Vspominaya minuvsheye', *Zvezda* (1966) no. 5, pp. 173–83. See also G. Kryzhitskiy, 'Vospominaniya. Laboratoriya smekha', *Teatr*, VIII (August 1967) pp. 110–20, and C. Moody, 'The Crooked Mirror', *Melbourne Slavonic Studies*, vol. VII (1972) pp. 25–37.

7. Z. Kholmskaya, 'Neskol'ko slov o moem "detishche"', programme for *Teatr Krivoye Zerkalo* (1928) p. 13.

8. Kugel', *List'ya s dereva*, p. 200: 'Almost everything at the Crooked Mirror that was new in the sense of creative ideas came from Geyer and Erenberg.' Kugel' wrote this after he had broken with Yevreinov, but it is clear from Kugel''s earlier writings that his admiration for Geyer was sincere. Yevreinov, on the other hand, de-emphasised the significance of Geyer's contribution in his writings on The Crooked Mirror.

9. Kugel', *List'ya s dereva*, p. 201; N. N. Yevreinov, *Histoire du théâtre russe* (Paris, 1947) p. 397; Kugel' also provided a short obituary

biography of Geyer in *Teatr i iskusstvo*, XXVIII (1916) pp. 563–4 (henceforth *Til*).

10. B. F. Geyer, *Tayna solntsa, legenda v odnom deystvii* (St Petersburg, 1912) p. 9.

11. B. F. Geyer, *Khameleony, sharzh v 1 deystvii* (St Petersburg, 1912) p. 7.

12. E. de Goncourt, 'Préface à *Henriette Maréchal*', in E. and J. de Goncourt, *Théâtre* (Paris: Fasquelle, n.d.) p. 17. Stanislavsky, who read little science but absorbed ideas that were in the air, popularised Ribot's concept of 'affective memory' as 'emotional memory'. See E. Bentley, 'Who was Ribot? or: Did Stanislavsky Know Any Psychology?', *Tulane Drama Review*, vol. VII, no. 2 (Winter 1962) pp. 127–9.

13. Kugel', *List'ya s dereva*, p. 196.

14. S. Rafalovich, 'Evolyutsiya teatra', in *'Teatr' kniga o novom teatre* (St Petersburg, 1908) pp. 219–42. Curiously, in the same year as Geyer's parody the literary historian B. V. Friche published an essay, 'Evolyutsiya teatra i dramy', which cited the cabaret as the latest avatar of theatrical development (*Iz istorii noveyshey russkoy literatury* (Moscow, 1910) pp. 61–148).

15. In M. Ya. Polyakova (ed.), *Russkaya teatral'naya parodiya XIX nachala XX veka* (Moscow, 1976) p. 569. *Evolyutsiya teatra* is the only one of Geyer's plays to be published in the Soviet era. Pictures from the original production appear in *Til*, v (1910) p. 111.

16. *Don Carlos an der Jahrhundertwende* was published in M. Reinhardt, *Schall und Rauch*, Part I (Berlin and Leipzig, 1901) pp. 11–126. Its Part II, *Karle*, as well as Bernauer's *Nora*, are reprinted in H. R. Schatter (ed.), *Scharf geschossen. Die deutschsprachige Parodie von 1900 bis zur Gegenwart* (Berne, Munich, Vienna, n.d.). A translation of *Nora* will appear in L. Senelick (ed. and trs.), *Cabaret Performance: Europe 1890–1920* (New York, 1989).

17. One reviewer did think the dialogue in the Ostrovsky spoof more reminiscent of the language of the comic journalist Nikolay Leykin: 'S.', 'Krivoye Zerkalo', *Til*, IV (1910) p. 87.

18. Polyakova, pp. 579–83.

19. In the 1920s, a fifth scene was added to mock Constructivism.

20. Vas. Bazilevskiy, *Rampa i zhizn'*, v (1910) pp. 79–80; *Rech'*, XXI (22 Jan.–4 Feb. 1910) p. 5. For a discussion of Geyer in the tradition of Chekhovian parody, see L. Senelick, 'Stuffed Seagulls: Parody and the Reception of Chekhov's Plays', *Poetics Today*, vol. VIII, no. 2 (1988) pp. 285–99.

21. Alter, *Til*, xv (1910) pp. 309–10; production shot, XXIV (1910) p. 474; Deych, p. 175.

22. 'P. Orlovskiy', 'Neskol'ko slov o "Krivom Zerkale"', reprinted in V. V. Vorovskiy, *Sochineniya*, vol. II (Leningrad, 1931) pp. 373–5. The 'apoliticism' of the Crooked Mirror is such a party line that it is repeated even in the memoirs of contemporaries; see, e.g., A. G. Alekseyev, *Ser'eznoye i smeshnoye: polveka v teatre i na estrade* (Moscow, 1972) pp. 21–2.

23. For a detailed account of Yevreinov's contributions to the Crooked

Mirror, see S. Golub, *Evreinov: The Theatre of Paradox and Transformation* (Ann Arbor, Mich., 1984) pp. 145–90.

24. Quoted in Kryzhitskiy, p. 114.
25. 'A. B.', 'Krivoye Zerkalo', *Til*, LI (1910) p. 988; production shots, pp. 998–9.
26. *Rech'*, XLI (11 February 1911) p. 7; *Til*, VII (1911) p. 148.
27. A translation as 'Introduction to Monodrama', appears in L. Senelick (ed. and trs.), *Russian Dramatic Theory from Pushkin to the Symbolists* (Austin, Tx., 1981) pp. 183–99.
28. This is not generally understood, and Soviet historians are prone to garble the Crooked Mirror's chronology. For instance, Yevgeny Kuznetsov in his *Iz istorii russkoy estrady. Istoricheskiye ocherki* (Moscow, 1958), says, 'After this monodrama [Yevreinov's *V kulisakh dushi*] a series of others followed ("Vospominaniya", "Son", "Voda zhizni")' (p. 295). In fact, the first and third plays he cites *preceded* Yevreinov's comedy, the second *appeared on the same bill* with it.
29. B. F. Geyer, *Voda zhizni* (St Petersburg, 1917) p. 2.
30. See, for instance, Ye. Znosko-Borovskiy in *Russkaya khudozhestvennaya letopis'*, XV (1911) p. 23. Znosko-Borovskiy's usually harsh critiques of the Crooked Mirror are suspect, since he wrote for rival miniature theatres.
31. *Til*, LXIV (1911) p. 830.
32. A. Kugel', 'Monodrama', in *Utverzhdeniye teatra* (Petrograd, 1923) p. 198.
33. For contemporary reactions to the play, see P[etr]. Yu[zhnyy], 'Krivoye Zerkalo', *Til*, XLVII (1911) p. 900, and, in the same issue, A. Kugel', 'Teatral'nyye zametki', p. 915. For memories of *Memories*, see Kugel', *Utverzhdeniye teatra*, pp. 197–8; Ye. Znosko-Borovskiy, *Russkiy teatr nachala XX veka* (Prague, 1925) pp. 330–1; V. Polyakov, *Tovarishch smekh* (Moscow, 1976) p. 45. Geyer's 'polydramatic' approach seemed so liberating, it was adopted by the satirical journal *Novyy Satirikon* when the censorship prevented reportage of the visit of an English delegation to Russia in 1912. V. Azov invented descriptions of it as seen through the eyes of a liberal reformer, an illiterate reactionary, and the mayor of Petersburg. See L. Yevstigne-yeva, *Zhurnal 'Satirikon' i poety-satirikontsy* (Moscow, 1968) pp. 375–8.
34. B. F. Geyer, *Van'kina literatura. Protsess tvorchestva v 1 d.* (St Petersburg, 1916) pp. 2–3; an English translation will appear in Senelick, *Cabaret Performance: Europe 1890–1920*. For a review, see Petr Yuzhnyy, 'Krivoye Zerkalo', *Til*, V (1912) p. 101.
35. Noticed in Petr Yuzhnyy, 'Krivoye Zerkalo', *Til*, XXXIV (1912) p. 738.
36. V. Khovin, 'Teatral'naya zhizn': Krivoye Zerkalo', *Voskresnaya vecher-nyaya gazeta*, XXI (14 October 1912) p. 3; Petr Yuzhnyy, *Til*, XLIII (1912) p. 817; for production shots, see pp. 826–7.
37. A. Paulson (ed. and trs.), *Eight Expressionist Plays by August Strindberg* (New York, 1965) p. 343.
38. Quoted in A. A. Brill (ed.), *The Basic Writings of Sigmund Freud* (New York, 1938) p. 217.
39. Petr Yuzhnyy, 'Krivoye Zerkalo', *Til*, LXVIII (1912) p. 937.

40. 'N. N.', 'Krivoye Zerkalo', *TiI*, LI (1913) p. 1048.
41. *TiI*, XL (1914) p. 788.
42. *Chto govoryat – chto dumayut. Psikhologicheskiy opyt v 1 d. i 2 kart.* (St Petersburg, 1915) pp. 2–3, 6–7.
43. 'N. N.', 'Krivoye Zerkalo', *TiI*, LI (1914) p. 969.
44. Kugel', *Utverzhdeniye teatra*, p. 198.
45. Golub, *Evreinov*, p. 157.
46. 'N. N. . . . v', 'Krivoye Zerkalo', *TiI*, XLVII (1915) p. 875; *Rech'*, CCCXVIII (15 November 1915) p. 5; *Birzhevyye vedomosti* (17 November 1915) p. 6; Deych, p. 176.
47. *TiI*, XXXVI (1916) p. 77; *Den'*, LII (24 February 1917) p. 4. The number of Russian theatrical luminaries who died of typhus at this period is remarkable: it includes Geyer's musical colleague Vladimir Erenberg and the satirical clown Anatoly Durov.
48. Yevreinov, *V shkole ostroumiya*, pp. 40–1.
49. Ibid., ch. 3, p. 5.
50. H. Bergson, *Creative Evolution* (1907), trs. A. Mitchell (New York, 1911) p. 7.
51. W. James, *A Pluralistic Universe* (New York, 1909), see esp. pp. 233–74.
52. V. Chudovskiy, '"Krivoye Zerkalo" i monodrama', *Russkaya khudozhestvennaya letopis'* (supplement to *Apollon*), v (March 1912) pp. 75–6.

# 3

# Boris Pronin, Meyerhold and Cabaret: Some Connections and Reflections

## MICHAEL GREEN

*'Without Boris Pronin not one of the artistic enterprises of pre-war Petersburg is conceivable.'*

G. Lugin, *28° 14' 30"* (Riga, 1933)

*'We (Mandelstam and I and many others) began to have the illusion that the entire world was actually concentrated in the "Dog" – that no life, no interests existed apart from "doggy" ones.'*

V. Pyast, *Encounters* (Moscow, 1929)

Given the nature of Russian cultural life at the turn of the twentieth century, it was inevitable that Konstantin Stanislavsky's Moscow Art Theatre – which rapidly gained prominence as the triumphant exponent of a theatrical realism that some called naturalism – became, equally rapidly, the target of anti-naturalistic broadsides. So vocal was this opposition that there came a time when Stanislavsky himself felt that it could no longer be ignored. Yet his efforts to accommodate the anti-realist trends within the Art Theatre have provided some of the least impressive pages in the history of that illustrious institution. When, in 1904, the director had allowed himself to be persuaded by Anton Chekhov to stage a triple bill of plays by Maurice Maeterlinck (*Les Aveugles, Intérieur* and *L'Intruse*),[1] the result was disappointing. The productions were unimaginative and served only to demonstrate the unreadiness of the Art Theatre to join the Symbolist avant-garde. But such was Stanislavsky's resolve to maintain the primacy of his theatre in contemporary

Russia, that he was prepared to experiment again, even at the price of 'novelty for novelty's sake'.[2] Thus it was that he hit on the notion of establishing the Theatre Studio, an experimental mini-theatre to be attached to the main Art Theatre, and of recalling Vsevolod Meyerhold to the capital from the provinces, where he had been attempting to enlighten theatre audiences with his 'Fellowship of the New Drama'. Was not Meyerhold just the man to take charge of this new venture? (It was, after all, a younger Meyerhold who had taken the role of Treplev, that seeker after 'new forms', in the Art Theatre's crucial 1898 production of *The Seagull*, and whose exclusion from the theatre's newly-formed joint stock company in 1902 had caused Chekhov much concern.) But, once again, the flirtation with experiment ended unsatisfactorily. The uprising of December 1905, combined with Stanislavsky's lack of enthusiasm for the dress rehearsal of another Maeterlinck play, *La Mort de Tintagiles*, brought about the untimely demise of the Theatre Studio. Yet, in one respect at least, the ill-starred venture had one positive result: it brought into contact two men of the theatre whose well-nigh symbiotic relationship in the succeeding years was to change the Russian theatre – Vsevolod Meyerhold, the future Dr Dapertutto, acquired a 'double' in the person of Boris Pronin, the future Hund-Director.

Although Boris Pronin was at the very hub of the Russian theatre for more than a decade, his achievement has remained sadly unsung, at least in the groves of academe. (It would not be difficult, however, to assemble an anthology of prose and poetry that owe their inspiration to Pronin and his cabaret, 'The Stray Dog'.) Born in Chernigov in 1875, Boris Pronin completed college in Kiev in 1897. He was an unsettled youth, making the rounds of university departments – from philosophy to mathematics, from mathematics to jurisprudence – without completing his studies. He was prone at this period to the urban mysticism that marked the century's beginning. As one of his contemporaries recalled: 'He invited us all to make a sortie to the Nikolayevsky Bridge with the purpose of leaning back against its parapet – the bridge's vibrations would give us the most extraordinary sensation!'[3] During his student *Wanderjahre* Pronin sampled life in the old capital as well as the new: in the spring of 1900 his involvement in student rioting at Moscow University led to a period of exile from that city, as a consequence of which he briefly studied medicine as far afield as Lyons. When he was in his mid-twenties, however, his destiny at last found him out: he enrolled in a course of stage management offered by the Moscow Art Theatre, where a fellow student recalled him as a 'free spirit' (*ptitsa bozhiya*) with a 'restless, sparkling energy'.[4]

Boris Pronin was a charmer, if the word 'charm' is sufficient to convey a power to captivate that was not peripheral but central to his nature – and to his career:

> When I first met Pronin he was over thirty, but he gave the impression of an eighteen-year-old. Of medium height, unusually well-proportioned, graceful, with small, beautiful hands, a delicate, almost girlish face with a radiant smile that never left it, eyes that radiated inspiration and welcome to those in any degree capable of devotion to someone or something. . . . Pronin enchanted everyone.[5]

Such are the memories of Aleksandr Mgebrov, actor and charter member (along with Aleksey Remizov, Nikolay Yevreinov, Mikhail Kuzmin and Nikolay Sapunov, to name but a few) of the 'Artistic Association of the Intimate Theatre' (*Khudozhestvennoye obshchestvo Intimnogo teatra*), a select 'club' which played no small part in the history of the Russian cabaret. Not everyone was as susceptible to the Pronin charm, however. Georgiy Ivanov, in his *Petersburg Winters* ('Peterburgskiye zimy') draws a less appealing portrait:

> 'Boris Konstantinovich Pronin – Doctor of Aesthetics, Honoris Causa' – such was the inscription on Pronin's visiting card. . . . Making an appearance with some project in his head, Pronin would shower his interlocutor with words. Any attempt to make an objection, to interrupt, to ask a question was hopeless.[6]

Although Ivanov too notes the 'unceasingly smiling mouth', for him Pronin was a machine that gyrated ceaselessly to very little purpose.

But let us return to 1905 and the Art Theatre's still-born Theatre Studio. This was, of course, a period of unparalleled cultural ferment in Russia, a ferment that found one outlet in the *jours-fixes* – the famous 'Wednesdays' – of the poet and classical scholar Vyacheslav Ivanov. 'The crisis of the theatre' was undoubtedly a favourite topic of discussion at these weekly get-togethers of the capital's cultural élite. As a classicist, Vyacheslav Ivanov was a passionate advocate of the rebirth of the Dionysian spirit of the theatre. As he put it in an article of 1906: 'The stage must step across the footlights and draw the community into itself, or the community must absorb the stage. This is an aim already acknowledged by some; but where is the means by which it is to be realised?'[7]

But if Russian Symbolism had an organising spirit, it was surely Valery Bryusov. Poet, novelist, translator and editor, Bryusov was present at the 'Wednesday' held on 18 January 1906, of which he observed in a letter: 'Vyacheslav Ivanov's "Wednesdays" are a Noah's Ark where you often come across as many as fifty or sixty people'. An appended list, in Ivanov's own hand, of those present on that particular occasion reveals Meyerhold and Pronin to have been among their number.[8] There is no doubt that they would have found themselves very much at home in this company. It was Bryusov, for example, who in his article of 1902, 'Unnecessary Truth', had called the principles of the Moscow Art Theatre's stage realism into question, declaring: 'It is time that the theatre stopped counterfeiting reality.'[9] And it was to Bryusov – who was to have been the Theatre Studio's literary consultant – that Meyerhold had addressed a frantic note dated 24 October 1905, which read: 'We implore you to come to the "Prague" (private dining entrance). We must share with you the horror that grips our hearts now it's clear that everything is finished.'[10]

Boris Pronin was closely involved with the Theatre Studio project throughout, acting as Stanislavsky's secretary in matters relating to the new enterprise.[11] He was also among the select few to be present at the crisis meeting with Bryusov at the popular Moscow restaurant. But there was no rescuing the Studio, and, having reconstituted his 'Fellowship of the New Drama', Meyerhold again took to the road. This time he was accompanied by Pronin. A letter of 23 July 1906 confides a fantasy entertained by the two wanderers in the remote provincial fastness of Kherson in the southern Ukraine: 'What we have to do is to organise a Commune of Lunatics. Only such a commune will be able to transform our dream into reality.'[12]

An earlier letter of the same year affords us a picture of what must have been an effective working relationship between the two men. (The production referred to is of Ibsen's early (1862) verse drama *Love's Comedy*, a play now rarely performed, but – as a

forerunner of *A Doll's House* – controversial enough in its day.)
This is what Meyerhold had to say:

> The first performance was a model from the production point of
> view, and for this I have Pronin's good taste to thank. There
> were many local colour spots, and the scenery was splendidly
> put together. I was responsible for that; Pronin worked on the
> Norwegian local colour.[13]

But such moments of creative satisfaction did not amount to
sufficient reward for exile in the provincial backwoods. 'But worst
of all', Meyerhold complained on another occasion, 'if I'm to labour
in the provinces I'll have to lower my standards. I can't stand the
local repertoire, and I can't stand their actors' temperaments, their
actors' voices.'[14] A new dream, something in the manner of a
Petersburg version of the ill-fated Theatre Studio, was taking
shape, this time in conjunction with the 'mystical anarchist' Georgiy
Chulkov, another patron of the Ivanov 'Wednesdays'. The new
theatre was to bear the name 'Torches' (*Fakely*), at once an
incandescence and a guiding light. (This was also the title of a
journal edited by Chulkov.) It was for 'Torches' that Aleksandr
Blok followed Chulkov's suggestion that he develop one of his
lyrics into a short play of the same name – *The Puppet Show*
('Balaganchik'). But although the play was written, the theatrical
project fell by the wayside due to the lack of financial resources.

Fortunately, there were other options on the horizon. Vera
Fedorovna Komissarzhevskaya was an actress who had a special
appeal for the Symbolists, an appeal which, according to Blok, lay
in what 'shimmered behind her restless shoulders, and what her
sleepless eyes and ever-thrilling voice summoned us to'.[15] A
discontented spirit, impatient with the entrenched routine of the
imperial stage, she had in 1902 resigned from the Aleksandrinsky
Theatre (where, in 1896, she had played the role of Nina in the
original production of Chekhov's *Seagull*). In 1904, using funds
raised by provincial tours, she was able to open her own independent theatre in the capital. Komissarzhevskaya did not open her
new theatre in St Petersburg until the autumn of 1904, but there
survives a carefully worded telegram from Meyerhold to Vera
Fedorovna dating from April or May of that year which leaves no
doubt that the actress had vainly envisaged collaboration with
Meyerhold well before the Theatre Studio debacle.[16] Again it was

Komissarzhevskaya herself who, in a letter of February 1906,[17] renewed the offer to Meyerhold to join her company as both actor and director. Although Meyerhold did not sign a formal contract with Komissarzhevskaya until the end of May 1906, it is clear that he did not hesitate this time. Most interestingly of all, as early as February we find him pressing the claims of Pronin: 'I'm asking you to take on Pronin as my stage manager. He was with the Studio, studied stage management with the Art Theatre. . . . He's well-educated, energetic, full of initiative.'[18]

Although Pronin was certainly employed at the modish theatre on Ofitserskaya Street during its first, 1906–7, season, he did not have any part in the second and (for Meyerhold) last season of that short-lived enterprise. The partnership between Meyerhold and Komissarzhevskaya, in fact, was not an easy one. Perhaps they represented irreconcilable extremes of the complex literary – and theatrical – phenomenon labelled 'Symbolism': she the idealist 'reaching beyond the blue boundaries of man's life *here*' (the words are Blok's),[19] he the scholar and experimenter obsessed with finding a modern form for past epochs and styles, with 'theatre for theatre's sake'. We can sense this rift in the *'fear'* and *'foreboding'* (the words are actually underlined by Meyerhold himself) of which he speaks in a letter of 22 May 1907 addressed to Fedor Komissarzhevsky, brother to the actress and a thoroughgoing aesthete who was to succeed Meyerhold as director at the end of 1907. The letter is filled with its author's unease at the need for compromise and at the conventionality of repertoire; its tone is hurt and uncomprehending. 'The world', Meyerhold complains, 'is a very complicated place – is there anything one can be certain of? Yesterday B. K. Pronin sent me a letter with the information that he is leaving your theatre.'[20] (Note that it is 'your', rather than 'our', let alone 'my' theatre.)

The same letter to Komissarzhevsky contains a mention of P. M. Yartsev, with whom Meyerhold had differed in his attitude to the Art Theatre. Petr Mikhaylovich Yartsev ('Yarchik' to his friends) is a curious and quixotic figure in the annals of the Russian stage. Boris Zaytsev has described him at this time of his life as 'profoundly bohemian', as 'one who lived as a bird of the air. A more carefree, penniless and unpractical individual I never encountered.'[21] Yartsev was a man of the theatre – critic, theorist and even dramatist: his play *In the Cloisters* ('V monastyre') took the fancy of Nemirovich-Danchenko and was mounted (albeit without much success) by the Moscow Art Theatre in their 1904–5 season. Yartsev and Pronin rented spacious garrets in what has been claimed to be 'one of the most original buildings in turn-of-the-century Russia'.[22] Pertsov House (*Dom Pertsova*) an ingenious combination of traditional Russian motifs and *style moderne* (*alias* art nouveau), stood on the Moscow River facing the church of Christ the Saviour. The garrets and cellars of this imposing building, above and below the apartments of solid citizens at its core, served as a centre of theatrical dissidence: from its opening on 8 February 1908 Russia's first popular cabaret, Nikita Baliyev's 'Bat' (*Letuchaya mysh'*) was located in the basement, while Pronin and Yartsev set up 'something between a club, a café and a theatre'[23] in their studios overlooking Christ the Saviour.

Let us consider what might be meant by 'dissidence' in this, the golden age of the Russian theatre. Baliyev's 'Bat' has been described as the *alter ego* of the Moscow Art Theatre;[24] but if Freudian terminology is to be used, perhaps *id* might be the more suitable term. Originating from the traditional 'cabbage parties' (*kapustniki*) preceding Lent (in imperial Russia a period of forced abstinence from theatrical diversion as well as voluntary abstinence from meat), the 'Bat' offered Art Theatre actors a unique opportunity for good-humoured self-parody. Still in costume, actors would arrive at the Pertsov cellars towards midnight and then proceed to 'send up' the roles they had just been performing with Stanislavskian commitment. Needless to say, there was a price to be paid for all this. Nikita Baliyev's role as Stanislavsky's 'court jester' did little to further his career as a professional actor: he was reduced to the odd walk-on part and discreetly manoeuvred out of the Art Theatre at the close of the 1911 season. (Meyerhold's fate a decade earlier comes to mind.) Pronin's garret complemented Baliyev's basement. In Mgebrov's words:

> Here all the latest developments in the theatre would be passionately discussed. . . . Here too were born the first storms and the first protests of youthful discontent that could not tolerate the role of silent witness to the magnificent theatrical banquet that resounded from the M.A.T., a banquet all but inaccessible to the mass of the younger crowd.[25]

A frequent hostess at these gatherings was Vera Kholodnaya, later to become the first great Russian star of the silent movies and, according to Jay Leyda, 'the only actress to command a salary even comparable to modern motion picture salares'.[26] If Kholodnaya had already assumed the guise which was to become familiar on the screen – the pallor of her face accentuated by dead white make-up – she must have added a welcome touch of the exotiç to these informal gatherings. However, relations with the Moscow Art Theatre were uneasy. To quote Mgebrov again:

> We were too much of a lure for many M.A.T. actors, especially the young ones: there were many who thought that Pronin with all his doings had sown the seeds of discord within the M.A.T. It was even alleged that he had created a kind of Montague and Capulet situation.[27]

For Vsevolod Meyerhold, in contrast – as always – to Konstantin Stanislavsky, cabaret theatre was to have a special and positive function. However, the naming of his first venture into cabaret seems to have presented something of a problem. In a note to Benois dated 18 November 1908 Pronin begged Diaghilev's designer to send Meyerhold 'a list of names (a nickname, a trademark) for our little theatre'.[28] Pronin himself had returned to St Petersburg after the Pertsov House enterprise had collapsed for lack of funds. He found in Meyerhold a collaborator more practical than Yartsev; and his prime task during the 1908–9 season was to be the organising of Meyerhold's new cabaret. The name eventually chosen – *Lukomor'e* – defies English translation. 'Strand', the customary rendering, fails sadly to convey the flavour of the Push-kinian archaism whose obscurity torments – and poeticises – Masha in Chekhov's *Three Sisters* ('Tri sestry'). It is clear that Meyerhold had high hopes of the 'Strand'. 'Just you wait and see', he wrote in a letter of December 1908, 'the group will build itself a little nook where the *cultured* St Petersburg theatregoer will find somewhere to relax.'[29] But when he wrote these words the 'Strand' was already doomed; opening at the St Petersburg Theatre Club on 6 December 1908, it closed three days later (surely a record of sorts) when the club's management announced that their premises would again be available for their usual customers – devotees of lotto and cards. The rapid closure of the 'Strand' provided a painful lesson. A mistake that was to be avoided in future was that of opening from eight to eleven thirty in the evening, a time which coincided with more conventional and better-established enterprises. The 'House of Interludes' (*Dom intermediy*) the successor to the 'Strand' and the final Meyerhold–Pronin foray into the uncertain world of cabaret, took care to cater to a sophisticated after-theatre audience, providing 'comfortable drawing rooms' where patrons could sit at little tables in an atmosphere of 'easy gaiety'.[30]

The repertoire of the 'House of Interludes' did not consist, as it had at the 'Strand', exclusively of one-act plays (another mistake), but was varied with musical numbers, burlesques and pantomime. Nor was the audience, seated at small tables rather than on rows of chairs, allowed to be entirely passive. In Znosko-Borovsky's *Transformed Prince* ('Obrashchennyy prints'), for example, members of the audience involuntarily found themselves playing the part of topers in the Spanish tavern where the musical had its setting.

One result of these 'extra-curricular' activities was that Meyerhold, as the director of an imperial theatre, was officially advised to adopt a pseudonym for his cabaret productions, which, not being state-sponsored, might constitute a breach of contract. At the suggestion of Mikhail Kuzmin, he borrowed the name of Dr Dapertutto, the sinister manipulator in E.T.A. Hoffmann's *Fantastiestücke in Callots Manier*. Regarding the cabaret productions themselves, these are characterised in a letter from A. N. Tolstoy to Valery Bryusov: 'What Meyerhold is after now is the fantastic, and he's putting on pantomimes; he's much taken with exaggerated absurdity and unexpected turns of event, both tragic and comic.'[31]

As for Pronin, Meyerhold, who was now director of the imperial theatres, did his best to secure an official post for his protégé, complete with pension. There are two versions of his ultimate failure to do so; each is illuminating and may contain an element of truth. According to Sergey Sudeykin, an artist who designed sets for the 'House of Interludes' and who was later to be a dominant figure in Pronin's 'Stray Dog':

> Pronin was considered politically unreliable and his name was in the appropriate files. He was nevertheless appointed to service with the imperial theatres, pension attached. The post Meyerhold managed to obtain for him was an odd one: it was Pronin's duty to indicate when the fire screen was to be raised. For a couple of months there was no talk of anything but of how Pronin had managed to fix himself up with a job. When the great day arrived for Pronin to indicate the raising of the fire screen he was nowhere to be found. He made an appearance towards the end

of the performance: 'I seem to be a bit late.' With that Boris Pronin's state service came to an end.[32]

The other account, which is more scholarly, if less immediate, offers a different version of Pronin's dismissal. It will be remembered that when Pronin was studying at Moscow University in 1900 he had been exiled from the city because of his involvement with student protest. Thus, in the words of two recent Soviet scholars: 'At the end of 1911, when as a result of the assassination of P. A. Stolypin the police were checking the political reliability of imperial theatre employees, this came to light and Pronin was dismissed from the Aleksandrinsky, where he had been taken on shortly before.'[33]

And so, at last, to the 'Stray Dog' (*Brodyachaya sobaka*). The 'Dog', together with its successor, the 'Players' Rest' (*Prival komediantov*) — the two are often undifferentiated — remains the most successful achievement of Pronin's life, a triumph of the *vie de bohème*. The 'Stray Dog' opened its doors on 31 December 1911 and was closed — officially for the illegal sale of wine — on 3 March 1915.

Let us begin by examining the name of this most famous of Russian cellars. This is what Pronin himself had to say in the remarkable shorthand record he made in 1939:

> And so I got the idea that I ought to create a romantic tavern where all of us 'stray dogs' would be able to squeeze in, get a cheap meal and feel that we – stray, homeless dogs – had a place of our own. I was afraid to call the 'Stray Dog' by that name, thinking that the name should be more striking, that a name would come to mind, but there was no getting away from it – homeless dogs. Then the concept developed of its own accord, I talked it over with I. A. Sats, S. Yu. Sudeykin, N. N. Sapunov, V. E. Meyerhold.[34]

The artist Sudeykin referred to here tells a rather different story (his recollections, dating from 1943, are even later after the event than Pronin's):

> 'Here's where our theatre will be,' said Boris, 'This is where you'll paint a wreath for Sapunov, this is where he would have sat, and here you can paint another one for Sats.' Sapunov had drowned in the Gulf of Finland during my absence and Sats had died of a heart attack. We felt sick at heart and made our

way to the Nevsky in silence. . . . On the way we came across a tramp who was trying to sell a shaggy dog of indeterminate colour. 'Splendid,' said Pronin, 'the stray pup, no, the future "stray dog". Buy it – that'll be a name for our cellar.'

I bought the 'stray dog' for two silver roubles. A name had been found.[35]

If there is any truth in Sudeykin's story (Sapunov, by the way, was drowned in 1912, *after* the 'Dog' had opened, so a wreath would seem a little premature), we have a pleasing parallel with the naming of the forerunner and exemplar of the literary (and painterly) cabarets that began to dot turn-of-the-century Europe, 'Le Chat noir', set up by Rudolfe de Salis in Montmartre in 1881. Harold Segel tells the story as follows: 'While pondering what to call his establishment, Salis happened upon a short-haired black cat perched atop a street lamp. He took the cat home with him and then hit upon the idea of naming his café after it.'[36]

Unlike its two predecessors, the 'Stray Dog' was not a joint venture. As Pronin proudly asserts in his 1939 recollections, 'the idea of the "Dog" belonged entirely to me'.[37] As its surviving programmes bear witness, from first to last the 'Stray Dog' claimed to be the organ of the 'Artistic Association of the Intimate Theatre'. It is something of a paradox, therefore, that Meyerhold – who was in many ways the spiritual father of the 'Dog' – should have chosen to absent himself *on principle* from the creation of his old friend and comrade-in-arms. Pronin offers the following explanation: 'Meyerhold was in a huff because he always had a very jealous attitude to anything he didn't think up himself: he felt that it was good but not his.'[38] This is not implausible. Indeed, there is an earlier instance of similar professional jealousy on Meyerhold's part. In 1909 the editor of *Apollon*, Sergey Makovsky, had requested a letter from Meyerhold evaluating the qualities of Pronin as manager, together with Yevreinov, of a miniature theatre under the magazine's auspices. Meyerhold's response of 18 June is a revealing document. Here are a few salient passages:

You ask about Pronin. I know him very well and cannot recommend him at all. . . . He won me over with that charm of his: his face, his hairstyle, his stylish necktie. . . . He was with Komissarzhevskaya as 'stage manager' for a year – and just couldn't *do anything*. He was with Stanislavsky for a year (also as stage manager) – and used to turn up late for work and just had to be got rid of. . . . he started to expound to Yevreinov all the ideas that had arisen from *intimate* research in my 'Studio', and Yevreinov started to make practical use of these ideas.[39]

It is also quite possible, however, that a decisive factor in Meyerhold's rejection of the 'Stray Dog' may have been a fastidiousness that disdained the motley entourage of an enterprise which turned out to be a successful business venture. As O. N. Vysotskaya put it: 'Vsevolod Emil'evich was suddenly indignant: "Boris has let the pharmacists loose and I'll never be a frequenter of the 'Stray Dog'"'.[40] It should be added at this point that the term 'pharmacists' (*farmatsevty*) had come to be used in the sense of 'philistines' among Meyerhold's set. In his unpublished memoirs V. I. Kozlinsky defines the typical 'pharmacists' as 'dentists with tables covered in pressed velvet upon which a volume of Vrubel is casually displayed, as if it were in constant use'.[41]

In the glorified literary salon that the 'Dog' became, elegance and social adroitness were at a premium. For some, the encounter with well-to-do fashionable St Petersburg society in which art served above all as a status symbol was embarrassing and intimidating. Thus the response of Klyuyev to Yesenin, as one fêted peasant poet to another: 'My blood runs cold when I recollect the humiliations and patronising endearments I had to endure from the 'Dog' customers.'[42] And the 'pharmacists' themselves were not in ignorance of the soubriquet applied to them: 'No pharmacists allowed' – Sapunov's testament was on prominent display; and on 26 November 1914 a presentation 'Concerning pharmacists' ('*O farmatsevte*'), complete with musical and visual illustrations, was given by one of the 'Dog's' most eccentric denizens, N. S. Tsybul'sky, a pianist and composer who preferred to be known as 'Count Aucontraire'.[43] Looking back on events many years later, Pronin himself took a resignedly pragmatic view of this compromise with Mammon:

It has to be said that without the pharmacists we just couldn't have got by – it was they who provided us with an income. Somehow we got used to them. Bauer used to send along the wine together with the bill. I always used to tell Kuz'ma the bartender not to bother the poets and artists with bills. It was the pharmacists who paid the bills.[44]

The sovereignty of the creative (and interpretative) artist was also reflected in the carefully differentiated fees customarily attached to each programme: 'Entry exclusively on written recommendation of Messrs the Actual Members of the Association of the Intimate Theatre. Price three roubles. Actors, Poets, Artists, Musicians and Friends of the "Dog" – one rouble.' As for this last-named category, 'Friends of the "Dog"', 'with a capital letter', Pronin informs us that these were 'people who had done important things for the "Dog"', and the example he gives is of an engineer who had climbed out on to the roof in a tail-coat and white shirt in order to repair the chimney flue.[45]

To complete the account of Meyerhold's relations with the 'Dog', it should be recorded that early in its existence he did not disdain to make use of its resources for a project of some importance in his own creative biography. Meyerhold transferred his enthusiasm from the parent organisation of the 'Stray Dog', the 'Artistic Association of the Intimate Theatre', to his own newly-formed 'Fellowship of Actors, Musicians and Artists' (*Tovarishchestvo akterov, muzykantov, pisateley i zhivopistsev*). In the spring of 1912 he recruited a number of leading 'Stray Dog' personalities – including Pronin, Sapunov and Mgebrov – to take part in a trial summer season at Terioki on the north shore of the Gulf of Finland. Although it was only about thirty miles from St Petersburg, this fashionable resort enjoyed a rare privilege in the Russian empire: plays could be mounted there without prior submission to censorship. Meyerhold did make an appearance in the 'Dog's' cellar to co-ordinate this enterprise, and the dwelling occupied by the 'Dog's' contingent in Terioki was known as the 'Dog dacha'.[46]

The 'Stray Dog' lasted a little more than three years before its forcible closure under the harsher censorship brought about by wartime conditions. Best remembered as a legendary haunt of the literary avant-garde, it ceased to be preoccupied with the theatrical experimentalism of Meyerhold–Dapertutto. In order to gauge the nature of its achievement, it will be illuminating to consider the relationship of three poets (two of them also dramatists of some consequence) to the 'Stray Dog' – Aleksandr Blok, Anna Akhmatova and Vladimir Mayakovsky. Each had a very different attitude, for reasons both aesthetic and sociological, to Pronin and his enterprise. As the most famous representatives of the three main literary 'schools' of a period much given to warring literary factions – Symbolism, Acmeism and Futurism – their views take on a significance which exceeds the purely personal. It should be added that the very fact that the 'Stray Dog' brought these literary rivals into contact is perhaps its most characteristic (and positive) achievement. Pronin's own position was one of good-natured eclecticism – he was certainly not one to man the aesthetic barricades. A partisan such as the Futurist poet and artist Benedikt Livshits assures us that 'Pronin was wary of too close a friendship with the Futurists, from whom some unpleasant surprise was always to be expected'.[47] We would do well to note, however, that Livshits goes on to grant that 'it would be a mistake to imagine Symbolists, Acmeists and Futurists as three warring camps entrenched in impassable ditches and who rejected once and for all the possibility of interaction'.[48]

It has long been the convention to assume that Blok was a regular patron of the 'Stray Dog'. Thus, in a recent study of the European cabaret theatre, we find Blok included in a 'list of habitués' together with Akhmatova, Mayakovsky and many others.[49] However, a pair of Soviet scholars who have had enviable access to rich archival material, as well as contact with the surviving members of the Pronin family, have demonstrated that there is not a shred of documentary evidence to prove that Blok even so much as set foot in the cellar.[50] Blok himelf seems to have experienced a growing distaste for what increasingly bore the brand of a successful commercial enterprise. Here is what Pronin has to say on the subject:

> Gumilev, Akhmatova and Kuzmin came along, but there was no tempting Blok. . . . Although we had been close and he did have some affection for me (from the days of Vera Fedorovna Komissarzhevskaya's theatre), he wouldn't have been at his ease in the 'Dog', and so he stayed by himself in his apartment, melancholy and unsociable.[51]

The poet's actress wife, Lyubov' Dmitriyevna, had participated in the Terioki summer season of 1912 and was thus on friendly terms with some of the 'Stray Dog' personalities; this would appear to have confirmed Blok in his disinclination to have any dealings with the 'Dog'. The poet himself recorded a conversation of November 1912 with Aleksey Remizov 'about the "Stray Dog" (I did my best to persuade him not to go there and not to give them any encouragement), about how people don't know how to enjoy themselves in Russia'.[52] His notebook for 11 February 1913 contains a similar refrain. After complaining at length of those who attach themselves to the world of true creativity, people who 'bestow a word of praise here, a word of discouragement there' on the artist and thus 'drink . . . the artist's blood', he concludes: 'Tears to us are toys to them. Private viewings, "Stray Dogs", theatrical premières – that's all they live for.'[53] But for all that, Blok had once almost contributed to the repertoire of the cabaret he held in such low regard. The previous year had marked the centenary of Napoleon's invasion of Moscow, and Lyubov' Dmitriyevna had asked her husband to write a monologue for her to deliver at an evening the 'Dog' intended to devote to the anniversary. In fact, the evening never took place, and Blok got no further than the following sketch: '(a gambling house in Paris a hundred years ago). I had the notion of writing a monologue by a (mad?) woman reminiscing about the revolution. She puts those assembled to shame.'[54] One can only regret that this monologue, eternally *à propos*, was never written.

In any anthology of writing inspired by the 'Stray Dog' the work of Anna Akhmatova, both early and late, would certainly occupy a prominent place. The poetess, whose piquant angular beauty attracted the pencil of Amedeo Modigliani, was an habituée of the 'Dog'. As Livshits writes:

> Wrapped tightly in black silk, great oval gems about her waist, Akhmatova would drift in, lingering at the entrance to write in the 'piggy book' (*svinaya kniga*) at the insistence of Pronin, who would always rush forward to greet her and her latest verse, concerning which the simple-minded 'pharmacists' would make conjectures that tickled their curiosity still further.[55]

Akhamatova's familiar lyric of January 1913, 'Cabaret artistique', has served the 'Dog' as both epigraph and epitaph: 'All of us here are revellers and whores, / Joyless the company we keep.'[56] But it is in the lyrical and fragmentary *Poem without a Hero* ('Poema bez geroya'), which was not given its final shape until after the Second World War, that the 'Stray Dog' provides the most extensive subtext. Of the poem's three dedications, the first is 'To the memory of Vs. K.', the second 'To O. A. G.-S.'.[57] It is no secret that Vs. K. are the initials of Vsevolod Knyazev (1891–1913) the 'dragoon Pierrot'[58] whose verse provides an epigraph to the 'Fourth and

Final Chapter' of the poem's first section.[59] As for O. A. G.-S., these are the initials of Olga Glebova-Sudeykina, the poem's 'muddle-headed Psyche' (*putanitsa-Psikheya*), an enchantress who was both the cellar's leading lady and the wife of its chief decorator, Sergey Sudeykin. The 'tragic event of 1913 of which the tale is told in *Poem without a Hero'*, to quote the letter to 'N' with which Akhmatova prefaces her poem,[60] was the suicide of Vsevolod Knyazev. He had been the lover of Mikhail Kuzmin, who had himself made a significant contribution to the 'Stray Dog', especially in its early days. However, Knyazev later gave his heart to Glebova-Sudeykina, for whom he was just one of many: 'Love has passed – distinct / And close become death's features / . . . My dreams are still of you alone', to quote from a poem Knyazev wrote in December 1912.[61] He persisted in his infatuation, she in her indifference, and on 5 April 1913 Knyazev is reported to have put a revolver to his head in front of Glebova-Sudeykina's very door.[62] In her own notes to the *Poem*, Akhmatova constantly reminds the reader of its connection with the 'many-hued, smoky "Stray Dog", with its invariable touch of mystery'.[63] Recalling her first reading of the work at the Union of Soviet Writers in 1941, the poetess indicated that her audience included 'those to whom it is dedicated'. Since Pronin was among those present, it has been not unconvincingly argued that he was the person honoured as the *Poem*'s dedicatee.[64]

It was in the 'Stray Dog' that Vladimir Mayakovsky gave his first public reading on 17 November 1912 – a month before his debut in print with 'A Slap in the Face of Public Taste' ('Poshchechina obshchestvennomu vkusu'). Although he became something of an habitué of the 'Dog' ('Mayakovsky would often drop by, he would sit for hours, and he would write there too – at the fireside'),[65] the young Futurist had mixed feelings about the cellar and its clientèle. He behaved as a barbarian in a refined aristocratic salon, putting on a deliberate show of coarseness as if to emphasise the contrast between himself and more typical patrons. A dramatic encounter took place between Mayakovsky and the 'pharmacists' in February 1915, at the height of the First World War, an encounter that no doubt was one of the primary reasons for the decision by the wartime censorship to close down the cabaret the following month. The scandal was caused by Mayakovsky's reading of one of his most virulent attacks on the bourgeoisie, 'You There!' ('Vam!'). Just before mounting the platform, Mayakovsky had turned to Pronin ('Borichka', as he called him) with the words: 'Just let me get up on that stage and give .'em a bit of shock treatment. I'll stir those bourgeois bastards up a bit!'[66]

The effect of 'You There!' ('with your bathrooms and warm WCs') was of a thunderbolt: there was turmoil; ladies fainted. An attempt to mollify the outraged 'pharmacists' was made by Prince Mikhail Nikolayevich Volkonsky (who has added a word to the Russian language with his '*Vampuka*', an immortal skit on operatic absurdities). Pronin has recorded, to the best of his memory, the words of this old-style aristocrat:

> I'm here for the first time, it's the first time I've ever set eyes on any one of you, including the young man who just read that splendid, if somewhat eccentric poem. It seems to me that if only another word could be found for the unprintable one in the last line, the verses of this unusually gifted poet would be quite remarkable! Why did the young fellow choose you for an audience – that's what I can't understand![67]

It should be noted that the 'unprintable' word appears in the penultimate line, and is not worse than *blyad'* – 'whore'. Akhmatova recorded her recollections of the same evening in 1941:

> The pharmacists were yelling at the top of their voice, but Mayakovsky stood there on the stage, perfectly calm, motionless, smoking an enormous cigar. . . . Yes. And that's how I remember him — very handsome, very young with those great eyes of his, surrounded by howling bourgeois.[68]

An exchange that took place on this occasion reveals Mayakovsky's gift for repartee. A woman in the audience yelled out: 'Why aren't you at the front?' 'Because a poet's quill is as much needed by the homeland as the soldier's sword', was the reply. 'But not *your* quill', the woman persisted. 'I see no point in discussing that with you, madam', responded Mayakovsky, 'because the only quills that interest you are located on feather hats.'[69] It is worth recording that it was during his one and only visit to the 'Dog', two weeks after the events described above, that Maksim Gorky delivered himself of the famous verbal shrug that would serve as moral support to one who was subject to the badgering of the yellow press: 'You know, the Futurists *do* have something.'[70]

Pre-revolutionary Pronin was irrepressible and, undiscouraged by the closure of the 'Dog' in March 1915, organised a new Petrograd cabaret, 'The Player's Rest', the following year. This new venture, which lasted until 1919, still awaits the painstaking research that recent Soviet scholarship has at last allotted to the 'Stray Dog'. It was here that Lyubov' Dmitriyevna Blok gave many public readings of her husband's 'The Twelve' ('Dvenadtsat''), and it is certain that here, at least, the famous poet did make an appearance, sharing a unique poetry reading with Mayakovsky on 20 February 1919. Other projects came to nothing. One such was the Chamber Theatre of 1918, over the artistic council of which Blok was invited to preside.

In the early 1920s Pronin was back again in Moscow, where, as Lugin tells us, 'his thoughts were of the creation of a new society. This society would be called the "Wandering Enthusiast" ("Stranstvuyushchiy entuziast")'.[71] The 'Enthusiast' was housed in another cellar, but Pronin himself inhabited a tiny attic room in the same building, something between an artist's and a photographer's studio. Here is Lugin's description of it: 'The only thing that lodges in the memory is a plenitude of glass – a glass wall, a glass window in the ceiling – and paintings by Sudeykin. Pronin has more pictures than he has chairs. Whether the chairs had gone into the stove and the studio was heated by furniture or whether there never had been any chairs, I don't know.'[72] Another memoirist recalls sitting in the 'Enthusiast' itself several years later (although he calls it 'The Enthusiast's Rest', confusing Pronin's old Petrograd cabaret with the new Moscow one) with Vadim Shershenevich, the leading theoretician of Imaginism. A sunken-eyed and languid Sergey Yesenin seemed not to recognise them at first. 'He was gloomy, nothing was left of his old bravado', we are told.[73] Soon after, they heard the news of the poet's suicide.

It will be apparent from this compilation of dates and data pertaining to the life and career of Boris Pronin that he had ceased to be a central influence in Meyerhold's creative life even before the Revolution. He did not share Meyerhold's splendours and miseries of the 1920s and 1930s; but neither did he share Meyerhold's ultimate grim fate. This does not mean, however, that no reparation needs to be made. The words of Olga Berggolts, who first met Pronin in 1941, will serve as a fitting conclusion:

84     *Russian Theatre in the Age of Modernism*

in almost every article about Mayakovsky and almost every piece where mention is made of the 'Stray Dog' and Boris Pronin, he is spoken of in slighting terms, at best with a kind of lordly condescension – and this is an obvious injustice. . . . The impression he made on me was of a lively and intelligent man, and – this is the main thing – a man boundlessly in love with art, so much in love, so dedicated, especially to poetry, that God grant such love and dedication to the administrators of our writers' or composers' centres.[74]

## Notes

1. On the subject of Chekhov in relation to Maeterlinck, see M. Green (ed. and trs.), *The Russian Symbolist Theatre* (Ann Arbor, Mich., 1986) pp. 10–11.
2. Ibid., p. 10.
3. A. Ye. Parnis and R. D. Timenchik, 'Programmy Brodyachey Sobaki', in *Pamyati kul'tury. Novyye otkrytiya* (Leningrad, 1983) p. 162.
4. I. V. Lazarev, 'O sozdanii Narodnogo Khudozhestvennogo teatra', ibid., p. 244.
5. A. A. Mgebrov, *Zhizn' v teatre*, vol. I (Leningrad, 1929) p. 265.
6. G. Ivanov, *Peterburgskiye zimy* (New York, 1952) pp. 61–2.
7. V. Ivanov, 'The Need for a Dionysian Theatre', in Green, p. 116.
8. *A. Blok. Novyye materialy i issledovaniya*, vol. III (Moscow, 1982) p. 236.
9. V. Bryusov, 'Against Naturalism in the Theatre', in Green, p. 28.
10. V. E. Meyerkhol'd, *Perepiska, 1896–1938* (Moscow, 1976) p. 58. Meyerhold's initial reaction to the loss was a horrified incredulity far different from the reasoned calm he was later to affect: 'The failure of the Studio was my salvation, because it really wasn't the right thing' (N. Volkov, *Meyerkhol'd* (Moscow, 1923) p. 23).
11. Parnis and Timenchik, p. 162.
12. Meyerkhol'd, p. 67.
13. Ibid., p. 62.
14. Ibid., p. 63.
15. A. Blok, 'Vera Fiodorovna Komissarzhevskaya', in Green, p. 43.
16. Meyerkhol'd, pp. 44, 360.
17. Ibid., pp. 61, 364.
18. Ibid., p. 63.
19. Green, p. 43.
20. Meyerkhol'd, p. 96.
21. B. Zaytsev, *Moskva* (Paris, 1939) pp. 136–7.
22. Mgebrov, p. 267.
23. Zaytsev, p. 139.
24. H. B. Segel, 'Cabaret in Russia', in his *Turn-of-the-Century Cabaret* (New York, 1987) pp. 261–2.

25. Mgebrov, p. 269.
26. Jay Leyda, *Kino: A History of the Russian and Soviet Film* (London, 1960) p. 79.
27. Mgebrov, p. 271.
28. Parnis and Timenchik, p. 163.
29. Meyerkhol'd, p. 123.
30. G. Auslender, 'Peterburgskiye teatry', *Apollon*, 1910, no. 10, p. 123.
31. Parnis and Timenchik, p. 163.
32. S. Sudeykin, 'Brodyachaya sobaka', in *Vstrechi s proshlym*, vol. v (Moscow, 1984) p. 189.
33. Parnis and Timenchik, p. 244.
34. Ibid., p. 162.
35. Sudeykin, p. 190.
36. Segel, p. 4.
37. Parnis and Timenchik, p. 162.
38. Ibid., p. 169.
39. Meyerkhol'd, p. 126.
40. Parnis and Timenchik, p. 247.
41. Ibid., p. 238.
42. K. M. Azadovskiy, 'Yesenin i Klyuyev v 1915 godu', in *Yesenin i sovremennost'* (Moscow, 1975) p. 239.
43. Parnis and Timenchik, p. 237.
44. Ibid., p. 238.
45. Ibid., p. 166.
46. Ibid., p. 170.
47. B. Livshits, *Polutoraglazyy strelets* (Leningrad, 1933) p. 262.
48. Ibid., p. 263.
49. Segel, p. 303.
50. Parnis and Timenchik, p. 168.
51. Ibid.
52. A. Blok, *Sobraniye sochineniy*, vol. vii (Moscow and Leningrad, 1963) p. 184.
53. Ibid., p. 219.
54. Ibid., p. 161.
55. Livshits, p. 26.
56. A. Akhmatova, *Sochineniya*, vol. i (Munich, 1968) p. 87.
57. Ibid., vol. ii, p. 101.
58. Ibid., p. 115.
59. Ibid., p. 119.
60. Ibid., p. 97.
61. J. E. Malmstad, 'Mikhail Kuzmin: A Chronicle of his Life and Times', in M. A. Kuzmin, *Sobraniye stikhov*, vol. iii (Munich, 1977) p. 184.
62. Ibid., p. 185.
63. Parnis and Timenchik, p. 249.
64. Ibid.
65. Ibid., p. 165.
66. Ibid., p. 166.
67. Ibid., pp. 166–7.
68. Ibid., p. 167.

69. Ibid.
70. Ibid., p. 171.
71. G. Lugin, *28° 14' 30" vost. dolgoty* (Riga, 1933) p. 32.
72. Ibid.
73. V. P. Komardenkov, *Dela minuvshiye* (Moscow, 1972) p. 87.
74. Parnis and Timenchik, pp. 164–5.

# 4

# Leonid Andreyev's *He Who Gets Slapped*: Who Gets Slapped?

## ANDREW BARRATT

Leonid Andreyev is at once one of the most prominent and yet one of the most enigmatic figures in the rise of the Russian modernist theatre. Of his prominence little needs to be said. A prodigious writer of plays, Andreyev achieved dubious celebrity in a career which encompassed both spectacular successes – of which the Meyerhold production of *The Life of Man* ('Zhizn' cheloveka') was the undoubted highlight – and a growing coolness on the part of audiences and critics towards the works of his later years, in which he came to experiment with a perplexing variety of styles and forms. To this public story of Andreyev's fall from grace first the gossip columnists, then the memoirists and biographers have added the poignant account of the private man, whose life became poisoned by a sense of injustice at the often vitriolic attacks of his critics and increasingly burdened by the symptoms of the grave illness which was to result in his premature death in 1919. The famous dacha, built in Finland at the height of Andreyev's fame, but which fell rapidly into disrepair and eventual ruin, has somehow become an emblem of a writer whose name is almost invariably invoked as a case study of the rise and fall of the popular man of letters in early twentieth-century Russia.[1]

These circumstances would not warrant particular attention were it not that they have left an indelible mark upon the scholarly assessment of Andreyev's significance as a dramatist. Just as contemporary critics – especially in the 1910s – began to suggest that his early successes were a sort of confidence trick, as much a product of the times as of any real gift on the part of the writer himself, so subsequent commentators too have displayed an unwillingness to assign a place for Andreyev amongst the great theatrical talents of his day. For better or worse, Andreyev has been remembered above all as the author of *The Life of Man* and the other pseudo-morality plays, such as *Anathema* ('Anatema') and *The Ocean* ('Okean'), which followed in its wake, plays which have earned him the reputation of a Symbolist *manqué*. 'The whole problem with Andreyev', as Andrey Bely wrote at the time in a review of *Anathema*, 'is that he wants to be Symbolist, but that he is becoming a sensationalist instead'.[2] As for Andreyev's subsequent flirtation with naturalism (in *Days of Our Lives* ('Dni nashey zhizni') and other plays), his attempt to invent a new type of drama, the so-called 'pan-psychic' drama, and his later experiments with markedly different modes of writing, from the stylised historical drama of *Samson Enchained* ('Samson v okovakh') to the Pirandello-like metadrama *Requiem* ('Rekviem') – all of this has been treated in much the same spirit of critical condescension.

There can be little doubt that the sheer variety of dramatic idioms represented in Andreyev's works for the theatre has been the crucial factor in the general devaluation of his achievement as a playwright. In the eyes of his detractors, this served as proof of an incurable literary opportunism; it was a desperate search for a style which would ensure the author's place in the limelight. Even his more generous-minded commentators have tended to view this aspect of his work as an inevitable product of an innate instability both as a man and a writer.

These preliminary comments are intended both to suggest the need for a reassessment of Andreyev's contribution to the Russian theatre and to indicate the terms in which such a reassessment might be conducted. Instead of working within a framework which tends to ensure that he will remain a victim of his reputation, I believe that it would be better to begin by taking the writer at his word, and to insist that he was above all a man sincerely committed to the notion of perpetual experiment. Despite his status as one of Russia's most popular writers of the early part of the century – his only real rival being his erstwhile friend, Maksim Gorky – Andreyev was never content simply to repeat the literary formulae which had brought him success. As A. L. Grigor'ev has suggested, it is above all in his work as a dramatist that this experimental imperative found its fullest expression.[3] The evidence of this is to be found everywhere. From his bold statement in a letter of 1906 to Serafimovich that he intended nothing less than to achieve a total 'reform' of the drama,[4] to his sad acceptance in his diary of 1918 that the writing of a great dramatic work may have ultimately eluded him,[5] Andreyev was constantly engaged in a conscious quest for new modes of dramatic expression. What is more, in his well-known *Letters on the Theatre* ('Pis'ma o teatre'), in private letters to Stanislavsky and Nemirovich-Danchenko,[6] as well as in the numerous interviews which appeared regularly in the periodical press of the day, Andreyev made a contribution to the public discussion of the problems confronting the modern theatre which has yet to receive the careful treatment it deserves.

Andreyev's scattered theoretical statements are every bit as diverse and contradictory as his dramatic practice itself, yet one may discern in them two central ideas which constitute a 'credo' of sorts. The first is a distrust of the division of contemporary writers into clearly defined groups with fixed aesthetic or ideological objectives. 'Who am I?', Andreyev wrote to Gorky in 1912. 'To highborn Decadents I am an accursed Realist, to hereditary Realists I am a suspicious Symbolist.'[7] We should not be misled by the jocular tone of this remark; Andreyev's insistence on his independence as a writer is his strongest drive, perhaps even to the point of obsession. It was this same fierce determination to find his own way in literary life that had made him suggest some years earlier in a letter to Georgiy Chulkov that he would have liked to publish each new work under a different name.[8] And even as late as 1918, although he now writes with undisguised bitterness, we find a pointed reference to what Andreyev describes as his 'loneliness' as a writer and the 'hatred' towards him displayed by 'literary life'.[9]

The second distinguishing feature of Andreyev's position is, in a sense, a corollary of his desire to assert his independence from the competing literary schools of his day. This is the urge to create a type of play which would achieve a *synthesis* of dramatic styles. His statement in a letter to Nemirovich-Danchenko of his desire to avoid the excesses of naturalism, on the one hand, and mysticism, on the other,[10] is just one example of what a number of recent critics have considered the essence of Andreyev's theatrical experiment.[11] The scathing comments on the failings of both Realists and Symbolists which one finds in the first of the *Letters on the Theatre* have their source in the same urgent sense of the need to create a drama which will transcend what the author saw as the fatal dichotomy afflicting the contemporary Russian theatre.[12]

The student of Andreyev's drama is confronted, therefore, with two basic tasks. The first is to monitor carefully his changing practices as a playwright, relating these to the theoretical concerns voiced in his various statements on the theatre. The second is to place both the theory and the practice against the background of developments within the European modernist theatre. It remains to be added, however, that the best place to begin some sort of review of his achievement is at the end. As I have already suggested, it is the products of the writer's later period which have fared worst at the hands of his critics. 'During the last years of his life (1912–1919)', Alexander Kaun wrote in his path-finding study, 'Andreyev created nothing that was new in form or in motive.'[13] Although later writers have been less extreme in their rejection of the works of Andreyev's final years, the balance of their attention has still tipped very much in favour of his pre-1910 writings. The same emphasis is to be discerned in the work of Soviet critics, although here the explanation is to be found in politics rather than aesthetics. The intense interest in the writer's more socially-oriented plays of the period following the 1905 Revolution (especially *To the Stars* ('K zvezdam') and *Savva*) reflects the general tendency amongst Soviet commentators to vaunt Andreyev the 'Realist' over Andreyev the 'Modernist'.[14] More recently, however, there has been a concerted effort by critics within the USSR to reconceive Andreyev's career as a dramatist by concentrating in particular upon his place within the development of European Modernism, thereby emphasising the significance of his later plays in that process. By suggesting Andreyev's proximity to the ideas and practice of expressionism, existentialism and other movements within the Modernist theatre, these critics have provided a valuable starting point for a more thorough reinterpretation of his career as a writer of plays.[15] My purpose in the present essay is necessarily more modest. Never the less, in offering a new reading of *He Who Gets Slapped* ('Tot, kto poluchayet poshchechiny') I am seeking quite deliberately to shift the focus of critical interest in Andreyev to the much-neglected last period.

*He Who Gets Slapped* is, in several respects, something of an anomaly among Andreyev's later plays. To begin with, it is undoubtedly the best-known product of these years: indeed, it is perhaps the only one of Andreyev's dramas to have won for itself a permanent place, however tenuous, in the world theatrical repertoire. It is also the play which has most consistently defeated the efforts of those who have sought to classify it.[16] The section on Andreyev in a recent Soviet study, whilst it offers a most useful overview of his last plays in the context of contemporary dramatic styles, conspicuously omits any mention of *He Who Gets Slapped*.[17] The uniqueness of the play has not often been recognised. Perhaps the only critic to do so quite explicitly was G. Kryzhitsky. Writing in 1922, he expressed his opinion as follows: 'This is the only play in which [Andreyev] rises to true *theatricality*, combining the most profound philosophical content with a vivid theatrical form.'[18] It might be added that *He Who Gets Slapped* is also the work in which Andreyev achieves, perhaps more successfully than anywhere else, the elusive ideal of a 'synthetic' drama. In the discussion which follows, I shall attempt to show the manner in which philosophy and theatre are combined in this remarkable play. In so doing, I shall argue that its central idea is rather more complex than has usually been acknowledged and that the play as a whole sheds important light on the author's attitude towards Russian Symbolism.

A note in Andreyev's diary for 9 August 1915 reports that the process of work on *He Who Gets Slapped* led to a temporary cessation of the painful symptoms of his illness. Such was the author's mood, in fact, that he even found himself typing the text to a tango rhythm.[19] Andreyev's spirits were still high the following month, when he wrote to his good friend, the theatre critic Sergey Gouloushev, that his new play would be a treat for actors and audience alike (*'budet zdorovo igrat'sya i smotret'sya!'*).[20] Given this enthusiasm, it was perhaps inevitable that when the play came to be performed, it failed to live up to the author's expectations. Boris Zaytsev, who met Andreyev for the last time during the Moscow première, records the playwright as saying: 'They've ruined the play. . . . The main role has been misunderstood.'[21] As for the response of audience and critics, this too gave little cause for satisfaction. V. Beklemisheva, who attended a performance of the play at the Aleksandrinsky theatre in St Petersburg later recalled: '*He Who Gets Slapped* was incomprehensible for the audience of the Aleksandrinsky theatre. I remember the perplexed questions during the intervals, the requests to explain who the gentleman was who came to see He. And when I said that it was immaterial whether this was He's "double" or a real person from his past, that the sense of the play is not affected in either case, my interlocutors responded with a mistrustful smile.'[22] This incomprehension was largely shared by the critics, whose reviews served only to increase Andreyev's suspicion that they were involved in a conspiracy against him. 'My dear friend, what asses the local reviewers are!', he complained to Gouloshev from St Petersburg, 'You should see what they have written about He! They're probably even worse than the Muscovites!'[23] For once, at least, he was not exaggerating: such was the chorus of bafflement from the critics that one of their number was inspired to devote an entire pamphlet to an explanation of the play's meaning.[24]

Given the confusion generated by *He Who Gets Slapped* among Andreyev's contemporaries, it is curious to note that his more recent commentators seem to have experienced very little difficulty with the play and have even displayed a striking unanimity in their interpretation of it. Two approaches have been dominant in these modern readings. The first is an autobiographical approach, according to which the story of He and his circus act is viewed as a metaphor by means of which Andreyev has dramatised his own predicament in Russian literary life.[25] According to this view, He's abortive attempt to bring serious ideas to the circus, to raise it from the level of pure entertainment, translates into a straightforward parable of the artist as prophet scorned. This theme is also prominent in the scene of He's encounter with the Gentleman at the beginning of Act 3, in which several critics have detected a veiled statement of Andreyev's disdain for those of his contemporaries who took up his own ideas only to debase them.[26] These arguments are persuasive, and all the more so when the play is placed alongside the playwright's letters and diaries. Consider, for example, the following extract from a letter to Belousov of 1914 (Andreyev is describing the hostile reaction of the Moscow audiences to the dramatisation of *Thought* ('Mysl'')): 'I even like it when they whistle: I shall soon become a sado-masochist and demand that I be beaten – what are whistles after all?'[27] It is difficult to avoid the suspicion that one is privy here to the idea which was to become the seed of what Alexander Kaun has termed He's 'bizarre revenge'.[28]

The second line of approach favoured by modern critics has been to draw upon Andreyev's own statements about the play. Although these are well-known, it is worth quoting the salient passages from them here. The first is from a letter to Ye. A.

Polevitskaya, the actress who played the part of Consuella in the Moscow Dramatic Theatre production of the play. 'The real centre of the play is not in He', Andreyev explained, 'but in Consuella. . . . The play contains an argument between Hellenic paganism and Christianity, which has poisoned love; in this fairytale play I tell of beautiful gods, tormented by earthly dominion, lost in petty human labyrinths and their painful passions.'[29] Writing to I. Ye. Duvan-Tortsov, the theatre's director, at about the same time, Andreyev expanded further upon this view:

What Consuella might become on the stage will be seen, but I shall say what she ought to be. First and foremost, in her appearance she must be a *goddess* – in accordance with the strict laws of classical beauty. Tall, slim, with regular and stern features, softened by an expression of almost childlike naïvety and charm; everything circus-like and crass, from her costume down to her expressions and a certain vulgarity of gesture – all of this is only on the surface, *on the outside*. And this is one of the main tasks for the actress and the director: to show the goddess beneath the tinsel of the horsewoman and acrobat.

From the point of view of character and psychology, C[onsuella] is lofty, pure and unconsciously *tragic*. The latter is very important. And this is not the external theatricality of the splendid Zinida, but a deep and real *theatricality*, created by the contradiction between the divine essence of Consuella, and her external, *chance* form. She is a captive of life, she is enslaved by brute reality, the power of things, and she is *suffering*. Before the appearance of He, she had been in a dream, as it were – and he *awakened* her; and the moment when she wants to remember her native land and sky, but cannot, is full for her of the very greatest *sorrow*. In this sense, due to the force of her tragic experiences, which increase towards the fourth act, she is no less a *heroine* than Katerina in *The Thunderstorm*.

There is nothing simpler than the drama, in which all is on the outside: in movement, cries, tears, sobs, in clearly visible dramatic conflicts. But the difficulty of this role is terribly great, for all the tragicality is based externally on *half-tones, sighs, smiles, on the expression of sadness in the face and eyes, when the soul is hidden from the very person who is experiencing it all*. (p. 581)

The importance of these remarks requires little in the way of commentary. As a statement of authorial intention they are as clear as anything one could wish for. Indeed, in these few brief paragraphs, Andreyev has done nothing less than supply a succinct interpretation not only of Consuella's role but of the drama as a whole. It is certainly no wonder that so many readings of the play supply little more than a gloss on the author's own words.[30]

But perhaps the most interesting feature of Andreyev's remarks on *He Who Gets Slapped* is not their clarity, but the fact that they are couched in terms which derive quite unmistakably from the works of Russian Symbolist authors. The opposition of Hellenism and Christianity, to take the most obvious instance, was an idea borrowed from Nietzsche's *The Birth of Tragedy* and one which had proved a major inspiration for many of the writers of Russia's Silver Age, finding expression both in the historical trilogy of Merezhkovsky, and (more notoriously) in the erotic scenes between Lyudmila and Sasha in Sologub's *The Petty Demon* ('Melkiy bes'). Nor should we forget the example of Daryalsky, the hero of Bely's *The Silver Dove* ('Serebryanyy golub''), who imagined that 'in the depths of his native people there pulsed an age-old past, native to the people but not yet vitally experienced – that of ancient Greece'.[31] It is fully understandable, therefore, that when Sologub came to review Andreyev's play, he offered a reading of it which differed in no significant respect from what Andreyev himself had written in private. Describing He as a hero who has descended from the purer realm of a higher reality into the base world of the circus, he speaks of his treatment of Consuella as the rescue of Psyche from the mundane forces which theaten to hold her in thrall.[32]

These observations raise a number of interesting questions, not the least of which is the nature of Andreyev's relationship with Sologub at this time. We know from Beklemisheva's memoirs that Andreyev counted the author of *The Petty Demon* among his favourite writers during these years,[33] and the writer's eldest son, Vadim, reports on the 'truly friendly relations' that existed between the two men.[34] One might even wonder, given the fulsome praise contained within Sologub's article on *He Who Gets Slapped* and his particular concern to defend Andreyev from the criticism of those like A. Izgoyev, who had found the play to be 'tedious and unintelligible',[35] whether we are not dealing with a case of collusion.[36]

But it is the question of Andreyev's *treatment* of the Symbolist motifs in *He Who Gets Slapped* which is the most important to our present purpose. Even though the author's own statements and Sologub's article suggest quite plainly that the play should be read as an unproblematic (indeed, rather routine) statement of the neo-Romantic conflict between the higher and lower realms of being, there are a number of reasons to doubt that things are really that simple. It is certainly difficult to believe that a writer who had so fiercely insisted on his independence from Symbolism, as from all the other literary movements of his day, would have suddenly turned his dramatic talent to the production of an almost stereotypical Symbolist work. These suspicions are reinforced by the very *prominence* of the Symbolist theme in the play, which in itself suggests a self-consciousness which belongs more to the realm of parody than sincere imitation. On a few occasions it even appears that Andreyev is indulging in what might best be described as Symbolist 'in-jokes'. For example, when Consuella responds to one of He's speeches about the 'gods' with the typically naïve question: 'Do the gods really exist?' (p. 358), one may detect an oblique reference to *The Death of the Gods* ('Smert' bogov') and *The Gods Reborn* ('Voskresshiye bogi'), the first two volumes of Merezhkovsky's famous trilogy, a work of which it is known that Andreyev had a low opinion.[37] And when Jackson remarks with indisguised sarcasm of Bezano's madcap heroics in Act 4: 'Why does he run such risks. Or perhaps he has wings like a god?' (p. 389), the allusion to Mikhail Kuzmin's notorious novella *Wings* ('Kryl'ya') – in which the Hellenic theme again features significantly – appears quite unmistakable.

The presence of such playful elements in *He Who Gets Slapped* invites the suspicion that Andreyev's attitude to the all-pervasive Symbolist theme is perhaps not quite so serious as has often been assumed. What is most important, however, is that they raise certain doubts about the role of He as Symbolist hero. The main problem with the readings canvassed earlier is that they find no complexity or ambiguity in the behaviour of the play's central character. (This is as true, of course, of Andreyev's own remarks on the drama as it is of later critical statements.) Despite the author's dogged insistence, a year after the writing of the work, that the character of He should be numbered among the great 'heroic' personalities celebrated in his plays,[38] the fact is that He's presentation in the play is anything but unambiguously heroic. As the critic. A. R. Kugel' noted at the time, 'the play . . . shows He by turns as a phantom, a god, a madman, and a human being'.[39] Whatever we may come to think ultimately of his mission, we should not forget that He is often a figure of fun, especially in the early scenes where his unworldliness constantly finds expression in naïve hyperbole – witness the absurd inappropriateness of his response to Mancini's disclosure that Consuella's name was suggested by a George Sand novel: 'What a wonderful knowledge of books!' (p. 334).[40] But this is only to work at the surface. In order to appreciate fully the problematic status of He, it will be necessary to examine more carefully the dramatic action of the play, for it is here that his ambiguity is most deeply inscribed.

Let us begin with a question. What is He really up to? As the Gentleman puts it in Act 3, 'Knowing you as I do, I cannot admit that you are here without pursuing some idea. But what is it?' (p. 369). In suggesting an answer I shall, of course, explore the nature of He's activities in the circus, in particular his dealings with the 'sleeping gods', Consuella and Bezano. But I wish first to approach the problem somewhat tangentially, by considering He's place in the melodramatic structure of the play's action. We shall see later that these two elements are, in fact, most closely linked.

The melodramatic framework of *He Who Gets Slapped* is easily described. To be sure, Andreyev makes no effort to disguise what is, in effect, a rather crude example of the genre. No sooner is the action initiated than the characters are readily identified with the conventional formulae of this kind of writing. In Consuella and Bezano we have the young lovers, typically pure of body and soul, whose union is threatened, equally typically, by the evil designs of Baron Regnard and the complicity of Mancini. Regnard and Mancini are themselves the traditionally flat characters of the melodrama, almost grotesque in their villainy. Mancini is odiously hypocritical and utterly selfish; in everything he says and does – be it his aristocratic scorn for the mob, or his sordid misdeeds, for which he is prepared to condemn Consuella to a loveless marriage with the hideous Regnard – he is bound to arouse the moral outrage which is the *sine qua non* of the melodramatic method. As for Regnard, he is not so much a character as a cipher. Although James Woodward has referred to him as 'evil incarnate',[41] it should be noted that his evil attributes are never so specifically portrayed as those of Mancini. This very lack of specificity, combined with his ominous designation as the 'spider', is what allows him to function as the 'fate worse than death' which threatens the innocent heroine.

Even as he invokes this melodramatic pattern, however, Andreyev renders it problematic. He does so in the first place by causing us to doubt the ability of the young hero and heroine to conform to their traditional stereotypes. Thus, Bezano, although he is suitably strong and handsome, displays traits which ill befit his ostensible role. Although we will be encouraged by his forthright resistance to the advances of Zinida, there are times when his attitude to Consuella suggests less than the total devotion that is expected of the young lover. This is evident not only in his display of embarrassment at Consuella's lack of epistolary sophistication (p. 337), but also – and far more subversively – in his apparent reluctance or inability to challenge the evil intentions of Regnard and Mancini. Instead of the righteous indignation and purposeful action required for his part, Bezano displays only resignation and a willingness to sublimate his feelings in his dedication to the circus act in which he and Consuella perform.

Bezano's unsuitability to his role of hero is matched, if not surpassed, by the failure of Consuella to live up to our expectations of the melodramatic heroine. Although she is beautiful, naïve and vulnerable, these latter qualities derive from altogether the wrong source. From the outset, she displays not only her semi-literacy but also her vulgarity and embourgeoisement. It is significant that the first thing that she does when He appears on the scene is to show him a Venetian handkerchief of which she is so proud (p. 335). This attachment to material blandishments is what renders her so susceptible to Regnard's overtures. But this is not the worst of it. As the action moves towards its climax, Consuella appears quite unable to view Bezano as a potential alternative partner and even displays a disarming lack of concern at the prospect of her imminent marriage to the 'spider':

HE. And if the Baron asks you to be his wife, will you accept?
CONSUELLA. Certainly. That's all father and I are waiting for. Father told me yesterday that the Baron will not hesitate very long. Of course, I don't love him. But I will be his honest, faithful wife. (p. 357)

This is the moment of greatest generic subversion, all the more so to a Russian audience, who could hardly fail to detect in this exchange an almost blasphemously ironic echo of Tatyana's famous words to Onegin at the end of *Yevgeny Onegin*.

In short, this is a curiously off-key melodrama, in which the hero and heroine seem either unable or unwilling to act out their designated parts. This is where He comes in. Even before he has found his feet in his new environment, He displays an interest in the young couple. 'I suppose that good-looking bareback rider is in love with Consuella, isn't he?', he remarks to (of all people) Zinida, only to receive a predictably curt reply: 'It's none of your business' (p. 338). But He is made of sterner stuff than the young hero and heroine, and in the sequel he takes every opportunity to make their union his particular business. He tells Mancini that Consuella should marry Bezano, not Regnard (p. 350); he tells Consuella that Zinida loves Bezano, hoping thereby to arouse her jealousy (p. 356); he even resorts to direct exhortation: 'I do not want you to marry the Baron. I . . . shall not allow it. . . . I beg you!' (p. 378). And in a last desperate effort to avert the catastrophe, he turns to Bezano at the end of Act 3, telling him of Consuella's love and entreating him to 'save her from the spider!' (p. 380).

We have already reached the point where we can provide a provisional answer to our initial question. He's purpose – or at least *one* of his purposes – is to act as a traditional ally or facilitator figure in a melodrama which, due to no fault of his own, is destined to fail. This is his *dramatic* function, which no reader or spectator of the play could fail to appreciate. This dramatic function is all the more important, however, as it provides a paradigm for his *thematic* function as a quintessentially Symbolist hero. It is to this second function that we may now turn.

He's efforts to awaken Consuella and Bezano to the divine pagan spirit that lies with them has been discussed so regularly as to require little detailed comment here. From the occasion at the end of Act 1, when he remarks: 'Yes, they are dancing. How beautiful Consuella is, and how beautiful the youth. He has the body of a Greek god' (p. 343), the Hellenic theme features regularly in his dealings with the young hero and heroine. But, as it was with his attempts to facilitate their romance, so is it here: his efforts to alert Consuella and Bezano to their 'higher' nature meet with little success. Indeed, in Bezano's case, He's failure is total; their final exchange, at the end of Act 3, concludes with an angry outburst which constitutes a double rejection of He: 'And don't let me hear any more about Consuella, and . . . don't tell me I'm a god! Don't

you see . . . it's disgusting!' (p. 381). Here, as on so many occasions
in the play, He's dramatic function and his thematic function are
invoked simultaneously: Bezano clearly wants nothing to do with
He in either of his roles.

If Bezano is totally unamenable to He's powers of suggestion,
Consuella at least promises to be a more suitable subject for
persuasion. In the crucial scene towards the end of Act 2 – the one
to which Andreyev himself drew attention as a moment of 'the
very greatest sorrow' – Consuella appears to be on the brink of
rediscovering her 'divine' essence:

> HE.   Sleep, and then wake again, Consuella! And when you
> awake, remember the time when you emerged with the foam
> from the azure sea! Remember the sky, and the gentle wind
> from the East, and the whisper of the waves at your marble
> feet . . .
> CONSUELLA [*closing her eyes*]. Wait . . . I seem to remember
> something. Remind me some more.   (p. 359)

This is the moment when He comes closest to triumph; Consuella's
response, uncertain though it is, nevertheless seems to vindicate
his mission. It is essential, however, that we attend to the total
dramatic context in which this exchange takes place. For no sooner
has Consuella succumbed to the hypnotic charm of He's speech
then He displays a new, and hitherto unsuspected, side to his
character. Annoyed when the sound of music from the circus ring
intrudes to remind Consuella of Bezano, he bursts out angrily,
'Forget the boy!', and proceeds to declare his own love for her
(p. 360). For her own part, Consuella responds by dealing out a
slap which quickly brings He back to his senses and moves him to
declare that he was only 'play-acting'.

The importance of this brief interlude can scarcely be exaggerated,
and yet it has been consistently overlooked in discussions of the
play. Andreyev's strategy is clear: at the very moment when He
appears most unambiguously to play his role as Symbolist hero,
he deserts his dramatic function as the facilitator of the melodrama
and reveals himself, albeit only fleetingly, as a *rival for Consuella's
love*. He is careful not to declare himself so openly again, being
obliged by the circumstance of Consuella's angry reaction to retreat
behind the mask of the 'court jester', but the doubt inspired by
this most dramatic (and hence most memorable) scene casts its

shadow, nevertheless, over the remainder of the action.

Although He apparently manages to contain the competing motives in the remainder of his dealings with the hero and heroine, the contradiction again comes to the fore – and with far more devastating results – in the final scenes of the play. Here again, we might do best to begin with a question. Why does He find it necessary to poison Consuella? On the face of it, his motivation seems clear enough. Having reached the point where his efforts to ensure the success of the romance are threatened with inevitable failure, He finds it preferable to kill Consuella and himself than to witness her sacrifice to the forces of evil represented by the Baron. It is, in brief, the last act of a thwarted idealist, a romantic defiance of a world in which the Regnards and the Mancinis hold sway. But this is not the whole story. The fact is that although He appears to do everything within his power to facilitate the union of Bezano and Consuella, he actually stops short of using the one weapon which might conceivably have achieved this objective. I am referring to a vital piece of information regarding the matter of Consuella's parentage.

Our curiosity about Consuella's background is first aroused when her 'father', Mancini, admits to He that for three centuries the males of his line have fathered no children (p. 352). The implication is obvious, and yet when the subject is raised again more explicitly in conversation with Zinida, He reacts rather oddly:

> ZINIDA.   Yes, you are certainly no fool. You have guessed, of course, that Consuella is not Mancini's natural daughter?
> HE [*shocked*].   What do you mean? And does she know of this?
> ZINIDA.   Hardly. Anyway, what does she need to know for? Yes, she is a common girl from Corsica.   (p. 385)

Given that he was privy to Mancini's earlier admission, He's astonishment at Zinida's revelation is curious, to say the least. One can only conclude that this is knowledge which he would somehow prefer to ignore. Even more remarkable, however, is He's unwillingness to bring the secret out into the open at the end of the play. This is especially the case because, were he to do so, he would, of course, be *conforming perfectly to his dramatic role as facilitator of the romance.* Indeed, the disclosure of the true facts of the parentage of heroes and heroines is one of the most common traditional methods of removing the block to the proper resolution of the comic plot.[42] In the present instance, it is easy to see how the announcement of Consuella's humble background would transform the dramatic situation. Consuella would no longer feel obliged to save the fortune and honour of the Mancini family; Regnard would baulk at the prospect of marriage to a commoner; and Bezano, no longer discouraged by the barrier of social class, would at last be able to stir from his apathy. Yet He, who has the perfect means for this perfectly melodramatic solution presented to him, fails to avail himself of it. Why?

The most obvious answer, perhaps, is to be sought in He's love for Consuella, which was so inopportunely disclosed in the second act. Thus, his failure, when brought to the testing point, to provide for the happiness of Consuella and Bezano, may be ascribed to an unwillingness – possibly more unconscious than conscious – to give up his beloved to a rival. But there is more to it than this. For the revelation of the truth about Consuella's background has a devastating implication not only for his romantic aspirations, but also for his function as *Symbolist hero*. When one looks back at the crucial scene between He and Consuella in Act 2, it becomes apparent that the moment at which the 'pagan goddess' stirred within her may have been nothing more than the dim, and utterly mundane, recollection of her early childhood on the island of Corsica. This is to say, therefore, that He's perception of her as a goddess-like being may have been nothing more than the product of wishful thinking on his part.[43] To play his dramatic role to the end, therefore, would be to jeopardise entirely his mission as the envoy of a new spirit of paganism. It is no wonder, then, that He holds back from the act which would have been the natural culmination of his dramatic function.

It is time to draw some conclusions. In the light of the above analysis, it should be clear that I tend towards a very different reading of the play's dénouement from that found in most studies. 'In poisoning Consuella, He saves both her and himself from the clutches of vulgarity' – the words are those of Babicheva,[44] yet they express a view which is more or less universal in the critical literature on *He Who Gets Slapped*. The present interpretation places Andreyev's He firmly within the ironic tradition of Russian Symbolist writing which we associate above all with the names of

Bely and Blok.[45] Like them, Andreyev appears both attracted and repelled by the figure of the neo-Romantic prophet. In particular, the action of his play bears a marked similarity to the story of the 'false prophet' as it is encountered in many of Bely's prose works. Consider, for example, the following description of the predicament of Musatov, the hero of Bely's *Second Symphony* ('Vtoraya sim-foniya'): 'the people he had taken to be the "woman clothed in the sun" and her "man child, who is to rule all nations with a rod of iron" turn out to be an ordinary society lady and a little girl named Nina'.[46] Although Andreyev eschewed the unmistakably parodic manner so characteristic of Bely, *He Who Gets Slapped* is still recognisably a tale of defeat for the would-be prophet. And this is nowhere more evident than at the end of the play. The unexpected suicide of Regnard marks the collapse of He's fantasy and provides a signal to the audience that the entire course of his behaviour in the play stands in need of a fundamental review. No less than Bely and Blok, Andreyev discerns in the prophet-idealist a capacity for self-deception and a desire for self-aggrandisement which place his entire venture under suspicion. When He replays the part of the scorned prophet for the benefit of his circus colleagues backstage – 'I am great, I am wise, incomparable – what divinity lives within me' (p. 348) – one senses (and not for the only time) that He may not necessarily be playing a part. And there is no mistaking either the sinister ring to the words he utters as the poison begins to take effect on Consuella: 'Give yourself to my charms, o goddess!' (p. 397). Strange words indeed on the lips of a would-be saviour!

What, finally, are we to make of the suggestion that He is a sort of authorial self-portrait? Against those who have suggested that Andreyev has presented an uncomplicated dramatic metaphor of his own position as a writer unjustly maligned, let us consider a statement by Beklemisheva which suggests a different approach to the question of an autobiographical reading, and one which, significantly, takes account of He's essential ambiguity. Most importantly of all, it also offers a possible explanation of why Andreyev should have so resolutely ignored that ambiguity in his subsequent statements about his drama. Speaking of the autobiographical impulse which she detects in all Andreyev's plays, Beklemisheva comments: 'Leonid Nikolayevich realised that there was in himself something which prevented that living embodiment of love of which he dreamed.' And she remembers the author himself as saying: 'I dream of Psyche, but would Psyche find it possible to live with me?'[47]

## Notes

I wish to record my gratitude to the Russian and East European Centre of the University of Illinois, under whose auspices part of the work towards this article was conducted.

1. For a full account of Andreyev's life and career see Alexander Kaun, *Leonid Andreyev: A Critical Study* (New York, 1924); James B. Woodward, *Leonid Andreyev* (Oxford, 1969).
2. *Vesy*, 1909, no. 9, p. 105.
3. A. L. Grigor'ev, 'Leonid Andreyev v mirovom literaturnom protsesse', *Russkaya literatura*, 1972, no. 3, p. 199.
4. *Moskovskiy al'manakh*, vyp. 1 (Moscow and Leningrad, 1926) p. 295.
5. Vadim Andreyev, *Detstvo* (Moscow, 1966) pp. 221–2.
6. For a thorough discussion of Andreyev's dealings with Stanislavsky and Nemirovich-Danchenko, see V. I. Bezzubov, 'Leonid Andreyev i Moskovskiy Khudozhestvennyy teatr', *Uchenyye zapiski Tartuskogo gosudarstvennogo universiteta*, vyp. 209 (1968) pp. 122–242.
7. *Gor'kiy i Andreyev. Literaturnoye nasledstvo*, vol. 72 (Moscow, 1965) p. 351.
8. *Pis'ma Leonida Andreyeva* (Leningrad, 1924) p. 17.
9. Vadim Andreyev, p. 221.
10. *Uchenyye zapiski Tartuskogo universiteta*, vyp. 266 (1971) p. 282.
11. See, for example, Yu. V. Babicheva, *Evolyutsiya zhanrov russkoy dramy kontsa XIX–nachala XX veka* (Vologda, 1982) p. 75; V. Shcherbina, *Puti iskusstva* (Moscow, 1970) p. 92. It is interesting to compare Andreyev's statements on the theatre with the ideas of a more famous advocate of 'synthetism' in the arts – Yevgeny Zamyatin.
12. Leonid Andreyev, *Pis'ma o teatre* (reprint, Letchworth, Herts., 1974), pp. 11–12.
13. Kaun, p. 303.
14. See Yu. V. Babicheva, 'P'esa L. Andreyeva "Tot, kto poluchayet poshchechiny"', *Uchenyye zapiski Moskovskogo pedagogicheskogo instituta*, no. 456 (1971) pp. 27–44 for further details of Soviet responses to Andreyev's drama.
15. See, in particular, Grigor'ev; Shcherbina; N. Guzhiyeva, 'Dramaturgiya Leonida Andreyeva 1910-kh godov', *Russkaya literatura*, 1965, no. 4, pp. 64–79; V. A. Keldysh, *Russkiy realizm nachala XX veka* (Moscow, 1975); and the section on Andreyev in *Literaturno-esteticheskiye kontseptsii v Rossii kontsa XIX–nachala XX veka* (Moscow, 1975).
16. See, however, Harold B. Segel, *Twentieth-Century Russian Drama* (New York, 1979) pp. 118–23.
17. The work in question is *Literaturno-esteticheskiye kontseptsii*.

18. G. Kryzhitskiy, 'Tsirk papa Brike (k postanovke p'esy Leonida Andreyeva "Tot, kto poluchayet poshchechiny")', *Yezhenedel'nik petrogradskikh gosudarstvennykh akademicheskikh teatrov*, 1922, no. 14, p. 5.
19. Vadim Andreyev, p. 223.
20. D. L. Andreyev, V. Ye. Beklemisheva (eds), *Rekviem. Sbornik pamyati Leonida Andreyeva* (Moscow, 1930) p. 117.
21. *Kniga o Leonide Andreyeve* (Berlin, Petersburg, Moscow) p. 145.
22. D. L. Andreyev and Beklemisheva (eds), pp. 240–1.
23. Ibid., p. 122.
24. A. M. Yevlakhov, *Kto poluchayet poshchechiny v novoy drame L. Andreyeva?* (Rostov-on-Don, 1916).
25. This argument is developed most fully in Babicheva, 'P'esa'.
26. Guzhiyeva, p. 70. Babicheva ('P'esa', p. 43) relates this scene quite specifically to some angry comments about Artsybashev contained in a letter from Andreyev to the critic Izmaylov.
27. D. L. Andreyev and Beklemisheva (eds), p. 70.
28. Kaun, p. 315.
29. L. Andreyev, *P'esy* (Moscow, 1959) pp. 581–2. All further references to this volume are contained in the text.
30. This is true even of those Soviet critics who have wanted to see in He above all the voice of social and political protest against the forces of the bourgeoisie. See, in particular, A. B. Rubtsov, *Iz istorii russkoy dramaturgii kontsa XIX–nachala XX veka* (Minsk, 1960) p. 63, where it is argued that the play is an unsuccessful attempt to weld social criticism to a philosophical theme which is alien to it.
31. A. Belyy, *Serebryanyy golub'* (reprint, Munich, 1967), vol. I, p. 174.
32. F. Sologub, 'Mechtatel' o teatre', *Teatr i iskusstvo*, 1916, no. 1, pp. 14–15.
33. D. L. Andreyev and Beklemisheva (eds), p. 257.
34. Vadim Andreyev, p. 255.
35. Sologub, p. 15.
36. It should be noted that the phrase 'hostages of life' in Andreyev's letter to Duvan Tortsov has a distinctly Sologubian ring. *Hostages of Life* was the title Sologub gave to a drama of 1912.
37. Beklemisheva reports the author as saying that he found Merezhkovsky's trilogy 'artificial' (D. L. Andreyev and Beklemisheva (eds), p. 257). For those who know Merezhkovsky's work, the conversation between He and Consuella in Act 2 could not fail to remind them of scenes like the following from *The Antichrist: (Peter and Aleksis)* ('Antikhrist. Petr i Aleksey'), in which Aleksis's mistress, Yefrosinya, appears in the guise of Venus: 'In the quadrangle of the doors, which opened on to the blue sea, her body appeared golden-white, like the waves, as though it had emerged from the sparkling blue of the sea' (D. S. Merezhkovskiy, *Polnoye sobraniye sochineniy*, vol. v (Moscow, 1914) p. 33). This is only one of many occasions on which this motif appears in the trilogy.
38. Letter to Goloushev, 15 December 1916: D. L. Andreyev and Beklemisheva (eds), p. 132.
39. Article in *Teatr i iskusstvo*, 1915, no. 49, cited in Rubtsov, p. 264.

40. The novel in question is *Consuelo*.

41. Woodward, p. 251.

42. It is interesting to note that Andreyev makes use of this same traditional motif of unknown parentage – and in a similarly unconventional manner – in *The Black Masks* ('Chernyye maski'), where Duke Lorenzo discovers when reading some old manuscripts that he is the illegitimate product of a liaison between his mother and a steward.

43. These observations take on further interest in the light of a clash between the directors of the Moscow Dramatic Theatre over the choice of actress to play the part of Consuella. Whereas A. A. Sanin wanted the 'earthly' Yureneva for the role, I. F. Shmit considered the more 'ethereal' Polevitskaya as right for the part. Andreyev supported Shmit (Babicheva, 'P'esa', p. 40).

44. Ibid., p. 33.

45. In his memoir of Andreyev, Blok himself commented that 'certain Symbolists were much closer to him, in particular Andrey Bely and myself, of which he told me more than once. But, despite his proximity, nothing came of it' (*Kniga o Leonide Andreyeve*, p. 96).

46. Roger Keys, 'Bely's Symphonies', in John E. Malmstad (ed.), *Andrey Bely: Spirit of Symbolism* (Ithaca, N.Y., 1987) p. 54.

47. D. L. Andreyev and Beklemisheva (eds), p. 228.

# 5

# Kuzmin, Gumilev and Tsvetayeva as Neo-Romantic Playwrights

## SIMON KARLINSKY

### 1  RUSSIAN REALIST AND SYMBOLIST DRAMA

Historically speaking, the first Russian Symbolist playwright was probably Konstantin Treplev in Chekhov's *The Seagull* ('Chayka'). His poetic play about the Soul of the World and her enemy, the Devil, has occasionally been read by critics as Chekhov's satire on Russian Symbolist drama. However, in 1895, when *The Seagull* was first staged, there were no Russian Symbolist playwrights to satirise.[1] The earliest significant Russian Symbolist plays, such as *Alma* by Nikolay Minsky, *Sacred Blood* ('Svyataya krov'') by Zinaida Gippius and the first verse tragedies on Greek mythological themes by Innokenty Annensky all date from the first five years of the twentieth century.

Symbolist drama was preceded by the period traditionally characterised by Russian literary historians as that of Critical Realism. It encompasses the time between the plays of Nikolay Gogol in the 1830s and those of Anton Chekhov and Maksim Gorky that were contemporary with the early Symbolist drama of 1900–5. Although the word 'Realism' does not really suffice to describe the plays of either Gogol or Chekhov, it does provide a convenient term to characterise the playwrights who were active in the interim between them: Aleksandr Ostrovsky, Aleksey Potekhin, Ivan Turgenev, Aleksey Pisemsky, Lev Tolstoy and Aleksandr Sukhovo-Kobylin. All these playwrights, including Gogol, Chekhov and Gorky, complied with three uncodified rules of Russian realist drama that were observed as rigidly as the three famous unities of seventeenth- and eighteenth-century neo-classicism. All serious realist plays (1) were written in prose; (2) their action took place in Russia; and (3) they were set in the present. The exceptions we find in the nineteenth century serve only to confirm the prevalence of these rules. There were some neo-Shakespearean historical dramas written by A. K. Tolstoy, Ostrovsky and a few others in iambic pentameters in imitation of Pushkin's *Boris Godunov*; there were a few prose plays by Pisemsky set in the eighteenth century; and there were at least two poetic fantasy plays in verse: A. K. Tolstoy's remarkable *Don Juan* and Ostrovsky's pseudo-mythological *The Snowmaiden* ('Snegurochka'). Remote history, mythology, fantasy and stories set in non-Russian cultures were relegated to opera and ballet.

Symbolist drama of the early twentieth century was written by poets, such as Annensky, Gippius, Sologub and Blok. They felt free to write drama in verse, in prose and in a mixture of both. This new drama could be set in Russia or in any other country, real or imaginary; in the present or in any period of the past. It could (and did) treat contemporary social issues as the realists had done. But it also brought back fantasy, mythology, religion, Christian and pre-Christian mysticism – areas that were dealt with by playwrights of the Renaissance, of the Baroque and of the Romantic Age, but which were largely disregarded in realist drama.

Inherent in Symbolist drama was a view of life as a juxtaposition of two or more realities, as a simultaneous presence of other worlds in the experience of the play's characters. Such duality of existence could be treated seriously, as in Blok's *Incognita* ('Neznakomka') and *The Rose and the Cross* ('Roza i krest'), Gippius's *Sacred Blood* and Annensky's *Thamyris Kitharodos* ('Famira kifared'): or it could be presented ironically and even comically, as in Blok's *The Puppet Show* ('Balaganchik') and Sologub's *Nocturnal Dances* ('Nochnyye plyaski') and *Vanka the Butler and the Page Jehan* ('Van'ka klyuchnik i pazh Zhean'). The absence of this Symbolist multiple and mystical perspective in the plays of the three poets that I propose to discuss in this paper, Mikhail Kuzmin, Nikolay Gumilev and Marina Tsvetayeva, is what gives us the right to speak of their plays as post-Symbolist. The Symbolist world view is present in the plays of these poets only minimally. Far more dominant is a sensibility that goes back to the Romantic Age. This allows us to speak of some of these poets' plays as not only post-Symbolist, but also as neo-Romantic.

Another thing that unites the dramatic work of Kuzmin, Gumilev and Tsvetayeva is their resolute rejection of the usages of Russian realist drama that were formulated above. None of the plays of Gumilev and Tsvetayeva is in prose, none is set in Russia and, with the exception of Gumilev's *Don Juan in Egypt* ('Don Zhuan v Yegipte') none is set in the present time. In the case of Kuzmin, his last important play, *The Death of Nero* ('Smert' Nerona', 1929), is in prose and is set in part in twentieth-century Russia. But his other plays are written in a mixture of prose and verse and they all have foreign, pre-twentieth-century settings. The plays of these three poets do not concern themselves with the fate of Russia, with either the revolutionary or the mystical transformation of the world in the proximate future, and the texts of their plays (with the exception of Kuzmin's *The Death of Nero* and Tsvetayeva's *The Snowstorm* ('Metel'')) do not confront their reader or spectator with any veiled or arcane meanings. Therefore, even though Kuzmin's plays coincided chronologically with the heyday of Symbolist drama in Russia, they are not a part of the Symbolist movement, as Blok authoritatively pointed out in one of his letters to Andrey Bely.[2]

## 2   ROMANTIC AND SYMBOLIST DRAMA

At this point we should establish the corpus of the plays to be discussed. Michael Green's tabulation of Kuzmin's works for the theatre lists almost forty items.[3] But the majority of these were cabaret skits, ballet librettos and texts for ephemeral operettas. Most of them disappeared or were never published. For our purposes, we can restrict Kuzmin's output for the theatre to the dramatic poem (possibly meant to be an opera libretto), *The History of the Knight d'Alessio* ('Istoriya rytsarya d'Alessio'), published in 1905; three brief one-act plays brought out in one volume in 1907; the three plays that are dramatisations of the *vitae* of Orthodox saints, published as *Three Comedies* in 1909; the comedy *Venetian Madcaps* ('Venetsianskiye bezumtsy') performed in 1914; a brief one-act comedy *A Prince from a Farm* ('Prints s myzy'), 1914; and the posthumous *The Death of Nero*.[4]

Gumilev's three one-act verse plays written in 1911–13, *Don Juan in Egypt, Actaeon* and *The Card Game* ('Igra') and his three longer plays dating from 1916–18, *Gondla, The Child of Allah* ('Ditya Allakha') and *The Poisoned Tunic* ('Otravlennaya tunika'), are all conveniently available in the third volume of Gumilev's collected works published by Gleb Struve and Boris Filippov in 1966.

Marina Tsvetayeva's dramatic output consists of the cycle of six verse plays she wrote in 1918–19, during the time of her association with the actors of the Third Studio of the Moscow Art Theatre.[5] The plays of this cycle, which the poet herself qualified as 'romantic', are, in the order of writing, *The Jack of Hearts* ('Chervonnyy valet'), *The Snowstorm, Fortuna, An Adventure* ('Priklyucheniye'), *The Stone Angel* ('Kamennyy angel'), and *The Phoenix* ('Feniks') (a section of which was also published separately as *Casanova's End* ('Konets Kazanovy')).[6] In the 1920s, Tsvetayeva wrote two neo-classical verse tragedies, *Ariadne* and *Phaedra*, which were intended as a part of a trilogy, the last play of which was never written.

Since the aim of this paper is to search for the romantic features in this group of plays, it would be best to exclude the final plays of all three poets from our discussion. Kuzmin's *The Death of Nero* happens to be the only authentically Symbolist play this poet ever wrote, built on a complex series of correspondences between the lives of Nero as described by Suetonius and of a twentieth-century Russian playwright who is writing a play about Nero.

It will also be hard to find truly romantic features in Gumilev's *The Poisoned Tunic* because this play is a neo-classical tragedy as it was practised in the seventeenth and eighteenth centuries, with careful observance of the unities of time, place and action. Tsvetayeva's neo-classical tragedies of the 1920s are couched in the manner of modernist neo-classicism in the drama and music of the 1920s and 1930s. Like Cocteau, Giraudoux and Stravinsky, Tsvetayeva borrowed the themes and gestures of antiquity to convey a new, twentieth-century conception of the classical myths.

Thus, romantic features will have to be sought in the remainder of the plays mentioned. These features may be classified under the following four headings: (1) the romantic revival of the genre of mediaeval mystery and miracle plays; (2) Romantic orientalism; (3) Romantic androgyny and reversal of sex roles; and (4) Romantic idealisation and poetisation of the past. The earliest play in our list, Kuzmin's *The History of the Knight d'Alessio*, happens to be a work that offers examples of all four of these categories.

## 3   ROMANTIC REVIVAL OF MEDIAEVAL MYSTERY AND MIRACLE PLAYS

Critics were not kind to *The History of the Knight d'Alessio*, either at the time of its first publication in 1905 or during the recent revival of interest in Kuzmin in the English-speaking countries. As John Malmstad indicated in his biography of Kuzmin, both the utilitarian hack Nikolay Korobka of the Gogolian name (his speciality was baiting the Symbolists) and the great poet Aleksandr Blok agreed that Kuzmin's dramatic poem was an imitation of *Faust* and A. K. Tolstoy's *Don Juan*.[7] Michael Green in his indispensable study of Kuzmin and the theatre also sees this work as 'immature', 'derivative' and 'poorly constructed'.[8] To my mind, the qualities that these commentators saw as imitative are actually inherent in the work's genre. In both its theme and structure, *The History of the Knight d'Alessio* belongs to the romantic variant of the mediaeval mystery play. The revival of this genre was initiated in modern times by Goethe's *Faust*, whose progeny included Byron's *Manfred* and *Cain*, Shelley's *Prometheus Unbound*, Mickiewicz's *Forefathers' Eve* and, in Russian literature, the insufficiently valued *Izhorsky* by Wilhelm Küchelbecker.[9]

All these works are dramatic poems (Kuzmin listed his characters not as *dramatis personae*, but as *poematis personae*). Their central character is always a man who moves through various environments on a personal quest for knowledge, for redemption, or, as in Kuzmin, for identity and self-understanding. Supernatural characters who communicate with the protagonist are the rule in this genre of dramatic poems. Kuzmin's Astorre d'Alessio leaves his ancestral castle and the preceptor who educated him, setting off on a journey under the influence of his guardian spirit, who appears to him as a handsome, green-eyed youth. His travels, which take place in the age of the crusades, bring him into contact with three women: Helena, an English novice in an Italian nunnery; a sultana in Turkey; and the fickle courtesan Bianca in Venice. Each time, just as Astorre is about to succumb to the woman's charms, the guardian spirit intervenes and removes either the woman or Astorre from the scene. In two later scenes we see the failure of two of Astorre's friends who chose other options for fulfilment, one in military glory and the other in monastic self-mortification in the Thebaid. In the final scene, patterned on the finale of Mozart's opera *Die Zauberflöte*, Astorre d'Alessio enters a

Masonic lodge that is also some kind of all-male heaven, the kind that was much later described by Tsvetayeva in a poem written in 1922:

> Помни закон:
> Здесь не владей!
> Чтобы потом — —
> В Граде Друзей:
>
> В этом пустом,
> В этом крутом
> Небе мужском
> — Сплошь золотом —

[Remember the law: / Own nothing here! / So that later, / In the City of Friends: / In that empty, / In that steep / Masculine heaven / — Totally golden —][10]

Those who have studied Kuzmin's work know that his eroticism is exclusively male. Commentators have repeatedly pointed out that the Knight d'Alessio's search for identity is a poetic restatement of the similar but realistically depicted search of the protagonist in Kuzmin's semi-autobiographical novel *Wings* ('Kryl'ya'). His early mystery play is thus a deeply personal work. But Kuzmin also wrote plays patterned on earlier forms of religious drama where the personal element was not quite so prominent.

This is the case with three plays in prose and verse, styled 'comedies', written in 1908 and published in 1909. They are modern versions of the earlier religious miracle plays, a genre otherwise not known in Russia in the nineteenth and twentieth centuries, except possibly the moralising plays for peasant audiences by Lev Tolstoy and the unclassifiable plays of Aleksey Remizov. In France, however, this genre recurred steadily in the nineteenth century, as for example, in Théophile Gautier's *Une Larme de diable*, 1839 (a slightly blasphemous story about the averted seduction of two pious sisters by Satan, with Virgo Immaculata, Christus, Othello, Desdemona and a chorus of rabbits among the characters); in Flaubert's dramatised novel *La Tentation de Saint Antoine*, 1874; and all the way to Edmond Rostand's neo-Romantic *La Samaritaine*, 1897.

Kuzmin's three miracle plays are *The Comedy of Eudoxia of Heliopolis, or the Converted Courtesan* ('Komediya o Yevdokii iz Geliopolya ili obrashchennaya kurtizanka'), *The Comedy of Alexis the Man of God, or the Lost and Converted Son* ('Komediya o Alekseye cheloveke bozh'em: ili poteryannyy i obrashchennyy syn') and *The Comedy of Martinian* ('Komediya o Martiniane'). The term 'comedy' is used in the sense it had in Russian school drama of the seventeenth and eighteenth centuries, meaning 'a religious and edifying play', the meaning it had in *The Comedy-Parable of the Prodigal Son* by Simeon of Polotsk, published in 1685, or *The Christmas Comedy* ('Komediya na den' Rozhdestva Khristova') by St Dimitry of Rostov. In all three plays, Kuzmin followed scrupulously the accounts found in the Orthodox calendar of saints (Nastol'naya kniga). But Blok was quite right when he described *The Comedy of Eudoxia* as a 'sacred farce', a judgement that applies to all three of these plays. In the same review, Blok also wrote:

> The melody of the mystery tinkles like a silver bell in the fresh evening air. This is the most perfect work in the area of *lyrical* drama in Russia, permeated with some kind of enchanting sadness and drenched in the subtlest poisons of the irony which is so typical of Kuzmin's work.[11]

*The Comedy of Eudoxia* treats a theme that was popularised at the end of the nineteenth century in *Thaïs*, both the novella by Anatole France and the opera that Jules Massenet based on it – the courtesan who becomes a saint. The *vita* of Eudoxia is the story of a woman who begins by selling her love and ends up by converting a young man in love with her to the ways of chastity. *The Comedy of Martinian* deals with another theme common in religious writing. Saint Martinian is obsessed by a desire for women and mortifies his flesh so as to resist the temptation. In the course of his various adventures he manages to convert two women who attract him and they become saints in their own right. One of the episodes of his *vita* and of Kuzmin's play based on it corresponds closely to an episode of Lev Tolstoy's story 'Father Sergius' ('Otets Sergiy').

The *vita* of Saint Alexis the Man of God enjoyed tremendous popularity in both the Catholic and Russian Orthodox traditions. Unlike Eudoxia and Martinian, Alexis was not tempted by the flesh or, apparently, by anything else. He was married so as not to disobey his parents' wishes, but he walked out on his wife and parents the same day, leaving all of them bereaved for many years. He became a saint simply for abandoning his wealthy family. He survived by begging for alms. His is a story which may be hard to sympathise with in the twentieth century. As the well-known American writer Eleanor Clark put it, 'the virtues of solitude and self-abnegation have never had a more grotesque embodiment'. She called this saint 'a hero of personal filth and general uselessness'.[12] But the same author also wrote that the 'self-centeredness of fifth-century Christianity' may only be grasped through revelation, not reason. This, surely, was Kuzmin's own attitude to the protagonist of his miracle play.

In the remarkable prayer written in 1916 and included in Kuzmin's collection *The Guide* ('Vozhatyy') we read:

Еще мне скучно быть справедливым,
Великодушьем хочу гореть.

[I am still bored by justice, / I'd rather be aflame with magnanimity.][13]

It is this kind of magnanimity that we find in Kuzmin's treatment of both Alexis and the situation of his parents and wife, forced to pay for his saintliness by years of anxiety and pain. One can't help feeling some sympathy for the final outcry of the wife, Mastridia, 'I won't have it! I won't have it!' ('*Ne khochu! Ne khochu!*'), when she learns that the man who ruined her life and deprived her of the joys of love and motherhood has now become a saint. Nor can one agree with Michael Green when he writes that Mastridia is 'the dreadful Natasha of [Chekhov's] *Three Sisters* in Roman garb'.[14]

Features of romantic reinterpretation of a miracle play are also present in Marina Tsvetayeva's *The Stone Angel*, written in June and July 1919. Like most of the plays of her romantic cycle, this one was intended to provide roles for her actor-friends, Yury Zavadsky and Sophia Holliday. In her memoir 'The Tale of Sonechka' ('Povest' o Sonechke'), Tsvetayeva mentioned that many women were drawn to the tall and exceptionally handsome Zavadsky and that she wrote for him a play in which he would be shown as a stone angel, indifferent to all the female adulation. This is indeed the situation in the first scene of the play, set in Germany in the sixteenth century. But as the play proceeds, its main theme turns out to be the battle between the evil and good forces for the soul of the heroine, Aurora, who was meant to be played by Holliday. The play is a highly idiosyncratic fusion of the myth of Psyche and Eros with the final scenes of both Part One and Part Two of Goethe's *Faust*.

The evil is represented here by Venus, shown as a witch, a hypocritical abbess and a procuress. Her son, Eros, unlike his earlier incarnations in Lafontaine or, in Russia, in Bogdanovich's *Psyche* ('Dushen'ka'), is here a spoiled mama's boy and a heartless seducer. Eros puts a spell on Aurora causing her to think that the stone angel she loves has become human. She yields to Eros and bears his baby, after which he casts out both her and the child. The stone angel does come to life and tries to protect Aurora, but fails. When Venus, in her guise as the procuress, tries to turn Aurora into a prostitute, the Mother of God appears. She encloses Venus in a mountain on the bank of the Rhine for eternity and promises Aurora to remove her and her child to Paradise, where her beloved stone angel will await her.

*The Stone Angel* was originally published from a defective copy, with gaps and alternative readings of many passages.[15] With the appearance of the authoritative volume, Marina Tsvetayeva, *Teatr* (Moscow, 1988, with an introductory essay about Tsvetayeva by Pavel Antokol'sky and annotations by Anna Saakyants) we can get a better conception of this unusual play.

## 4   ROMANTIC ORIENTALISM

Scenes 4, 5 and 6 of Kuzmin's *The History of the Knight d'Alessio*, set in Smyrna, Turkey, and Gumilev's *The Child of Allah* exemplify the revival of Romantic Age orientalism in twentieth-century poetry and art. The fashion for depicting the Near East, made internationally popular by Byron and Chateaubriand in the early nineteenth century, was unselective to the point of eclecticism. In his highly informative dissertation *Les Ballets de Théophile Gautier*, Edwin Binney III has shown that by the early 1840s, when Gautier put together the libretto for his very successful ballet *La Péri*, European poets and playwrights who depicted the Near East piled up together, with no discrimination, elements from Arabian, Persian, Egyptian, Turkish, Greek and Moorish (prior to their expulsion from Spain) cultures.[16] Pushkin seemed to be aware, when writing 'The Fountain of Bakhchisaray' ('Bakhchisarayskiy fontan'), that the tradition he was following existed more in the imagination of Western poets than in the real Near East, introducing into his verse-tale settings and words popularised by Byron: harem, eunuch, fakir, sherbet and chibouque. Adam Mickiewicz, travelling in the mid-1820s in the Crimea, where he could observe the impoverished and poorly educated Crimean Tatars, wrote in his *Crimean Sonnets* of djinnis, caravans, harems and the wells of Cairo.[17]

By the time of Kuzmin and Gumilev, this synthetic 'Near East' was a well-established convention. The Smyrna scenes in *The History of the Knight d'Alessio*, with their unfaithful sultana who bribes a eunuch to smuggle a man she covets into the harem, dances seductively before the man and is then punished by the jealous sultan, are remarkably close to the plot of the Fokin-Bakst ballet done for the Diaghilev troupe, *Scheherezade*, 1910. As for Gumilev's *The Child of Allah*, possibly his most beautifully written work in dramatic form, with its mixture of humour, fantasy and elegant stylisation, one should not perhaps ask for authenticity from a play intended for a puppet theatre. But the subtitle is 'An Arabian Folk Tale in Three Tableaux'. The action is set first in the desert where caravans move toward Baghdad. That city is presumably the place of the action in the second and third scenes. The protagonist is a Peri, a Persian angelic being, popularised in Europe by Thomas Moore's poetry and Gautier's ballet. Hafiz, whose wife the Peri becomes after her various adventures, was a Persian poet who lived in the fourteenth century. A unicorn, which is also prominent in the play, is a Western European creation that resulted from artists trying to depict a rhinoceros from verbal descriptions only. Some of the verse dialogue is couched in the form of *pantoum*, which originated in Malayan poetry; other parts of the text are *ghazals*, a verse structure common with mediaeval Persian poets. What are they all doing in an Arabian folk tale? Should anyone wish to know what comes from where, I would recommend that they re-read *The Child of Allah* with Edwin Binney's chapter on the sources of Gautier's *La Péri* open in front of them.

## 5  ROMANTIC ANDROGYNY

In 1979 Olga Matich published two valuable articles, 'Androgyny and the Russian Religious Renaissance' and 'Androgyny and the Russian Silver Age'.[18] In them she cited considerable material from the religious writings of Vladimir Solov'ev, Nikolay Berdyayev and Dmitry Merezhkovsky, and from poetry and novels of Fedor

Sologub, Zinaida Gippius and Andrey Bely. She showed that they were all interested in either a mystical fusion of the male and the female to form one person, presumably a hermaphrodite; or in situations where the male and the female exchange their expected functions or at least put on clothing appropriate for the other sex (like Sasha Pyl'nikov disguising himself as a geisha in the costume-ball section of Sologub's *The Petty Demon* ('Melkiy bes')). Particularly striking is Professor Matich's analysis of the poem 'Thou' ('Ty') by Gippius, where the two words of different gender for moon, *mesyats* and *luna*, enable the poem's persona to be simultaneously in love with a male and with a female. The essays also point out the antiquity of the notion of androgyny in literature as well as in religious thought.

Androgyny was an important theme in French literature of the Romantic Age. In 1835, Honoré de Balzac published his mystical novel *Séraphita*, where the title character, an angelic being, is perceived by some as a young man and by others as a woman; and, a year later, came the best known treatment of the androgynous theme in French literature, *Mademoiselle de Maupin* by Gautier. Gautier wrote this novel on a commission and he did not dare to do full justice to the historical prototype on which his book was based. The real-life Mademoiselle Maupin (no *particule nobiliaire*) was born Mademoiselle d'Aubigny. Maupin was her married name. She was a singer at the Paris Opéra who lived from approximately 1673 to 1707. She liked to dress as a man, fought many duels, abducted a nun from a convent and took a wife away from her husband.[19] All this was too much for Gautier to handle in a nineteenth-century novel. He reduced the situation of the historical Maupin to a comedy of disguises in the manner of Shakespeare's *As You Like It*, the text of which is featured prominently in Gautier's novel.

In his essay on Gautier and his Acmeist manifesto of 1913,[20] Nikolay Gumilev told us how much Gautier's poetry and novels meant to him. He further demonstrated his devotion by his translation of Gautier's collection of poems *Emaux et camées* (1914). For his part, Mikhail Kuzmin was also involved with Gautier's writings. Gennady Shmakov's study of Kuzmin's relationship to Blok mentions at several points Kuzmin's fondness for Gautier.[21] It is in plays by Kuzmin and Tsvetayeva, however, and not by Gumilev, that we find instances of cross-dressing, similar to those in Shakespeare's comedies and Gautier's novel. The closest we come to role reversal in a Gumilev play is the contrast in *Gondla* between the weak male protagonist, a hunchbacked poet who disdains war and hunting, and the woman he marries, an Amazon longing for power and violence in her daytime personality as Lera (but soft and compassionate at night, when her name is Laik).

But Gumilev was by no means indifferent to the idea of androgyny and to conditions tangential to it such as hermaphroditism and homosexuality. In his verse collection *Pearls* ('Zhemchuga'), 1907–10, we find the poem 'Single Combat' ('Poyedinok') (possibly inspired by the battle between Tancredi and Clorinda in Tasso), where one of the combatants is a woman who kills her male opponent and then tells him that she will be his for ever. Also included in *Pearls* is 'The Androgyne' ('Androgin'), in which two lovers, a man and a woman, perform an ancient rite that will fuse their bodies into one androgynous being. A similar androgyne made up of a male and a female body appears in Gumilev's short story 'Journey into the Land of Ether' ('Puteshestviye v stranu efira'). In Gumilev's next collection, *The Alien Sky* ('Chuzhoye nebo'), there are two adjacent poems, 'To a Cruel Woman' ('Zhestokoy') and 'Love' ('Lyubov''). In the first of them, a man pleads in vain for reciprocity from one of Sappho's female disciples of the island of Lesbos; the second is about a man who against his will falls under the spell of a mannered and perfumed dandy.[22] Finally, in his Russian version of Gautier's *Emaux et camées*, Gumilev translated with great virtuosity Gautier's poem 'Contralto', a paean to the timbre of a woman's low-pitched voice, which Gautier likens to ancient statues of hermaphrodites to which both women and men could be attracted.

The androgyne, both in the poem of that name and in the story, is related to the religious symbolism of androgyny, which Olga Matich has found in Solov'ev and Berdyayev. But the themes and imagery in the other cited Gumilev poems were treated earlier by Gautier and Baudelaire and revived by Russian Symbolists. If, despite his interest in this entire thematic complex, Gumilev did not use transvestite situations in any of his plays, there are striking uses of them in plays by Kuzmin and Tsvetayeva.

In the first play of Kuzmin's 1907 volume of three dramatic miniatures, *The Dangerous Precaution* ('Opasnaya predostorozhnost''), set, as Michael Green has suggested, not too far from Shakespeare's Forest of Arden, a young man falls in love with Prince Floridal thinking that the prince is a woman in disguise.

Shown that his love is really a man, he is prepared to go on loving him just the same. The one change he asks for is that the musicians play in the finale not the gavotte he requested when he thought he was in love with a disguised woman but a jig, as being more suitable to be danced by two men.

A sly touch of androgyny is also present in the last scene of Kuzmin's brief prose comedy *A Prince from a Farm*. The rustic upbringing of the title character makes him uncomfortable at the refined, quasi-Shakespearean court over which he is unexpectedly called to preside. He refuses to take an interest in women or to marry his cousin Arsinoe, as had been arranged by his family. In an effort to win him over, the enamoured Arsinoe offers to dress as a man and to learn to be a master huntsman. The prince agrees to accept her on these terms, but with a proviso: 'But even so, promise that you will never try to kiss me.'

Tsvetayeva's verse comedy *An Adventure* is based on an episode from the memoirs of Casanova (as was her play *The Phoenix*). In her source, she found the character of a modest young Frenchwoman, Henriette, who wore male attire to escape from the custody of her repressive family. Tsvetayeva turned Henriette into one of the most thoroughly androgynous characters in the whole of Russian literature, who reminds one of the historical Mademoiselle Maupin far more than the heroine of Gautier's novel does. Tsvetayeva's character is called Henri-Henriette, described as 'lunar ice' ('lunnyy led'). In the first scene she is a male, a brawling young hussar who has just fought a duel over another woman and who speaks of himself in the masculine gender. Later, smitten by love for Casanova, Henri-Henriette becomes feminine and reveals herself as a virtuoso musician. After she leaves Casanova, he mourns losing her with the words: 'My love! My moonlit boy!'[23]

## 6    ROMANTIC IDEALISATION OF THE PAST

The Romantic Age in the early nineteenth century had a great deal to do with rediscovery and re-evaluation of the past. Periods previously considered cruel and barbarous, especially the early and late Middle Ages, came to be seen in a new light: exciting, picturesque and, yes, romantic. Russian writers in the age of Realism were not particularly interested in the past. The great exception was, of course, Lev Tolstoy, who invariably saw the past as superior to the present. The rediscovery of the past in the early twentieth century was due to the influence of the 'World of Art', both the journal of that name (*Mir iskusstva*, whose work in that area was later taken up by the journal *Staryye gody*) and the cultural figures associated with that group.

After the impact of the 'World of Art', the eighteenth century and the Romantic Age, so despised by the Russian utilitarian critics of the nineteenth century, became themselves objects of retrospective idealisation. Kuzmin's *Venetian Madcaps*, with its colourful action and its sudden tragic dénouement, brings to life, as the poet himself wrote, the eighteenth-century Venice 'of Goldoni, Gozzi and Longhi'. Gumilev's *Don Juan in Egypt* modernises one of the favourite myths of the Romantic Age. His brief play *The Card Game*, with its entwined themes of gambling and death, takes us back to Pushkin's 'The Shot' ('Vystrel') and 'The Queen of Spades' ('Pikovaya dama'). His *Gondla*, as Vsevolod Setchkarev pointed out, has a great deal to do 'with Ossian, with the music dramas of Richard Wagner and with such works of Symbolist theatre as Blok's *The Rose and the Cross*'.[24]

*The Rose and the Cross*, odd as this may sound, may have served as the prototype for the first play of Tsvetayeva's romantic cycle, *The Jack of Hearts*. All the characters are face cards (including the somewhat androgynous Jack of Diamonds, who introduces himself with the words: 'I am both a young man and a maiden').[25] Their interactions seem to anticipate such ballets of the 1930s as Igor Stravinsky's *Jeu de cartes* and Arthur Bliss's *Checkmate* (1937). But the love drama, where the Queen of Hearts betrays her elderly husband with the unworthy King of Spades and does not notice the selfless service of the Jack of Hearts, who loses his life while guarding her secret – all this has unmistakable parallels with the faithful Gaetan and the faithless Isaure of Blok's play. Tsvetayeva's next play, *The Snowstorm*, was also a variation on a theme by Blok. This time the model is *The Incognita*, even though the play is set in the forests of Bohemia and the action takes place in 1830. The situation of the male and female protagonists is reversed, so that in place of Blok's fallen star Mariya we have the Prince of the Moon. But his foreordained encounter with a unique clairvoyant woman has clear correspondences with Mariya's non-encounter with the poet in Blok.

The eulogies to the eighteenth century voiced in *The Snowstorm* by the character called the Old Woman (much in the manner of the Countess in Modest Tchaikovsky's libretto for his brother's opera *The Queen of Spades*), are the first instance for Tsvetayeva's play cycle of the poetic idealisation of that century. It becomes central to the three plays that Tsvetayeva based on historical sources: the two Casanova plays, *An Adventure* and *The Phoenix*, and the best play of the sequence, *Fortuna*, a dramatisation of the memoirs of the Duc de Lauzun. The taste for the rococo elegance of the eighteenth century was, of course, very much in the air in all Russian arts in the pre-revolutionary decades. But Tsvetayeva, writing her verse plays that glorified the spirit and style of that century during the Russian Civil War, had a clear contemporary purpose. Just as the memoirs of Casanova and Lauzun passed on to posterity a seductive view of the Age of Enlightenment, so did Tsvetayeva strive in her plays to show the value of the past to her contemporaries who proclaimed as their aim the oblivion of all earlier ages and the destruction of all traditional cultural values.

The neo-Romantic strain in the drama of early twentieth-century Russian modernism did not get the exposure on the stage that it merited. Very few of plays of this genre were produced. (Kuzmin's *Venetian Madcaps* was performed by amateurs when it was written and Gumilev's *Gondla* had a brief run shortly after his death in 1921.) The stage designers of the neo-Romantic school, such as the Russian-born Eugene Berman and Pavel Chelishchev and the Frenchman Christian Bérard, whose visual conceptions would have been perfect for the neo-Romantic playwrights discussed, made their mark in the West only in the 1930s and 1940s, by which time Russian Symbolist and post-Symbolist drama was no longer played anywhere. For the time being, the drama of Kuzmin, Gumilev and Tsvetayeva remains within the realm of Russian poetry. Their stage incarnation is at present unlikely, but by no means inconceivable.[26]

**Notes**

Another version of this paper will be published in a forthcoming issue of *Wiener Slawistischer Almanach*.

1. George Kalbouss, *The Plays of the Russian Symbolists* (East Lansing, Mich., 1982), dates the beginnings of Russian Symbolist drama from the 1880s because of an early dramatic poem by Nikolay Minsky, *The Sun* ('Solntse'), written in 1880. It is seen as Symbolist because it 'used the vocabulary of the Orthodox church' (p. 7). This book is a good guide through the Symbolist period of Russian drama. But the author's lack of discrimination leads him to discuss such dubious 'Symbolists' as Yury Belyayev and Teffi.
2. A. Blok, *Sobraniye sochineniy*, vol. VIII (Moscow and Leningrad, 1963) p. 386.
3. M. Green, 'Mikhail Kuzmin and the Theater', *Russian Literature Triquarterly*, vol. VII (Winter 1974) pp. 285–6.
4. Ibid. for publication data on the plays by Kuzmin mentioned here. *The Death of Nero* was not published at the time Green drafted his list; it appeared subsequently in M. Kuzmin, *Sobraniye stikhov*, ed. J. Malmstad and V. Markov, vol. III (Munich, 1977) pp. 569–613.
5. On the circumstances of Tsvetayeva's association with the actors of the 'Third Studio', see her memoir 'The Tale of Sonechka', in M. Tsvetayeva, *Stikhi, teatr, proza* (Paris, 1979), and my book, *Marina Tsvetaeva: The Woman, Her World and Her Poetry* (Cambridge and New York, 1985) pp. 83–91.
6. For publication dates on Tsvetayeva's verse plays of her romantic cycle, see M. Razumovskaya, *Marina Tsvetayeva* (London, 1983) p. 395.
7. J. Malmstad, 'Mixail Kuzmin: A Chronicle of his Life and Times', in Kuzmin, vol. III, p. 76.
8. Green, p. 247.
9. See my essay 'Trilogiya Kyukhel'bekera *Izhorskiy* kak primer roman-ticheskogo vozrozhdeniya srednevekovoy misterii', in V. Terras (ed.), *American Contributions to the Seventh International Congress of Slavists* (The Hague, 1973) pp. 307–20.
10. M. Tsvetayeva, *Posle Rossii* (Paris, 1928) p. 11.
11. Blok, vol. v, pp. 183–4.
12. E. Clark, *Rome and a Villa* (New York, 1956) p. 246.
13. Kuzmin, vol. II, p. 13.
14. Green, p. 256.
15. Tsvetayeva, *Stikhi, teatr, proza*, pp. 135–201.
16. E. Binney III, *Les Ballets de Théophile Gautier* (Paris, 1965). See esp. ch. v, 'Gautier et le Proche-Orient: les Sources de *La Péri*'.
17. See my essay 'The Amber Bead of Crimea: the Image of Crimea in "The Fountain of Bakhchisaray" by Alexander Pushkin, and in the "Crimean Sonnets" by Adam Mickiewicz', *California Slavic Studies*, vol. II (1963) pp. 108–20. See also Pushkin's letter to Vyazemsky of March and April 1825, where he criticised Thomas Moore for imitating 'in a childish and ugly way the childishness and ugliness of Saadi, Hafiz and Mahomet' and goes on to say that 'A European, even when he is intoxicated by the luxury of the Orient, must retain his European taste and outlook' (A. Pushkin, *Polnoye sobraniye sochineniy*, vol. x (Moscow, 1958) p. 135).
18. O. Matich, 'Androgyny and the Russian Religious Renaissance', in

A. M. Mlikotin (ed.), *Western Philosophical Systems in Russian Literature* (Berkeley, Calif. and Los Angeles, 1979) pp. 165–75; 'Androgyny and the Russian Silver Age', *Pacific Coast Philology*, vol. xiv (1979) pp. 42–9.

19. 'Maupin (madame, connue sous le nom de mademoiselle)', in J. Michaud, *Biographie universelle ancienne et moderne* (Graz, 1968), vol. xxvii, pp. 331–2.

20. N. Gumilev, 'Teofil' Got'e', *Sobraniye sochineniy v 4-kh tomakh*, vol. iv (Washington, 1968) pp. 386-94; 'Naslediye simvolizma i akmeizm', ibid., 171–6.

21. G. Shmakov, 'Blok i Kuzmin', *Blokovskiy sbornik*, vol. ii (Tartu, 1972) pp. 341–60.

22. The poems by Gumilev mentioned are in volume i of his *Sobraniye sochineniy*, pp. 111–12, 174–6. The story is in ibid., vol. iv, pp. 68–80.

23. M. Tsvetayeva, *Izbrannyye proizvedeniya* (Moscow and Leningrad, 1965) p. 622.

24. V. Setchkarev, 'Gumilev-dramaturg', in Gumilev, *Sobraniye sochineniy*, vol. iii, p. xxi. See also the discussions of Gumilev as playwright in S. Driver, 'Nikolaj Gumilev's Early Dramatic Works', *Slavic and East European Journal*, vol. xiii (1969) pp. 326–45; and E. Sampson, *Nikolay Gumilev* (Boston, Mass., 1979) pp. 164–70.

25. M. Tsvetayeva, 'Chervonnyy valet', *Novyy zhurnal*, vol. cxv (1974) p. 25.

26. With the advent of *glasnost'*, the popularity of Tsvetayeva in the Soviet Union has reached the level of a tidal wave, as is confirmed by the unprecedented increase in the publication of her work and of literature about her. During a visit to Moscow in January 1989, I became aware that her plays have now been taken up by Soviet theatres. The Vakhtangov Theatre was presenting *The Three Ages of Casanova* – a montage of Tsvetayeva's plays *An Adventure* and *The Phoenix*. Every Tsvetayeva scholar I met strongly disliked this adaptation. The Taganka Theatre was on tour with a production of Tsvetayeva's *Phaedra*. I was informed by a Soviet colleague that a new opera based on a play by Tsvetayeva has been announced for production by the Bolshoy Theatre in the spring of 1989. If the present trend continues, there should be stage productions of every play by Tsvetayeva within the next year or two.

# 6

# Mortal Masks: Yevreinov's Drama in Two Acts

## SPENCER GOLUB

*I always ask myself: What is the 'self' other than a succession of masks? Once you destroy them, the personality disappears.*

Nikolay Yevreinov

There are few figures in the history of the modern Russian theatre who are at once so representative of its central concerns and yet so unmistakably idiosyncratic as Nikolay Yevreinov. While not a Symbolist, Yevreinov combined the movement's pre-revolutionary tendencies toward Godseeking and life-building into a fully performative 'theatre-in-life' philosophy. In the years of 'derealised reality' (*c.* 1905–17), Yevreinov the extreme subjectivist defined the world as a text to be closed or left open according to his whim. In 1917 the seductive maskings, double realities, romantic fictions and adulterous betrayals of *commedia dell'arte*, his preferred form, were eclipsed by the 'unalterable betrayal' of the Revolution. To employ a quintessentially Yevreinovian literary analogy, the Gyntian storyteller became the Gyntian traveller, settling in Paris in 1925, the beginning of his permanent exile. From there he conducted a dialogue with a new Soviet authority that was in the process of defining itself, with both 'authors' recreating history as a mask for the story they wanted to tell. For Yevreinov the story was 'Paradise Lost'; for the Soviets, it was 'Paradise Achieved'.

Drawing upon previously unpublished play manuscripts and other materials from the archive Yevreinov and his wife assembled in exile, this article illustrates how the two halves of his career – his pre-revolutionary 'theatre-in-life', and his post-revolutionary and post-emigration 'afterlife' – filter and magnify one another.

I

Yevreinov's years of wandering outside of Russia are prefigured
in the roles upon which he modelled himself. He rehearsed his
exile by mastering the modern artist's self-sufficiency and self-
deification. This, Frank Wedekind had said, was made necessary
by the absence of social coherence and an inner legitimacy based
on myth.[1] Yevreinov was by definition displaced and estranged,
like his literary models Don Quixote and Robinson Crusoe and
like his performative model, Harlequin. The danger to which he
often fell prey in his splendid isolation masquerading as engage-
ment was the tyranny of Self.

But perhaps the most important of Yevreinov's literary models
was Peer Gynt, the archetypal combination of irrationalism and
wanderlust, whom Eric Bentley has called 'the Don Quixote of free
enterprise'.[2] In Yevreinov's hands the Gyntian credo was developed
into the notion of 'transformation through transfiguration'.
Constant transformation constituted for Yevreinov, as for Peer, a
liberation from the burden of selfhood and from death. In this
view Ibsen's hero, the solipsist with the impulse to conquer the
world, is also a subjective disorderer of reality, what Mikhail
Bakhtin would call a 'joyful relativist'.[3] He is audacious, childlike
in his egoism and yet strangely egoless, a teller in service to the
possibility of an infinite number of tales which spring forth once
reality is defamiliarised. Fittingly, Ibsen composed *Peer Gynt* while
in self-imposed exile from his native Norway. Although Yevreinov
planned to direct *Peer Gynt* during his émigré period, he never
did. In a sense a production would have been redundant. He had,
like Peer, already peeled the onion, lived the life.

A liar like Peer whose life's story constitutes a trying-on of
masks and styles, whose audacious spirit confronts the periods of
serendipity and uncertainty – to borrow Ibsen's own words – 'goes
roundabout'.[4] He becomes like the artist, who rather than being
defeated, is buoyed, even defined by the difficulty of creating art
and thereby finding a path through life. He is a formalist who
makes something, in fact everything, out of art's difficulty.[5] 'The
way of art', wrote Viktor Shklovsky, 'is a round-about way, a work
that makes us feel the stones on it, a way which returns on itself.'[6]
It is a story that, aside from being open-ended, is endlessly self-
consuming. It purposely mystifies and frustrates, retards and

obfuscates, defamiliarises itself, lays bare its own devices at every turn.

The method by which Yevreinov sought to defamiliarise death was likewise roundabout. He did so by making a fetish of life which he accomplished by embracing the childhood of men and of cultures. He expressed the former not only in his 'theatre of five fingers', the prototype for his later and better known 'theatre for oneself'; but also in *What Is Theatre?* ('Chto takoye teatr?', 1921), which was written for children; in 'The Merry Theatre for Grown-up Children' ('Veselyy teatr pozhilykh detey'), which he co-founded with Fedor Komissarzhevsky (1908–9); as well as in his many harlequinades and dramatised fairy tales at the 'Crooked Mirror' Theatre ('Teatr "Krivoye zerkalo'", 1910–17). It is manifest also in his adopted persona, Harlequin, who trumpeted his originality with a child's sense of grandiloquent self-discovery.

Yevreinov sought to promote his ideas through his work at the Ancient ('Starinyy') Theatre, an attempt to capture the 'childhood' of cultures. The same aim is to be discerned in his various historical works, *Peasant Actors* ('Krepostnyye aktery', 1912); *The Origin of Drama* ('Proiskhozhdeniye dramy', 1921); *The Primordial Drama of the Germanic Peoples* ('Pervobytnaya drama germantsev', 1922); *Azazel and Dionysus* ('Azazel i Dionis', 1924), and in his consistent attempts to discover and reinvent a Russian folk theatre. His studies of actors and acting, including those of the *commedia dell'arte*, the Middle Ages and the Spanish Golden Age (*The Spanish Actor of the XVI–XVII Centuries* ('Ispanskiy akter XVI–XVII vv.', 1909), reinforced his efforts to return to the essence and the beginning of theatre. His claim for the prepotency of the theatre argues for it as man's earliest and most distinctive impulse.

Armed with his studies of primitive ritual and child's play, Yevreinov sought to explode the fairy tale myth of death, that shadowy figure which in fiction and reality dims youth, beauty and happiness. In *The Golden Bough*, Sir James Frazer tells how the Carnival King, in a purposeful profanation of the *pharmakos* ritual (the origin of which Yevreinov discussed in *Azazel and Dionysus*), was buried under a dung-heap.[7] This strange yet hopeful juxtaposition between death skull and fool's cap appealed to Yevreinov because it offered a powerful alternative to the morbid neo-Romantic preoccupation with death among the Russian Symbolists. In devising the 'monodrama', the dramatic form and theory with which his name is most commonly associated, Yevreinov took the first step in making death performative and part of his overall theatricalisation of life.

Yevreinov's dramatic exploration of these ideas is present as early as 1902, in *The Foundation of Happiness* ('Fundament schast'ya'), a play which displays the marks of Symbolist influence. In this work death, in the guise of the Dark Lady, appears in a dream to a drunken coffin-maker. This incident, almost certainly borrowed from Pushkin's story 'The Undertaker' ('Grobovshchik') from *The Tales of Belkin* ('Povesti Belkina') also owed much to the work of E. T. A. Hoffman. In the later monodrama *Backstage at the Soul* ('V kulisakh dushi', 1911) the mock transcendence of the dream state gives way to visionary guidance to the afterlife. A conductor with a lighted lantern, probably meant to symbolise Yevreinov himself, appears to convey the unseen and recently deceased protagonist's eternal Self to the hereafter. Here Yevreinov seems to quote another romantic source, Christian Dietrich Grabbe's *Jest, Satire, Irony and Deeper Significance* (1827), which ends with the lantern-bearing author locked out of his text.[8] The ironic tone of Yevreinov's pre-revolutionary plays, with their *commedia* and romantic influences, suggests that, aside from being a healthful tonic, laughter may be the only means by which we can defeat and transcend death.

In his pre-revolutionary work, Yevreinov makes a great show of lowering curtains which are then passed through by characters who refuse to die or to see the play end. While these characters are wont to yell *'Finita la comedia!'*, they do so in order talismanically to forestall the end. They are dreamers who dream of no-end, of immortality.

Yevreinov's prototypical pre-revolutionary play in this regard is *The Beautiful Despot* ('Krasivyy despot', 1905) whose protagonist prefers to live in his dream of the distant past rather than confront the tasteless present. He represents the attempt to embody boundary-less time, in which past, present and future are interchangeable. In the harlequinade *A Merry Death* ('Veselaya smert''), Pierrot's turning back the hands of the clock, so as to forestall the arrival of Harlequin's appointed hour of death, represents another attempt to trick time into becoming infinite. This action is superfluous, because by living life to the full, Harlequin has already defamiliarised and vanquished death. Time's passage becomes irrelevant in relation to the revelation of meaning.

As a lifelong primitivist, the paradigms for Yevreinov's literary and performative arts owe much to two forms which Shklovsky

argued predate the novel – linking and framing tales.[9] Those most
pertinent to Yevreinov's *oeuvre* are *Don Quixote* in the first category
and *The Tale of the Thousand Nights and One Night* in the second.

Tzvetan Todorov equates framing with embedding
(*enchâssement*), with positioning stories within a story, truth within
a lie and vice versa. Framing/embedding dissolves absolute truth,
transforms storytelling into the ultimate and only virtue, reason
for and mode of being. Scheherezade tells stories to stay alive.[10]
Similarly, the story which Yevreinov made of his own life and of
history was a part of the war he waged against death.

Yevreinov's pre-revolutionary plays contain many instances
where a framing device is employed. Often it is embodied by a
loquacious lecturer whose compulsive rambling interrupts the
ostensible story of the play and in fact becomes the story. These
characters include so-called experts in the employ of the theatre
that is presenting the play. Sometimes these conveyors of framing
information are themselves characters in the play's central plot,
who find themselves thrust through the curtain which separates
stage from audience – Pierrot in *A Merry Death*, the Assistant
Director in *The Fourth Wall* ('Chetvertaya stena', 1915). The same
device carries over into the revolutionary period, witness Harlequin
in *The Chief Thing* ('Samoye glavnoye', 1921). All uses by Yevreinov
of the framing device are parodic, the objects of his parody
being theatrical conventions, recent innovators and innovations
(especially, Stanislavsky and his Art Theatre 'MKhAT-ism'), and
current trends, including those embraced by Yevreinov himself.
In this last case, Yevreinov mocks his own tendency to enlist
scientific or historical authority to contextualise and validate his
theatrical productions at the Ancient Theatre. Yevreinov's 'authori-
ties' are invariably exposed in his plays as being quacks, poseurs,
actors, prototypes for which can be found in the *commedia dell'arte*
in the persons of the chameleon-like, opportunistic survivor Harlequin and the Bolognese windbag *Il Dottore*. Even *The Chief Thing*,
with its 'theatre-in-life-as-salvation' premise, unmasks itself in the
end to reveal its 'true' identity as a harlequinade.

The ultimate frame in a Yevreinov play is the unseen presence
of the author himself, lying to, manipulating and mystifying his
characters, even those representing his surrogate selves. In reaction
to this perceived inequity in the author–character relationship,
Yevreinov's deflated poseurs illuminate the artificiality of the play
world with their self-referential questions and their abnegation of

responsibility for the play in which they appear. 'And what is the author of the play trying to say?', Pierrot asks the audience at the conclusion of *A Merry Death*. Harlequin in *The Chief Thing* asks the audience to finish the play for him.[11]

Yevreinov's narrators begin by believing themselves to be imbued with greater consciousness of the overall artistic design than their fellow characters. However, as they trace this design, they come to realise that the author's intention for the design has become no clearer, perhaps even more confusing to them. But of course the characters' confusion and discomfiture are only as real as they are.

The use of transformation, like that of the framing device in Yevreinov's plays, does more than argue for relativism and life's improvisatory nature. It dramatises Yevreinov's compulsion to change his mind in public so that he may continue to talk through newly minted possibilities, thus engaging us in a continuous dialogue with himself. Art becomes the essential life-affirming act, so long as it continues to reinvent itself and becomes a story without end. Thus, at the Crooked Mirror Theatre, Yevreinov wrote plays whose premise was often to reinvent themselves from different authors' or directors' perspectives.[12]

What French critic Charles de Saint-Cyr called Yevreinov's 'maddeningly incomplete genius' may in part be ascribed to his unwillingness to finish a story.[13] Closure for Yevreinov symbolised artistic and physical death. Instead of meticulously amassing life's sensate bits and pieces as an end in itself ('MKhAT-ism'), Yevreinov explored the sensory qualities of endlessly transforming consciousness in his 'theatre of the mind'. By defamiliarising life's discrete parts, which realism sought to mimetically render, Yevreinov in his monodrama, 'theatre for oneself' and 'theatre in life', took what had been the means and made it into the end. 'The act of perception in art', Viktor Shklovsky writes, 'is an end in itself and must be prolonged.' Monodramas, which are invariably short in duration, suggest the limits to which the act of perception as the object of art can be prolonged without this focus itself transforming into something else.

In many of his pre-revolutionary plays, Yevreinov contemplated and manifested the dangers of the very ideas he seemed to be promulgating: the lure of incompleteness; the paradox of aestheticism; the artist's self-seduction by the new certainty of his own omniscience and the sanctity of his inner experience. It is no wonder, then, that so many of these plays parody the idea of authority, including the author's, as well as reinvent the romantic metaphor of eros as death.

Yevreinov's major pre-revolutionary dramaturgical theme, adultery or the betrayal of love, was the perfect vehicle for expressing his concerns and defining his artistic ends: the defamiliarisation of perceived reality; the doubleness of masking and the mystery of identity; the power and peril of seduction to the self as well as to others. 'Betrayal', writes Peter Brooks, 'is a personal version of evil', made necessary 'in the post-sacred universe, where personality alone is the effective vehicle of trans-individual messages.'[14] Betrayal of the God of Love in the form of the story of Christ is treated metaphorically by Yevreinov in his tales of adultery, in which Woman most often plays the role of Judas. This is consistent with the infernality-of-Woman theme prevalent in the work of *fin-de-siècle* artists Felicien Rops and Aubrey Beardsley, on whom Yevreinov wrote monographs (1910 and 1912).

Adultery is likewise a central theme in *commedia dell'arte* scenarios and in *The Tale of the Thousand Nights and One Night*. The Infernal Woman, seductive in both her Dionysian carnality and in her Apollonian ability to spin a story and create an illusion with intimations of authority, even of immortality, conflates the images of the real Isadora Duncan (whom Yevreinov admired) and the fictional Scheherezade, as well as of Columbine and Salome. Her image appears in Yevreinov's pre-revolutionary plays: *The Foundation of Happiness* (in which she appears as Death); *Stepik and Maniurochka* ('Stepik i Manyurochka', 1905); *A Woman Like That* ('Takaya zhenshchina', 1908); *A Merry Death; The Performance of Love* ('Predstavleniye lyubvi', 1910); *Backstage at the Soul; A Columbine of Today* ('Kolumbina segodnya', 1915)'; and *The Eternal Dancer* ('Vechnaya tantsovshchitsa', 1916). She wears a mask of authoritative sensuality, yet remains sexually ambivalent, like Harlequin and Yevreinov himself.[15]

In Yevreinov's adaptation of Mohammed El Bassri's *About Six Beautiful Woman who Don't Resemble One Another and She Who Was the Most Beautiful of All* ('O shesti krasavitsakh ne pokhozhikh drug na druga i ona kotoraya byla samaya krasivaya iz vsekh'), which he staged at the Crooked Mirror Theatre in 1910, a Prince turns away six beauties sent to him by his beloved 'Clear Eyes' in order to test his love for her. She learns that the Prince loves her not for the attributes embodied individually and collectively by the 'six beauties' but because of the irrational, empathetic response which she inspires in him. Yevreinov took this adaptation with him when he emigrated.

Yevreinov projects not only Woman but the Self as Other, while asserting via self-publicity the openness of his persona to the world. Furthermore, by defining art as a function of the force of personality and as a hypnotically seductive medium (*The Revelation of Art* ('Otkroveniye iskusstva'), unpublished), Yevreinov is likewise positing the Otherness of art itself. Art betrays not only its audience but its maker. It is a treacherous fairy tale, promising transcendence which can beautifully and dangerously make something out of nothing. Like Woman, it engages us totally and irrationally. This theme was mitigated by the intervention of a different Other, the Revolution, which for a time made all of Russian history and society double and transformative, while exacerbating Yevreinov's sense of betrayal and having been betrayed.

## II

In his *Lectures on Theatre* ('Lektsii o teatre', 1917–20), Yevreinov called for a theatre that is based not so much on aesthetic feeling as on the instinct of transformation.[16] This tendency was reinforced by his emigration and reinvention as a citizen of the world.

Yevreinov's post-revolutionary plays are mostly concerned with history and science, technology and technocracy in relation to humanism, in particular the issues of love and faith. They are also largely anti-Utopian, although they often project the mask of Utopia. They tell us that while science and technology can bring us the future and ideology can give it definition within a narrow scope, none of this can return us to paradise nor can it reinvent it. The characters in these plays, although often dreamers, are no longer aesthetes. They must, more than ever, cut a spiritual path through the world's misery. The confusion and experimentation of the pre-revolutionary years have been replaced by the numbing certainty of the great Bolshevik experiment. It was no longer possible to live outside of history.

Yevreinov had always been interested both in the judgement of history and in history as a creative shaping agent. He echoed Taine in asserting that 'we have no absolute criteria for judging things – apart from the thing's relationship to its epoch, the people among whom it developed, etc.'[17] Yet in his late plays written on contemporary historical subjects and themes such as emigration, for example, *The Nameless* ('Chemu net imeni', written 1935–7, published 1965) and *The Steps of Nemesis* ('Shagi Nemezidy', written 1936–8, published 1956), and in his *History of the Russian Theatre* ('Istoriya russkogo teatra', 1955), Yevreinov's compulsion to judge and even to correct history becomes evident, reflecting a growing sense of social responsibility and personal frustration. Yevreinov now struggled with a no-longer-fashionable apocalypticism, succinctly articulated by one of *The Chief Thing*'s American translators in 1925, the year of his emigration: 'The Manager of the Universe, whoever he may be, is managing His Stock Company very badly. Two thousand years ago He put on a beautiful play, but this having had such a long run it is time to build a new theater.'[18]

Yevreinov was not only nervous about the future, he was desirous of the past, wanting to relive it so as to repossess it. The past had been taken from him, not naturally by time and evolution, but unnaturally by war and revolution, leaving him with a sense of disjointedness and incompleteness. He saw the contemporaneous development of Soviet history as an unreality parallel to his own in emigration. His post-revolutionary plays are purposeful misreadings of the evolving textual codes of the new Soviet drama, attempts to render paradoxical a regime which was quickly being purged of self-doubt.

As Marxist ideology worked its way toward happy endings and conflictless art, Yevreinov continued to assert the reality and viability of conflicting perspectives and endings and to question even the possibility of achieving sufficient singleness of purpose to imagine an end. In *Le Triangle immortal* ('The Eternal Triangle') or *Le Mari, la femme, et l'amant* ('Husband, Wife and Lover') (date unknown; unpublished), we are told a story from the perspectives of the three different characters listed in the play's alternate title. The audience must judge which version is best; 'best' rather than truest, because, like *The Chief Thing*, the play has a theatrical setting. The performers continually 'break character' to discuss the style and tone of the developing play and the meanings of their individual actions.

The 'multi-author' approach suggests Boris Geyer's and Yevreinov's earlier experiments with 'polydrama' – a sort of multiple monodrama – at the Crooked Mirror Theatre. A stagehand interrupts the action, echoing the many interrupted actions featured in

Yevreinov's pre-revolutionary plays. The characters are intermittently and ultimately distracted from the play by their hunger, which they openly discuss. While one does not want to claim too much for this slight play, the implications of a lingering hunger which distracts from one's ability to fulfil the prescribed programme are evocative in reference to Soviet society. This distractedness, along with the confusion over ends, suggests a lingering lack of faith in and commitment to the means. It says as well that the true, happy end has not yet been achieved, that the text is still open to individual initiative and interpretation.

Utopias are, according to Yevreinov, the invention of false messiahs, echoing the pretender theme manifested historically in the Time of Troubles and artistically in plays from Gogol to Gorky. In place of certainty, Yevreinov offered 'transformation through transfiguration', the beneficence of the 'theatricalisation of life'. This embraced both the naïve boastfulness associated with Gogol's Khlestakov and Don Quixote's love of humanity. It blended two of Yevreinov's major themes, philanthropy and betrayal, predicated on the paradox of belief. These themes come together in one of his best-known plays – *The Chief Thing*.

The anonymity of Yevreinov's philanthropist characters is a condition derived from a profusion of identities, as in *The Chief Thing*. This captures the essence of Yevreinovian masking and of his post-emigration predicament as a displaced celebrity bereft of the audience which had helped to define him. The theme of humble, philanthropic life-building was already at work in Yevreinov's early plays. The 'hero' of *Backstage at the Soul* is anonymous, the typicality of his *commedia* mask mixing exhibitionism with anonymity. The protagonists in the plays of the Ancient Theatre's mediaeval cycle are also largely generic. While Yevreinov's spirituality did not allow for the concreteness of a new paradise on earth, it did manifest itself in the form of a theatricalised social mysterion, a 'theatre-in-life' trilogy beginning with his play *The Chief Thing*.

*The Chief Thing* is, among other things, a riposte to Maksim Gorky's *The Lower Depths* ('Na dne'), the socialist ideologue's attempt to expose the 'theurgic fallacy' in contemporary Russian thought. In Gorky's play the broken and bankrupt faiths of art and religion – symbolised, respectively, by the Actor who cannot remember his lines and eventually commits suicide, and by the suspicious pilgrim Luka who inspires the downtrodden only to abscond – are eclipsed by the tramp Satin's vaguely articulated faith in material reality and the concrete will of the people.

In *The Chief Thing* the philanthropist/would-be messiah is called Fregoli after the famed Italian quick-change artist and is first revealed in the guise of a lady fortune-teller with a talent for hypnosis – the talent which the Symbolists of the preceding generation had ascribed to art. There is a correlation via symbol between art and fortune-telling. Yevreinov chose the name 'Fregoli', in part because etymologically *fregola* derives from *frigare*, which in Italian means 'to dupe, 'to adorn', 'to embellish'.

Yevreinov's original idea was to show Jesus Christ as a divine Harlequin bringing happiness to the unhappy via amusing illusions, guided by the truth that 'there is a divine sanctity in the Good'. A French critic likened Fregoli to both Don Quixote and Judas.[19] Fregoli brings hope to the residents of a boarding-house, who have been disappointed in life, via a 'theatre-in-life' experiment. For this he enlists the aid of some second-rate local actors who are ironically in the process of rehearsing a spectacle of consummate self-absorption, the Roman orgy scene from *Quo Vadis?* Aside from offering a Crooked Mirror-style parody of provincial theatre production, the *Quo Vadis?* scene serves a vital purpose in the play. The very messiness of this scene comically suggests the Roman Saturnalia, the December festival of misrule, reversal and mock kingship. In *The Chief Thing*, we are given a mock king and Lord of misrule in the figure of the Harlequin-Christ (the play's original title). The Carnival King may be a direct successor to the old Saturnalian King, much as Yevreinov's Act III Lenten Carnival succeeds his Act II Saturnalia. A feigned suicide in Act III follows the mock deaths of a symbolic god in Act II. *Quo Vadis?* or 'Whither Goest Thou?' signals rebirth, the seasonal cycle, changes in tonality, the revival of a dead god.[20]

In *The Chief Thing*, Yevreinov resolved the modernist theatre's pre-revolutionary identity crisis – captured in the competing images of the temple and the puppet-show – by making theatre's talent for deceit and diversion synonymous with its holiness: as it jests so it saves. *The Light in the Window* ('Ogonek v okoshke', written 1946, unpublished),[21] Yevreinov's second response to *The Lower Depths*, has as its setting a sort of church-restaurant (temple/puppet-show). It is operated by an ex-Salvation-Army officer who, together with a chemist-turned-holy man, Brother Maksim (the Gorky reference is clear), is marketing heaven to bourgeois patrons via a portfolio of 'actual' still photos.[22] The 'Unclean', the poor for whom this refuge was ostensibly built, are relegated to the bottom floor, while the monied elect occupy the top floor, much closer to heaven. While the elect converts see this divine 'light in the window' (this is also the restaurant's name), the play's protagonist, a publisher of spiritual books who is among them in a drunken stupor, sees his deceased wife with Saint Peter at the Heavenly Gates (a reverse echo of the undertaker's drunken vision in *The Foundation of Happiness*). The revelation of there being a material life beyond death leads to the spiritual conversion of some characters but to a new disregard for this life on earth by many more. Fires are set all over town, magnifying and transforming the 'light in the window' into an apocalyptic metaphor and the Utopian dream of social mysterion into a nightmare. In the end, Brother Maksim absconds. A character in the play states that in the history of peoples, everything happens twice: once as tragedy and once as farce.[23] Yevreinov extends this doubleness to include the truth and sham of story.

As in so many of his post-revolutionary plays, Yevreinov here depicts a conflict between, on the one hand, science and rationalism and, on the other, art, religion and irrationalism. Not uncharacteristically, the opposing camps are located within a single family, with the younger generation embracing science as the new religion. 'Unbelievable people these artists', opines the son of religious parents, who is a medical student. 'They're so inclined towards mythology in art that in life they believe it's real.'[24]

The idea of myth underlies this play, as it does Yevreinov's later work *The Nameless*. The two plays can, in fact, be read in tandem as contrasting images of the world after the Fall, life as a magic lantern show in which faith and reason are but two of the shadows projected upon the blank cosmos above. Both plays discuss nostalgically and hopefully the existence and possible persistence of heaven. The smallness of the Soviet conception of paradise-on-earth is contrasted with the romantic grandeur of the evangelical idea. For true believers, heaven and hell is within, an idea which Yevreinov had been developing since *Backstage at the Soul*. In a sense, *The Light in the Window* continues the story which ended in *Backstage* with the eternal Self's travelling on to 'Newville'. In the later play, the artist figure, again suggestive of Yevreinov, is denied entry into heaven by Saint Peter for drinking, and for committing adultery and suicide, the very sins of which the protagonist in *Backstage* is guilty.

*The Light in the Window* was Yevreinov's rehearsal for death. It captures as well the futility of trying to discern and describe the face of God. In many ways, Yevreinov had spent a lifetime trying to do just that. During his period of failing health (1945–53), he habitually quoted Tyutchev's verse, 'Life, like a wounded bird / Attempts to rise and cannot.'[25] Mortality was no longer an affectation in Yevreinov's work, as it had been in the pre-revolutionary years. Yevreinov's disillusionment and depression may have also stemmed in part from his at least partial perception of a point of similarity between himself and his Soviet antagonists. Like the Soviets, he had tied his aspirations for society to a credo which others perceived as reductive. His earnest attempt to establish a dominion of happiness based on the ruling principle of 'theatre-in-life' had become for some artistic totalitarianism. His constant hectoring in Harlequin's motley smacked of demagoguery. By the time he wrote *The Steps of Nemesis*, Yevreinov saw that 'theatre-in-life' could easily become the tool with which the State could suppress rather than liberate and heal the masses.[26]

In *The Ship of the Righteous* ('Korabl' pravednykh', 1924), the second play in Yevreinov's 'theatre-in-life' trilogy, the ship *Anchorite*, the gift of an unseen philanthropist, sets sail with a small entourage to found a paradise on earth. However, this enterprise is inspired not by any real collective faith or philosophy but rather by the desire of separate individuals to seek an end to personal pain and hardship. Rather than acting on the experiential evidence of the Symbolist mysterion or on the secular faith of Marxist ideology they have been taught by experience that the only viable alternative to faith is escape, self-preservation. The journey is a series of unmaskings of the characters' personal motives, in part instigated by the stowaway Vitalius who may represent the life force and/or the new Soviet man. At play's end, the passengers return to port, save for the Madman and 'The One Called Dream', the Artist and Muse figures, who again set sail for parts unknown.

*The Ship of the Righteous* was the first of Yevreinov's plays to be staged abroad and for a non-Russian audience.[27] It was taken to be a satire on the failure of emigration by many in the émigré press and as a satire on the failure of Bolshevism by others. Ironically, on the basis of this play, some foreign and émigré journalists labelled Yevreinov a 'devout Bolshevik', a fanatical propandist for the cause. The play was read both politically and non-politically as a satire on idealism in general, with the role of Vitalius likened

to that of Satin in *The Lower Depths*. There were also those who
cited the play's lack of satire as proof of its Bolshevik orthodoxy.
The émigré artist David Burlyuk wrote, after seeing the New York
production (at the Irving Place Jewish Art Theatre, 1926), that far
from supporting a particular programme, the play captured the
spiritual and moral confusion engendered by the Revolution.[28]

Yevreinov's anti-Utopian disillusionment had intensified by the
time he wrote the third part of the trilogy, *The Theatre of Eternal
War* ('Teatr vechnoy voyny', also called 'The Unmasked Ball',
1928). The socio-spiritual revolution promised in *The Chief Thing* has
devolved into continuous and cynical play-acting to no discernible
positive end. The pursuit of an earthly paradise which characterises
the two preceding plays in the trilogy is here visited upon
the director of a Theatrical Institute while in an opium-induced
reverie.[29] It is an illusory paradise gained not by striving but by
submission.

In *The Nameless*, the folkloric myth of a harmonious world
splintered by an angry God – such as the biblical Garden of Eden –
is carried within the racial memory of the play's young protagonist,
Shura. The play's events are refracted through her dream, and
leapfrog between 1915 and 1945.[30] In Shura's vision, each of her
traumatic experiences – be it war, the deportation or execution of
a loved one – takes on an apocalyptic significance, yet on each
occasion both the world and those whom she shepherds revive,
as in the Polish dramas of Witkiewicz and particularly those of
Wyspianski which Yevreinov admired.

The quasi-Utopian ending of *The Nameless*, in an American
skyscraper (the modern reworking of the angel's nests which myth
says once sat above paradise-on-earth) suggests a perfect union of
science and humanism. The play has been read as the émigré's
Proustian attempt to retrieve lost time and space.[31] Indeed, the
presence on stage of a giant calendar and the dreamer's structuring
of events suggest a wish-fulfilment fantasy of mastery over things
which no human being can really control. Yevreinov transports
his characters out of harm's way but to a world that really exists,
not to some dreamed-of paradise. He seems to be suggesting the
latent potential of existing reality rather than the vain hope of a
new beginning. If this is true, his vision has sobered considerably,
and he has become, of all things, something of a realist.

Consistent with the historical perspective of his later work,
Yevreinov here wants to judge the influence of the Revolution,

and in particular of its reign of terror, over the course of a half-century. *The Nameless* shows how Bolshevik terror grew out of the pre-revolutionary ideology of Marxism–Leninism and how this terror was exacerbated first by War Communism and later, in 1937–9, by Stalin in preparation for the Second World War. According to Yevreinov, the Russian revolutionaries who asserted their humanism turned out to be grotesquely lacking in humanity.

This fact is understood only in the future (that is, by the play's readers) and not in the present tense (that is, by the play's characters).[32] Yevreinov depicts in this play how the Bolsheviks trampled not only upon the ceremony but on the humanism of Christian belief. He was here influenced by his wife, who made much of religion.[33] Via the play's protagonist, the bookbinder and old revolutionary Lutokhin, Yevreinov hoped to show that for a socialist idea to work and to be true to itself, it must encourage men to reinvest in the principle of brotherhood.[34] In *The Light in the Window* Yevreinov had already shown this to be a negative capability of the Soviet regime.

Yevreinov's most anti-Utopian play is his most realistic. *The Steps of Nemesis,* or *I Do Not Know Another Country Like This One* treats the Stalinist show trials, drawing many of its characters and situations from the historical record.[35] Yevreinov's neo-Jacobean tragicomedy offers Stalin as the master practitioner of 'theatre-in-life', a continuation of the author's earlier theme of emperors (Napoleon) and mad kings (Ludwig II of Bavaria) as directors on the stage of world drama. Stalin is also portrayed as the Judas who crucifies the apostles of Lenin on the cross of the so-called 'common good'. This reworks both a major theme of *The Chief Thing* and the neo-Christian symbology of Yevreinov's 1920 mass spectacle *The Storming of the Winter Palace* ('Vzyatiye zimnego dvortsa').

The play depicts the transformation of the drama of Marxism–Leninism into the nightmare of Stalinism. It is the antistrophe to the choral movement of the idealised proletariat in *The Storming.* It fills in details of the Bolshevik reign of terror which had been treated more panoramically and more suggestively in *The Nameless.* Yevreinov's interest in masking and unmasking here extends to the 'social mask' which Soviet officialdom had compelled society to don. Role-playing was as pervasive after the Revolution as before, but the roles now played were less ostentatious and more homogeneous. The mask-like image of Stalin became as ubiquitous as Hitler's and as chilling in its monstrous buffoonishness as

Chaplin's 'Great Dictator'. After the Harlequin-Christ of *The Chief Thing* and after Jarry's 'Savage God', there came Yevreinov's 'Savage Harlequin'.

*The Steps of Nemesis* represents one of several attempts made by Yevreinov to 'counter-defamiliarise' history, the Soviets having already defamiliarised it once via the Revolution's recasting of the past as prologue. In balance Yevreinov hoped to capture some kind of truth.

The idea of an afterlife, alluded to in Yevreinov's earlier plays, is here transmogrified into a grisly, politically expedient concept. Two of Stalin's former allies, now enemies, Zinov'ev and Kamenev, are publicly declared to be dead so that they can be forced privately to endure a lingering death-in-life existence. This cruelly parodies the Christian belief in just reward beyond the grave and profanes the Christian attitude toward the dead by essentially burying men alive and above ground. It is equally uncompromising towards the quasi-Christian principles earlier espoused by Yevreinov. In Yevreinov's view, there is no higher human goal than happiness. It transcends even beauty.[36] As such, Stalin as the killer of happiness is the Anti-Christ incarnate.

The idea of an afterlife and of its corruption by the Bolsheviks is also symbolic of the condition of being an émigré, being forced to exist in a kind of shadow world parallel to your real life. The émigré figure in this play is a cynical woman now living in France (another Yevreinov mask), visiting her ballet-dancer sister who has remained in the Soviet Union and is loyal to Bolshevism. The idea of sisters, present as well in *The Nameless*, suggests doubleness of perspective. As a plot device, it allows Yevreinov, as it were, to revisit his homeland clandestinely and to comment upon the aftermath of the Revolution in disguise. Other by now familiar themes and devices abound. There is the murderous man of science – here the doctor who was rumoured to have poisoned Gorky; and the image of the modern world as madhouse/inferno (Zinov'ev, suffering the living death, says that 'hell is a reality . . . Dante's hell was a playground by comparison').[37] Also present are the quintessentially Yevreinovian motifs of masking and transformation. Stalin and his henchmen are described as being actors, and the representation in the Prologue of the tribunal conducting the show trials of the state's enemies suggests Blok's representation of the mystical symbolists in his harlequinade *The Puppet Show* ('Balaganchik'). The act of recantation, the centrepiece of the show trial, is another form of masking and transformation, as is the 'red baptism' of an infant which translates religion into the language of politics. The play is a further chapter in Yevreinov's ongoing 'History of Corporal Punishment'. Its 'theatre-in-life' design is dramatically captured in an unmotivated one-and-one-half-page play-ending speech by the chastened Yagoda, the nation's former political security head. Yagoda alludes to the government's enactment of the social ideals of service and justice, to the victims' impersonation of repentance, and to the acts of death and retribution as composing a comic spectacle for which the people must pay.

A group of Yevreinov's post-revolutionary plays, including *Radio-potseluy/Le Radio-Baiser* or *Le Robot d'amour* ('Radio-Kiss, or The Robot of Love', written 1925; unpublished), *Love Under the Microsope* ('Lyubov' pod mikroskopom', earlier called *God Under the Microscope* ('Bog pod mikroskopom'), written 1931; unpublished) and *La Comédie infernale* ('The Infernal Comedy', written 1928?; performed 1948; unpublished) parody the new Soviet drama just before and during the Socialist Realist eras (mid-1920s to early 1950s). Many of these are set in laboratories, academies and institutes and feature intra-departmental conflicts between forward-looking Soviet scientists, who wed politics to science, and the unregenerate, head-in-the-sand pre-revolutionary type of intellectuals.[38]

The important difference between Yevreinov's post-revolutionary plays and those of the Soviets is that, in Yevreinov's work, the issue is not the re-education of the intellectual by the new Soviet man (often of proletarian social origins) but the re-education of the scientist's heart by a woman in the ways of love. While both types of play maintain the importance of the scientist entering into real life and social relationships, Yevreinov has in mind something that is far more romantic and individualistic, more human.

In Soviet drama, the laboratory becomes the controlled environment in which perfect life/lives are made, using the metaphors of artificial insemination, eugenics and euthenics. However, children are not born. Adults are reborn. The experts trained in the science of social engineering are not-too-distant relatives of Yevreinov's *commedia* doctors. To the extent that they can be rehumanised, there is some hope of redemption. But first they must acknowledge that the prescribed 'cure' for society is the problem and not the solution.

Yevreinov had always considered himself to be an artist-sociologist. Much of his post-revolutionary inquiry into social and scientific questions was written directly into his plays of this period. His psychological farce *Radio-Kiss* was prepared in part on the basis of his investigation into robots, animal intelligence, colour and large-screen television, two-way radios and even an early prototype of the microwave oven. The play's title refers to a membrane which when kissed transforms nervous energy into radio energy. This energy can be transmitted over long distances. It is a part of the totally mechanised home-laboratory environment of a young American inventor. Yevreinov uses it to defamiliarise the present by placing the strange near-future in the familiar present. Science and technology sublimate the protagonist's sexual energy and Yevreinov's pre-revolutionary dramaturgical sensualism, hitting upon many of the author's favourite themes and devices, such as love and betrayal, antifeminism and Gyntianism. In the absence of his beloved 'Astra' ('star'), an actress playing the role of Ulysses' faithful Penelope in a film being directed by his father in Greece, Thomas Craig (the young inventor) devises a female robot in her image and with her recorded voice. This 'robot of love' is so responsive to male domination that another man actually falls in love with it.

*Radio-Kiss* also draws on other typical Yevreinov motifs, like dualism (the real versus the artificial, 'theatre-in-life', framing/ embedding). As in several of his other post-revolutionary works, Yevreinov embeds a play within a play and a locale within a locale in *Radio-Kiss*. Actual film projected on a giant television screen shows those who are shooting the film *Penelope* in Greece, while we remain in the laboratory depicted on stage. Thomas's father, the film director, has returned to nature, even as the son has subjugated it. 'In this positivist century', says Thomas, 'belief is not enough! One must have scientific proof.'[39] And so he shows us his beating heart filled with love via an X-ray machine and otherwise works to approximate real feeling artificially. In this play it is, ironically, a robot who speaks of the mutability of happiness and of man's inability to appreciate happiness, even when he accidentally finds it. This sense of comic inversion is further embodied in the set, whose ceiling is treated as if it were the floor of another room which could be (but is not) rotated to stage level. This play, which superficially resembles *Backstage at the Soul* in its pure theatricality, has never been staged.

The 'psychological buffonade' *Love Under the Microscope* (1931) again depicts the conflict between the worlds of science and of art. In it, the Professor, who is director of a surgical clinic, conducts a psychological experiment aimed at conquering the atavistic need for love. To this end, he and his secretary (whom he will eventually realise that he loves) enact the roles of the mediaeval knight Theobald (her male ideal) and his lady Nicolette. The Professor, who regularly visits a prostitute and views women as victimising men, is another of Yevreinov's protagonists (usually male) who would play God. In the course of his experiment, however, he discovers the Christian principle that God is love and that love must not, therefore, be pushed under the microscope. By surrendering to one's instinct, in particular to the sensation of love, Man becomes one with God. The 'theatre-in-life' experiment thus becomes a form of theatrotherapy for the doctor, transforming him at least partially into a man of art. Artists, as he knows from having treated them, believe in the efficacy of illusion. Love and God are healthful shared illusions whose persistence tells us that although man holds on to the rational, he prefers the irrational, the transformative, the truths which positivism cannot touch.

*Love under the Microscope* suggests several of Yevreinov's other works. The story of the Professor and his secretary, who not only play but in effect become mediaeval lovers in an artificially created mediaeval world, is reminiscent of *The Beautiful Despot* and of the mediaeval cycle of plays at the Ancient Theatre. Their process is that of the actors in *The Chief Thing*. The idea that faith (in God, love) needs no proof will later be echoed in *The Light in the Window*. The theme of science and rationalism versus art, love, faith and irrationalism is present in *Radio-Kiss* and *The Infernal Comedy*. It also harkens back to *Backstage at the Soul* whose structural metaphor for breathing it recasts. In *Backstage*, the unseen protagonist's giant onstage heart beats in accordance with his arousal and anxiety levels. In *Love Under the Microscope* each act is divided into two scenes, following one another without a break, which the author intends to suggest inhalation and exhalation.[40]

In *Microscope* and *Radio-Kiss*, Yevreinov embraces what is good in science and technology, while rejecting technocracy. Mechanisation and materialism must not be allowed to swallow the soul. Science should not be asked to 'cure' the irrational, because man the artist is ennobled by his irrationality. What distinguishes art, Yevreinov goes on to say in *Microsope*, is the eccentric individualism, the spiritual life of its creator. A man must create what is within him and not that which is prescribed and thought correct by society. The transformed Professor's statement on the matter, which intentionally employs a historical symbol of Religion, articulates the embedded anti-Soviet theme in this play: 'We have to combat the old prejudices, I agree! But that's not a reason for destroying the Cathedral of Reims. We have sentiments within us which are as old and as beautiful as the Cathedral of Reims!'[41]

*The Infernal Comedy* is a Yevreinovian compendium play, a compression of his life's work into a unified book of knowledge which finds its prototypes in both the mediaeval and modernist (for example, Joyce's *Ulysses*) canons. Subtitled 'a satiric suite in four acts, with a prologue and two interludes', this work was intended by Yevreinov to be an update of Dante's *The Divine Comedy*, with the new hell engendered in ourselves by science, technology, politics (Bolshevism) and feminism. 'Virgil' leads 'Dante' on a tour through the new infernal world, suggesting to him metadramatically that 'perhaps, in order to acquire a real existence, we must be incarnated as characters in the theatre, who are named after the originals'.[42] This reverses the notion expressed in Yevreinov's monograph *The Original on the Portraitists* ('Original o portretistakh', 1922), in which he attacked his portraits for having robbed him of his authenticity.

Dante tells Virgil that the twentieth century, a non-literary time, has become a sort of theatre in life. One such 'theatre-in-life' theme is the subjugation of the male by the female in the name of equality between the sexes. In the 'Artificial Insemination Institute' section, which begins the play, male sperm donors are presented to an audience of empowered masked women. In 'The Man of the Future' section which follows, a husband predicting future equality between men and women walks out on his wife. (This is the second conscious reversal of Ibsen's *A Doll's House* with which Yevreinov was associated. The first was Nikolay Urvantsev's *The Fate of Man* ('Sud'ba cheloveka'), produced at the Crooked Mirror Theatre in 1915, during Yevreinov's tenure as artistic director.)

A second of the play's 'theatre-in-life' themes is that of the failed Bolshevik Utopia. During the play's second interlude, Dante and Virgil come upon an iron curtain bearing the familiar legend, 'Abandon all hope, ye who enter here'. Virgil tells Dante that the inhabitants of the country behind the iron curtain 'tried to make this "paradise" like a sort of hell'. The play's third section, 'The Academy of the Music Hall', which recycles Yevreinov's *The School of the Stars* ('Shkola etualey', Crooked Mirror première, 1911), is similarly anti-Utopian. In the 'Academy' a totalitarian director controls the movements of a trio of singing and dancing women whom he denigrates, much as art itself is debased in this music-hall setting. Yevreinov here has his revenge upon Stanislavskian actor training, especially where applied to inappropriate forms (see also his *The Fourth Wall*), as well as upon women and the Soviets' debasement of art for the masses. The play's final section, 'Backstage at the Soul', expands Yevreinov's monodrama of the same name, explicating it within a wider dramatic context and via the running dialogue between Virgil and Dante. Dante argues that man's soul is immortal, while Virgil asserts that science has long ago negated the soul. They want to test the Professor's theory that hell is located in the human soul, which is 'not something indivisible but consists of several *Selves*'. The generic figures of the rational, emotional and eternal Selves – the Wife and the Songstress/Dancer from the original *Backstage* – here become specific characters introduced and developed in the preceding three sections of the full-length play. The unseen protagonist whose body and soul we explore in the original monodrama is now an alcoholic musician, a sperm donor from the 'Artificial Insemination Institute' and the beleaguered husband who declared his independence in 'The Man of the Future'.

Once again Yevreinov's agenda has become more personal and political. Contemporary life, his own as an émigré and that of his lost countrymen, is hell. The play's last line, *'Finita la Comedia!'*, with its Dante-like overtones, is at once a literary reference to its source and to Yevreinov's *commedia*-flavoured pre-emigration dramaturgy, as well as the playwright's impotent command to the modern age to cease its savaging of mankind's spiritual life. Dante, touring the modern hell, is a kind of émigré in disguise. His instruction to his co-traveller Virgil, 'Enough of politics. We're poets', is disingenuous on Yevreinov's part, given what he knows, but genuine, given what he feels.[43]

What Yevreinov liked best about technology was its ability to engage fully an audience's attention, to direct its perspective and to unify its consciousness, a goal to which his own theory of monodrama had aspired. Technology was the modern mythmaker, society's best chance at rediscovering the communal spirit lost in the past which the Symbolists and others in the pre-revolutionary period were unable to recapture. Like his role model, the Italian transformation artist Leopoldo Fregoli, Yevreinov sensed a natural aesthetic kinship between his art and the early cinema.[44] Yevreinov had said that the future of the theatre was in talking pictures, and that the libraries of the future would be enormous film stores. In his *The Theatre for Oneself* Yevreinov compared what we see in dreams to the frames of a film. In *The Storming of the Winter Palace* he had used the windows of the building in such a way as to make the scenes staged behind them resemble frames on an unwinding reel of film. In 1930 Yevreinov proclaimed the prospects of cinema to be unlimited.[45]

Perhaps the most pertinent cinematic device employed by Yevreinov in the later plays is a non-technological one. The giant calendar with its cascading pages, so prominently featured in *The Nameless*, creates what Sergey Eisenstein referred to as a 'montage of attractions' by conflating time and space.[46] It captures as well the dizzying sensation of life in a world which has spun off its axis, a body-less existence and the possibility of endless change. The fact of transformation remained for Yevreinov the most real of realities.

There is the sense in Yevreinov's later work that somehow technology was a metaphor for art's electrification of the senses, its ability to contact the soul in all things, animate and inanimate. Self-styled 'radio-futurist' David Burlyuk, a champion of Yevreinov throughout his career, wrote that the approaching 'Radio-Epoch' would, in Burlyuk's estimation, vindicate the scientific aestheticism of the pre-revolutionary artist.[47]

Yevreinov sought in science and technology what he had looked for hitherto in history and philosophy, namely, authority, authenticity, legitimacy, empowerment. Unsuited to the creation of 'useful' art – an idea captured in the notorious Stalinist notion of artists as 'engineers of the soul' – he could no longer embrace its 'uselessness' as the aesthete's offensive against the Platonic indictment. Sensitised to the experiential world, Yevreinov was ultimately unable to conquer it. His 'victory' lay in having held fast to the difficult path, forged in 'the spirit of contradiction', which 'led roundabout'.[48]

## Notes

This chapter was made possible by two grants from the National Endowment for the Humanities and by a Sesquicentennial Associateship grant from the University of Virginia.

1. Alan Best, *Frank Wedekind*, (ed.) R. W. Last, (London, 1975) pp. 24–6.
2. E. Bentley, *The Playwright as Thinker* (New York, 1987) p. 58.
3. K. Clark and M. Holquist, *Mikhail Bakhtin* (Cambridge, Mass., 1984) p. 309.
4. H. Ibsen, *Peer Gynt*, (ed.) R. Fjelde (Minneapolis, 1980) p. 64.
5. The similarity between Yevreinov and the Russian Formalists is exemplified in two dramatically similar statements made just two years apart. The first is by Yevreinov: 'We were born with a concern for our daily bread and for truth and justice – but with the complete atrophy of the feeling of theatricality, the instinct for the transformation of life, the will to the creation of the fantastic. And so it happened as it was bound to happen: the more people came to neglect theatricality, the more they turned from art to life, the more tedious it became to live. *We lost our taste for life* [my emphasis]. Without seasoning, without the salt of theatricality, life was a dish we would only eat by compulsion' (*Teatr kak takovoy* (St Petersburg, 1912) pp. 7–8). The second is by Shklovsky: 'By now the old art has already died, but the new has not yet been born. Things have died too: *we have lost the sensation of the world* [my emphasis]. We are like a violinist who has stopped feeling his bow and strings. We have ceased to be artists in our quotidian life; we do not like our houses and clothes and easily part with a life that we do not perceive. Only the creation of new forms of art can bring back to man his experience of the world, resurrect things and kill pessimism' ('Voskresheniye slova', as cited in P. Steiner, *Russian Formalism, A Metapoetics* (Ithaca, N.Y., 1984) pp. 48–9).
6. Viktor Shklovskiy, *O teorii prozy* (Moscow, 1929) p. 13.
7. Sir James Frazer. *The New Golden Bough*, (ed.) T. H. Gaster (New York, 1964) p. 321.
8. C. D. Grabbe, *Jest, Satire, Irony and Deeper Significance* (New York, 1966) p. 69.
9. R. Scholes, *Structuralism in Literature* (New Haven, Conn., 1974) pp. 83–4, 86.
10. T. Todorov, *The Poetics of Prose*, trs. R. Howard, (Ithaca, N.Y., 1977) pp. 21, 73–4. Among the works relating to the 'Arabian Nights' produced at the 'Crooked Mirror' between 1910 and 1917 were: *About Six Beautiful Women who Don't Resemble One Another*, a fairy tale by Mohammed El-Bassri, dramatisation and music by Yevreinov, 1 October 1910; *A Night in a Harem* ('Noch' v gareme'), a grotesque by Vep, 10 December 1910; *The One Thousand and Second Night* ('1002-aya noch''), an Arabian fairy tale in one act by Myurgit, no date given.
11. N. Yevreinov, 'A Merry Death' and 'The Chief Thing', in C. Collins (ed. and trs.), *Life as Theater: Five Modern Plays by Nikolai Evreinov* (Ann Arbor, Mich., 1973) pp. 18, 117.
12. Examples include *Æolian Harps* ('Eolovy arfy'), 1915, co-written with B. F. Geyer; *Kitchen Laughter* ('Kukhnya smekha'), 1913; *The Inspector General* ('Revizor'), 1913.
13. C. de Saint-Cyr, Review of *La Comédie du bonheur*, *La Semaine à Paris*, 9 November 1926, p. 11.

14. Shklovsky, quoted in Scholes, pp. 83–4; P. Brooks, *The Melodramatic Imagination: Balzac, Henry James, Melodrama and the Mode of Excess* (New York, 1984) p. 33. Betrayal is a particularly apt theme in Yevreinov's monodramas, whose very structure is built upon what Susan P. Compton, in relation to *The Performance of Love*, calls 'introverted eroticism': *The World Backwards, Russian Futurist Books, 1912–16* (London, 1978) p. 48.
15. Yevreinov, who was said to have been a great womaniser, may also have been bisexual. Whether or not this is true – at least one of his close acquaintances supports this claim – Yevreinov was artistically androgynous. His *alter ego* Harlequin, who produces and bears offspring, proclaims this, as do the many female protagonists in his plays who represent Yevreinov's embedded selves.
16. N. Yevreinov, 'Lektsii o teatre, 1917–20', *Tsentral'nyy gosudarstvennyy arkhiv literatury i iskusstva SSSR [TsGALI]*, fond no. 982, opis no. 1, yed. khr. no. 44.
17. Yevreinov is paraphrasing H. Taine, 'Introduction', *History of English Literature* [1864], trs. from the French by Henry von Laun (Edinburgh, 1873, rev. edn, New York and London, 1900).
18. W. L. Laurence, 'Quintessence', *The Harvard Crimson*, December 1925.
19. F. Ambrière, 'La Scène et l'écran: *La Comédie du bonheur*', *Clartés*, vol. VI, 3 August 1945, p. 10.
20. Frazer, p. 641.
21. A manuscript version of *The Light in the Window* is housed in the Yevreinov archive at the Bibliothèque de l'Arsenal in Paris. The same is true for all other unpublished Yevreinov plays cited in the text.
22. Scientific experiments by James Hazlitt are cited to substantiate the claim that heaven can be photographed. To this a cynical character in the play responds that, if this is true, he would like a snapshot of God, but in profile only, since he could not endure His direct stare.
23. N. Yevreinov, *The Light in the Window*, pp. 13–14.
24. Ibid., p. 1.
25. A. Kashina-Yevreinova, *N. N. Yevreinov v mirovom teatre XX veka* (Paris, 1964) pp. 70, 75.
26. G. Abensour, 'La Comédie du bonheur', in G. Abensour (ed.), *Nicolas Evreinov: L'Apôtre russe de la théâtralité* (Paris, 1981) p. 129.
27. The play premièred in Poland in 1925, the same year in which it was published in Leningrad under the title *The Commune of the Righteous* (W. and R. Sliwowski, 'Nicolas Evreinov et la Pologne', in Abensour, p. 90).
28. *Kurier Polski*, 25 April 1925, cited in ibid., p. 92; D. Burlyuk, 'Drama–Screen–Music: *Korabl' pravednykh*', *Russkiy golos* (New York), September 1926.
29. N. Yevreinov, 'The Theater of Eternal War (The Unmasked Ball)', in Collins (ed. and trs.), p. 272.
30. Attila Faj likens Yevreinov's use of a native popular myth 'to create a thing which did not have a name in the Russian family between 1914 and 1945' to Ibsen's work in *Peer Gynt*. A. Faj, 'Deux drames écrits en exil ayant la patrie pour sujet', in Abensour, pp. 140–1.

31. Sliwowski, p. 85; Faj, pp. 134, 141–2.
32. N. Yevreinov, 'Art and Literature', radio broadcast, Paris, 12–13 April 1965 (Yevreinov archive).
33. A. Kashina-Yevreinova, 'Introduction', in N. Yevreinov, *Chemu net imeni* (Paris, 1965) p. 3.
34. Lutokhin is suggestive of the old revolutionary Nikolay Morozov, author of a seven-volume study of Christ which was banned in the Soviet Union (Yevreinov, 'Art and Literature').
35. An English translation by Leon Savage of *The Steps of Nemesis*, entitled *Nightmare in the Kremlin*, or *Life Beyond the Grave*, can be found in the Yevreinov archive in Paris.
36. G. Welter, 'Preface', in N. Evreinov, *Histoire du théâtre russe* (Paris, 1947) pp. 7–19.
37. N. Yevreinov, *Nightmare in the Kremlin*, pp. 165–6.
38. A good example of the new Soviet drama, Aleksandr Afinogenov's *Fear* ('Strakh'), is set in an Institute of Physiological Stimuli. It concerns a professor's thesis that fear determines man's conduct even more than the basic stimuli of hunger, love and hate.
39. N. Yevreinov, *Radio-Potseluy/Le Radio-Baiser, Le Robot d'amour*. trs. G. Arout (unpublished) p. 33.
40. Synopsis of N. Yevreinov, *Bog pod mikroskopom/L'Amour sous le microscope* (unpublished).
41. N. Yevreinov, *L'Amour sous le microscope*, p. 23.
42. N. Yevreinov, *La Comédie infernale*, 'Prologue'.
43. Ibid., pp. 25, 55.
44. D. Gerould, 'Fregoli, Witkiewicz, and Quick-Change', *Theatre Three*. vol. III (Fall 1987) p. 52.
45. Yevreinov made several forays into cinema production. He wrote the screenplay for the silent film *Fecundity*, based on the Zola novel (1928) and for his own play *The Comedy of Happiness* (1939). He directed the film *Not on the Mouth* (1931) from a story based on Maurice Yvain's operetta of the same name.
46. Yevreinov likewise employs a number of 'magic lantern' effects to suggest battle scenes and other momentous offstage events. Eisenstein had Yevreinov's *The Storming of the Winter Palace* in mind when he filmed *October* (T. Q. Curtis, 'Evreinov Back in the Spotlight', *International Herald Tribune*, 11 January 1977).
47. D. Burlyuk, letters to Yevreinov, 22 August 1928, 7 April 1929.
48. N. Yevreinov, 'Otkroveniye iskusstva' (unpublished).

# 7

# The First Soviet Plays

ROBERT RUSSELL

It is an interesting and, perhaps, unexpected feature of the Russian Civil War that the Bolsheviks appear to have placed considerably more value than their opponents on art, using the term in its widest sense. In March 1919 at the 8th Party Congress the following resolution was adopted:

> It is essential to open up and make accessible to the workers all of the art treasures which were created on the basis of the exploitation of their labour and which have, until now, been available exclusively to the exploiters.[1]

It might be thought that at the height of the Revolution and Civil War there would be little time for the enjoyment of art treasures. Indeed, on 5 November 1917 the Union of Art Workers (*Soyuz deyateley iskusstv*), which numbered among its members such well-known figures as Fedor Sologub, Vsevolod Meyerhold, Vladimir Tatlin and Marc Chagall, anticipated a lack of concern for works of art during the military struggle and issued a printed broadsheet entitled 'An Appeal to the Entire Russian Nation' in which they demanded that 'palaces, museums and historical buildings should not be turned into places of military defence and billets for military units, which would give a possible pretext for the bombing, shelling and looting of the aforementioned buildings'.[2]

Some, at least, of the members of the Union of Art Workers remained unconvinced that the Bolsheviks would devote any resources to the preservation of Russian art. In the minutes of a general meeting of the Union on 17 November 1917 Fedor Sologub is quoted as saying:

> We do not wish to take anything away from the people, as Lunacharsky thinks, for Lunacharsky is not the people but just

148

a 'gentleman in a jacket' from whom it is necessary to protect art, the property of the entire nation.[3]

In fact, in the conditions of the Civil War, it was to prove difficult to protect and foster Russian art, but considerable efforts were made to do so, notably by Maksim Gorky and Anatoly Lunacharsky. Yet although Gorky, in particular, showed a concern for the welfare for all artists so long as they were not openly counter-revolutionary, there can be no doubt that the price of Bolshevik support for artists during the Civil War was a contribution of some sort to the Red cause. In many cases this was a direct contribution (such as the work of Mayakovsky); in others it was indirect though none the less real in the adversarial climate of the Civil War, in that the artist concerned continued to work in areas of the country controlled by the Bolsheviks, thereby giving them tacit support. For example, when Fedor Shalyapin continued to perform in Soviet Russia he was rewarded by the return of his requisitioned motor car and by the award of the title 'People's Artist' (the first to be so honoured).[4] The author of an article in the White newspaper *Vecherneye Vremya* noted wryly that when the Whites re-took Moscow the unprincipled Shalyapin would be the first to sing a welcoming anthem to Russia's liberators and the tickets to his concerts at the Bolshoy Theatre would continue to be sold out. In another White newspaper the poet Konstantin Balmont was criticised for accepting 'thirty pieces of silver' from the Bolsheviks (rumoured to amount in reality to a salary of 25 000 roubles a month) in return for some pro-Bolshevik verses.[5] It would appear that the propaganda value of art was quickly recognised. In October 1918 TEO, the Theatrical Section of the People's Commissariat of Enlightenment, resolved to organise theatrical events at the various Civil War fronts in order to mark the first anniversary of the October Revolution,[6] and throughout the war theatrical entertainment and propaganda (*agitprop*) was a regular part of the Red campaign. On 7 April 1919 Lenin signed Order No. 198, which enabled TEO or local Departments of People's Enlightenment to draft actors and other theatrical workers into front-line theatre units. Those who were unemployed were obliged to go, whereas those currently in work could be forced to participate only after agreement with local Theatre Committees. Outright refusal to go resulted in the case coming before a Revolutionary Tribunal which had extensive powers.[7] In this way companies of actors, directors and stagehands, generally about twenty strong, travelled to all of the major Civil War battlefields, performing a mixture of contemporary and classical plays and short propaganda pieces on topical issues (*agitki*). As the front line drew closer to Petrograd itself in November 1919, some of the permanent theatre companies made flying visits to perform for the troops on the outskirts of the city.[8] The value of theatrical work was recognised in a decree signed by Lunacharsky on 29 October 1918 transferring the actors in State theatres to the highest food ration category in view of the 'exceptionally intensive work-load borne by almost all groups of workers in these theatres'.[9]

In examining the development of Russian drama and theatre during the early Soviet period the impact of the Civil War and the particular pressures which it brought to bear on the arts can hardly be overestimated. As with other art forms, but to a greater degree than most, theatre was seen as directly useful in the military and political struggle, and the aesthetic and dramatic principles which underlie most of the plays written between 1918 and 1921 differ markedly from those of earlier years. As one critic has said, 'the living thread of the continuity of development was temporarily broken'.[10] Of course, this does not mean that there was no longer any place for the major theatre companies and for the classics of Russian and world drama. Some on the theatrical left, including the prominent Proletkult theorist Platon Kerzhentsev and – for a while – Meyerhold with his Theatrical October, sought to replace existing theatre with a totally new version in which the distinction between performer and audience would be minimised and the nature of theatrical experience would be fundamentally different from what it had been before the Revolution.[11] Fortunately for the existing theatres, Lunacharsky took a different view and vigorously defended the major theatrical companies from those who sought to destroy them. As he put it: 'I can charge Comrade Meyerhold with the destruction of the old and bad or the creation of the new and good. But the preservation of the old and good . . . I can not entrust to him.'[12] Lunacharsky also took a determined stand against a formidable opponent, Nikolay Bukharin, who had declared: 'It is necessary to smash the bourgeois theatre. Who does not understand that understands nothing.' Lunacharsky replied that

this slogan, if taken a little further, would lead to the slogan 'we must smash "bourgeois" libraries, we must smash "bourgeois" physics laboratories, we must smash "bourgeois" museums'. We hold a different opinion. We think that the libraries, physics laboratories and museums ought to be made the property of the proletariat.[13]

In fact, the repertoire was still overwhelmingly traditional, indeed more so than it had been before the Revolution, since the major theatre companies saw the production of the classics of world drama as more appropriate to the new era than some of the trivial works of the immediate past. According to one investigator, in the season 1919–20 Moscow theatres staged 105 plays by pre-revolutionary writers, of which 88 could be described as 'classics'. Productions of new plays were extremely rare: only four Soviet works were staged in Moscow during the 1920–1 season.[14]

There was a body of opinion which held that, far from being an irrelevance in a revolutionary age, the classical repertoire was a more effective means of conveying the spirit of revolution than contemporary plays with an overt political message. In Petrograd Gorky and Aleksandr Blok were among those instrumental in establishing in 1919 the BDT (*Bol'shoy Dramaticheskiy Teatr*) which was intended as a theatre specialising in plays of the classical repertoire as well as modern plays which could be described as tragedies, romantic dramas or high comedies.[15] Gorky expressed the belief that in order to counteract the hatred, spite and other base emotions brought to the surface by the Revolution, what was needed was 'a heroic theatre, a theatre which would have as its aim the idealisation of the individual, which would revive romanticism, and which would poetically embellish man'.[16] He saw the plays of the classical repertoire as fulfilling this aim, and so he supported the foundation of the new theatre. Even the organisers of shows for the Red Army stressed the value of the classical repertoire. In the list of plays officially recommended at the end of the Civil War by the Politico-Education Department of the Petrograd Military Region, the works of Shakespeare, Schiller, Cervantes, Molière, Beaumarchais, Gogol, Ostrovsky, Pushkin, Turgenev, Tolstoy, Chekhov and Gorky predominated, and the authors of the pamphlet even warned that 'one must not sacrifice the artistic value of a play for the sake of external revolutionary content. Therefore, when dealing with agitational plays, written for a particular occasion, extreme caution is necessary.'[17]

Nevertheless, a clear need was perceived for modern plays, both small-scale *agitki* and longer, more ambitious works reflecting contemporary events which could be staged by amateur and professional companies. Particularly in the provinces, the dearth of suitable material was having a serious effect on theatre groups, as the Historical and Repertoire Section of the TEO was made aware by a letter from an actor in a small town near Vitebsk which it received in July 1918. He asked for a list of 'sensible, comprehensible and simple plays' suitable for proletarian theatres and earnestly begged the committee not to 'extinguish our youthful impetuousness with your indifference'.[18]

Many of the short *agitki* on topical issues were written by the companies which performed them and were, by their very nature, ephemeral. Others, however, were published and from these, as well as from the accounts of participants and spectators an idea may be obtained of the nature of the Civil War *agitki*.[19] They were always concerned with topical issues, including military campaigns, the dangers of syphilis, desertion from the Red Army, or the reasons why the peasantry should co-operate with the proletariat. Since most of the *agitki* were aimed at the peasantry, a large number dealt with the issue of grain production and requisitioning. In 1920 the Commissariat of Enlightenment issued a pamphlet entitled *Theatrical Propaganda on the Food Question* ('Teatral'naya prodagitat-siya') in which P. S. Kogan explained that those provinces with a surplus of food must be persuaded to give up some of it in order to mitigate the effects of the bad harvest in other areas, and that theatre had a most important role to play in this process. In his words: 'The magic light of the theatre lamps melts down the crude ore of egoism and philistinism into the pure gold of sacrifice and romantic pathos.'[20] The examples of *agitki* in the pamphlet were preceded by a further introduction, this time much more down-to-earth, in which the actors were informed of the aims of the playlets, notably the need to explain to the peasantry the unavoidability of the policy of requisitioning. The *agitki* printed in the pamphlet are, for the most part, short verse plays with musical accompaniment in which simple slogans are chanted rhythmically. For example, in an anonymous *agitka* entitled *How They Grew Wiser* ('Kak oni poumneli') a peasant called Andrey and a worker called Vasily discover that only by voluntarily giving up the fruits of their labour can both prosper, for Andrey needs the scythe which Vasily produces while Vasily needs Andrey's corn. When Vasily appears reluctant to give up the scythe an actor planted in the audience shouts out:

Give Andrey what he asks for.
After all, his need won't wait.
And before his boots are worn out
He'll provide the bread.

Eventually Andrey and Vasily see sense and decide to work together and the *agitka* ends with the entire cast chanting:

Having finished our performance
In farewell we'll just say this:
Whoever hasn't got the message
Is either a traitor or a fool.
Strong is the plough and heavy the hammer.
We are all brothers for all time,
And our Red Star shines
On those who are young.[21]

There is no direct information on the effectiveness of *agitki* such as *How They Grew Wiser*, but they were performed hundreds of times by companies operating from the 'agit-trains', which, in general, were judged to be highly effective means of communicating Bolshevik policies to the peasantry, and one may therefore conclude that the *agitki* proved entertaining and useful.[22]

The *agitki*, together with the mass revolutionary festivals which were characteristic of the Civil War period, and which I have discussed elsewhere,[23] went some way towards satisfying the demands of critics such as Kerzhentsev for a new kind of Russian theatre. But even so determined an opponent of the professional theatre as Kerzhentsev still recognised the need for a new repertoire of longer plays, while others, including Lunacharsky, began to think of ways of encouraging a specifically Soviet dramatic literature. One widespread solution was the playwriting competition, of which there were a large number during the Civil War.[24] In many provincial centres, as well as Moscow and Petrograd, competitions were held for various categories of dramatic work, including plays for children, opera libretti, and – most notably – melodramas and revolutionary plays. In the view of Gorky, Lunacharsky and others, melodrama was one of the most appropriate dramatic genres for the new age, which demanded the simple, clear expression of heightened emotions. At the beginning of 1918 TEO announced a competition for melodramas in four acts set in any country and at any historical period. Among the advice to authors was the following point which helps to explain the relevance of melodrama to the Civil War situation in the eyes of the competition's organisers: 'Since melodrama is based on psychological primitivism, on the simplification of emotions and character relationships, it is desirable that authors should clearly and definitely emphasise their sympathies and antipathies to the various characters.'[25] Large prizes were offered, but of the entry of 41 plays none was considered worthy of the first prize by a jury containing Lunacharsky, Gorky and Shalyapin. Many of the plays failed to meet the criteria for melodrama, including the most significant entry, Aleksandr Vermishev's *Red Truth* ('Krasnaya pravda'), which was to become one of the most frequently performed plays of the Civil War era. In his comments on the entries Gorky singled out the ineligible *Red Truth* as the work of a talented though as yet inexperienced dramatist.[26]

Despite all his efforts to encourage the writing of plays, Lunacharsky remained dissatisfied with the results, declaring in September 1919 that there was not one that he could 'seriously recommend for production'.[27] Nevertheless, although only Vladimir Mayakovsky's *Mystery-Bouffe* ('Misteriya-Buff') is ever revived, the plays of this period are of considerable interest, for they shed much light on the nature and role of art in general in the Civil War as well as introducing to the Russian theatre some of the features which were to be developed in the Socialist Realist plays of the later 1920s and 1930s.

In the typology of plays of this period four categories may be identified. The first of these embraces plays by members of Proletkult, which, until Lenin's attack on it in October 1920, was a powerful body in the arts, particularly the theatre. By 1920 Proletkult had about 300 local branches and approximately half a million people were involved in some way in its various activities. The Proletkult leaders scorned professionalism, believing that only when actors remained genuine workers would they be able to create the new proletarian theatre.[28] In reality, though, the Proletkult actors in Moscow and Petrograd soon became full-time professionals, receiving a salary equivalent to the average for all categories of workers. They were taught by actors from companies such as the Moscow Art Theatre and the Maly Theatre, some of whom, such as A. A. Mgebrov and V. Smyshlyayev, became prominent in the movement.

The earliest Proletkult productions were dramatic readings ('instsenirovki') of the poetry of Aleksey Gastev, Vladimir Kirillov and Walt Whitman, among others.[29] Many Proletkultists were interested in the possibilities of mass recitation, since it offered artistic opportunities that accorded with their general ideological aims by transforming a number of separate voices into one mass chorus. Vasily Ignatov's dramatic work *Proletkult Dawns* ('Zori Proletkul'ta') represents an intermediate stage between evenings of mass recitation and genuine Proletkult plays, for it sets the verses of eleven Proletarian poets in a simple dramatic framework which follows a group of characters from a pre-revolutionary Workers' Mayday celebration through a factory strike and the October Revolution to a Utopian age when scientists under the leadership of Professor Timiryazev have allied themselves with the proletariat to create a heaven on earth.[30] Ignatov supplies only the skeleton of the work, for the majority of the lines are from the Proletarian poets, and include extracts from such relatively well-known works as Kirillov's 'We' ('My') and 'The Iron Messiah' ('Zheleznaya messiya') which illustrate, among other things, the important role of religious and mythological elements in Proletkult aesthetics. Ignatov's work also reveals a romantic view of revolution which appears to owe much to the mythology of the French Revolution and which is a common feature of the various art forms of the Civil War period. The publication of Russian translations of Romain Rolland's *Le Théâtre du peuple* and Julien Tiersot's *Les Fêtes et les chants de la révolution française* created considerable interest in the French experience of celebrating and mythologising revolution by, for example, using allegorical figures. Notable Russian examples include the mass festival entitled *The Mystery of Freed Labour* ('Misteriya osvobozhdennogo truda') which was performed in Petrograd on 1 May 1920.[31] Ignatov's personification of Revolution in *Proletkult Dawns* is a bare-breasted girl waving a red flag and carrying a rifle who bears an unmistakably close resemblance to the central figure in Delacroix's famous painting *Liberty on the Barricades*, the epitome of the romanticism of Revolution.

Platon Kerzhentsev's three-act *Amid the Flames* ('Sredi plameni') illustrates one of the central paradoxes of Proletkult drama: in spite of the Proletkultists' rejection of the culture of the past, important elements in their own work are derived from earlier literary schools, particularly Symbolism and Expressionism. Kerzhentsev's play draws on both of those schools (especially the latter), as well as the mass revolutionary festivals, in which he took a keen interest, and Meyerhold's production of *The Dawns*. The result is a highly eclectic drama which puts into practice some of the theoretical points raised in Kerzhentsev's important study *Creative Theatre* ('Tvorcheskiy teatr'). Characteristically, the *dramatis personae* lists groups before named individuals, and in an Afterword supplied by Kerzhentsev himself, it is emphasised that:

> The play's protagonist is the mass, the crowd. But this mass has its own particular face in each act and each scene and, most importantly, it comprises varied groups each with its own psychology and characteristic features (peasants, beggars, workers, youths, etc.).[32]

Each of the three acts depicts a stage in the revolution in an unnamed country. In Act One the peasants rebel against their landowners, burning and killing in an uncontrolled wave of elemental anger. Meanwhile in the town the workers, led by a certain Norman, are also rebelling, and some of the younger peasants try to persuade their fellows that the interests of workers and peasants are identical. Eventually, after some expressions of hostility towards the 'godless' workers, the peasants decide to go to the town to see for themselves what is happening. Act Two portrays the revolution escalating from a strike. The government has subverted the main trade union leader, Shtark, who tries to persuade his members to support the government against foreign enemies, but Norman's appeal to the soldiers and workers is heeded and the Act ends with the triumph of the revolution. By the beginning of Act Three Norman has been assassinated and the new revolutionary state is threatened by interventionist troops from the United Kingdom; on the other hand, some foreign workers have come to its aid. Norman's funeral is the occasion for an emotional call for commitment to the cause, and the play ends with the new leader, Ferst, appealing to the crowd, and to the audience, to save the revolution, an appeal which was as relevant to the actual situation in Soviet Russia as to the fictional state. Between each of the acts there are a number of short intermezzos (six in all) in which are presented, as Kerzhentsev again explains in the Afterword, 'slices of life which are most intimate, personal, hidden from view. The intermezzos cast light on the revolution from the other side. They give the psychology of individual participants in the struggle.'[33]

The basic idea of the play, according to the author, is the movement 'from chaos to organisation, from elemental revolt to class revolution, from the dissipation of strength to its powerful concentration in order to strike a victorious blow'.[34]

The influence of the Expressionism of Toller and Kaiser can be detected in the rhythmic speech, the chorus-like use of mass dialogue, the deliberate lack of individualisation, the imprecise locations (even the characters' names give no clue, for some appear Germanic while others could be French or English), and the unexplained presence of a madman who adds an air of unreality and menace to the play.[35] Act One ends with the madman's disturbing words: 'The nightingales are singing, singing, whistling. They'll fly over the whole earth, they'll whistle, they'll peck out eyes.'[36]

Kerzhentsev's play is one of the most notable dramatic works of the period, not so much for its artistic quality as for the fact that it acts as a clear statement of some of the aesthetic principles of Civil War art: it is openly agitational; its hero is the mass rather than any individual; its villains are portrayed in a cartoon style in the satirical intermezzos; and the author attempts to break down the barrier between performer and spectator and draw the audience into the action. In this respect it is significant that Kerzhentsev advised those who wished to produce the play to modify the normal proscenium stage by the addition of a stepped platform linking it directly with the auditorium.[37]

Other important aspects of Proletkult theory, notably cosmism and God-building, are exemplified in Pavel Bessal'ko's *The Mason* ('Kamenshchik'), also known as *Tower of the Commune* ('Bashnya kommuny'). The idea of man building his way out of his earthbound status and thereby challenging God had occurred earlier, for example in the works of Gastev, notably *The Tower* ('Bashnya') written between 1913 and 1917 and inspired by the sight of the Eiffel Tower.[38] This remarkable poem (perhaps 'poem in prose' would be a more accurate term) is about a gigantic iron and steel tower, built at great human cost, which rises higher and higher, quite overcoming its innate heaviness until it almost literally flies into the sky. By building it, man triumphs over his early limitations, even death, for it is the expression of that faith in himself and that ceaseless movement which is the guarantee of immortality. Only when those who climb to the top of the tower are seized by doubts about its reality do they plunge into the bottomless abyss that is the grave. This is a recurrent theme in early Soviet culture which is given by far its most significant expression in Tatlin's Tower.

The hero of Bessal'ko's play is a mason who has chosen that profession because it allows him to climb high buildings, leaving the earth far behind. As he says:

> I wanted to lay bricks beneath my feet, many bricks and stones so as to climb high above the earth. But people have stopped building high temples. Their god has become decrepit and has fallen to earth and they no longer raise their arms to heaven.[39]

The only person who shares the mason's vision is the wife of the architect on whose low-rise building he is currently working. She too dreams of flight, and the mason jokes that she has fallen in love with the skylark. In fact, she falls in love with him, leaves the earthbound architect (who falls to his death in a vain attempt to win her back), and marries the mason who himself becomes an architect so that he can turn into reality his dream of the Tower of the Commune. His creation is to be a new Tower of Babel which will unite mankind and harness the strength of his unity:

> If the people want a tower we will build it. We will excel ourselves. A million of us will work day and night. Fire, iron and stone we will forge into one. A great noise will resound through the city for a full year. At last the tower will touch the sky which will turn red from the wound inflicted by the steel spire of the tower.[40]

The third act is set at the foot of a fantastic tower. People have come from all over the world to see it, and although they speak different languages, one of them expresses the belief that now that the tower has been built they will begin to speak just one language. The references to the Tower of Babel are unmistakable. That story has particular appeal for the adherents of God-building ('bogostroitel'stvo'), for whom man himself is now the new god, and it is no surprise to find such obvious echoes of it in a Proletkult play. As one of the workers says: 'Whoever wishes to know that the old God is dead has only to climb up our tower.'[41] In his speech at the grand opening ceremony the President of the International

Commune declares that the building of the tower represents man's transition from a state of childhood, in which he had needed to create for himself the figure of God, to one of full adulthood in which he realised that he himself is greater than God.

The mason has the honour of performing the topping-out ceremony by climbing the tower and placing a red flag on the spire. The people on the ground wonder whether he will have the courage to climb up through the clouds on something which resembles a thread stretching between earth and heaven. Some doubt him, but as the clouds clear those with binoculars can see the red flag fluttering on the spire and the mason beginning his descent. The play ends with triumphant music and a series of explosions as man, victorious over nature, bends it further to his will by blowing up some nearby cliffs.

The première of *The Mason* took place in the Petrograd 'Arena of the Proletkult' on 29 December 1918, directed by A. A. Mgebrov. The first review, in the Proletkult journal *Gryadushcheye*, was full of praise for a play which 'evoked inexpressible rapture' in the audience.[42] Less complimentary reviews were to follow, however. Writing in *Zhizn' iskusstva* in April 1920, S. Garin referred to the play as 'hopelessly weak and completely unsuitable for the stage'. It was totally lacking in any sort of action and simply consisted of a number of *tableaux vivants*.[43] Indeed, the play *is* dramatically weak, and its organic links with the Proletkult recitation evenings are evident enough, but it remains an interesting and illuminating example of Proletkult art, the central concerns of which find some significant echoes elsewhere in early Soviet culture.

Even more obviously 'God-building' in its tendency than *The Mason* is P. Kozlov's *Legend of the Communard* ('Legenda o kommunare', 1919), described by its author as a 'play-poem'. This is a mystical allegory about the creation of the Communard, a Messiah-figure, by the forces of good, such as Thought, Happiness, the Son of Earth and the Son of the Sun. In a detail typical of Proletkult the Communard's heart is beaten out on an anvil by the Sons of Earth and the Sun while the forces of darkness leap around in rage and fear. The coming of the Communard has long been foretold, and mankind is waiting for him to lead them out of slavery to the land of happiness. A wise man reads from a scroll the following words about the coming of the Communard:

Tears glisten in the eyes of Mankind but he [the Communard] will dry them. He will lead the prisoners out of their cells, he will break the chains of slavery and will set Man free. Perhaps at first they will not believe in him and many will turn away from him, but he will be victorious. And the people will come to believe in him and will follow him, and he will lead them to the land of happiness.[44]

The biblical tone and references are maintained throughout the play. For example, in the second scene some workers are discussing whether the person who has come among them can possibly be the long-awaited Communard. On being told that he had been seen among the rubbish collectors one of the workers exclaims 'That's impossible! How could he bring himself down to the level of the dregs of society?' To this another replies: 'No, comrade! He is not bringing himself down, rather is he bringing all people up to his level, and the harder it is for them the more he helps them.'[45] Suddenly the stage is bathed in red light and the Communard, wearing a red cloak, appears at the window. He calls on them to assert themselves and claim the world that is theirs by right.

In the fourth scene, entitled 'The Rebellion', the crowd, exhausted and discouraged by the journey on which the Communard has taken them, begin to doubt him, but a woman reminds them that he is leading them 'to the land of freedom where all people are brothers, where there is neither hunger nor cold nor want'.[46] The Communard tells them that they are almost at their goal, and they press on. In the final scene, 'Victory', the promised land has been reached; the setting is that of a 'beautiful fantastic city' where the people are dressed in futuristic clothes. The Communard tells his flock that the time has come for individual identities to be dissolved in the new word 'we'. It was not he who brought them here; they came by themselves.

The use of biblical imagery and mythology in *The Legend of the Communard* is characteristic not only of Proletkult works but of the aesthetic principles of the Civil War period as a whole. Artists of all shades of political opinion turned to the Bible for images with which to convey the enormity of the changes that had taken place in Russia. In a fit of creative excitement the theatre director Yevgeny Vakhtangov noted in his diary on 24 November 1918: 'The Bible must be dramatised. The spirit of rebellion of the people must be put on stage.'[47] The author of an article in *Zhizn' iskusstva* in April

1920 declared that although people no longer needed religion they still needed its formal trappings which used to add a necessary theatricality to their lives. He therefore advocated the appropriation of religious symbolism for the art forms of the new age, particularly the mass festival.[48] A year later another article in the same newspaper urged the use of biblical imagery in the staging of opera (specifically Wagner) because of 'the allegorical significance of the Bible stories, not in the meaning given to them by the Talmud scholars or the Christian Church teachers but in a general human sense, a theatrical sense in the best meaning of that word'.[49] Thus, in structuring his play on biblical mythology Kozlov is very much in tune with the age.

*The Legend of the Communard* ends with singing and dancing, including the 'Dance of Labour', which stems from the general Proletkult attempt to stylise work movements into dance form. In Kozlov's words, the dance 'depicts labour in harmonious plastic movements'.[50] Similar stylised movements are characteristic of the mass festivals, especially *The Mystery of Freed Labour*. At this time many artists (mainly but not exclusively members of Proletkult) were interested in mass synchronisation and in the development of the natural movements of physical work into an art form. With the encouragement of Lunacharsky a special Institute of Rhythmic Education was established from which the first group of students graduated in 1920. Welcoming this development, Lunacharsky said that the institute met the growing need for rhythmic education. 'Its work is an expression of that "rhythmisation" of the chaos of experience which must follow after the first years of the Revolution.'[51] Similar work was being undertaken at the State Institute of Declamation under Professor V. K. Serezhnikov who organised a series of Sunday lectures by speakers such as Andrey Bely ('On rhythmic gestures'), Vyacheslav Ivanov, Balmont and Lunacharsky.[52] Some of the same people, including Serezhnikov, were simultaneously involved in an organisation called the Tonal-Plastic Association, the Central Bureau of which declared that: 'the tonal-plastic form of theatrical activity is a harmoniously complete synthesis of all art forms, being the fullest and clearest expression of the ideological essence of social outlook.'[53]

It is helpful to be reminded by such educational developments that the concern with rhythmic, stylised gesture and synchronised speech and movement, which is brilliantly satirised in Zamyatin's novel *We*, while largely the result of Proletkult theory, was also seen by others as a natural part of the aesthetic development of a revolutionary state.

The second category of play to be considered is the realistic drama with a contemporary, that is, Civil War, setting. Because of their theme, and because they were frequently performed at the front by mobile theatre companies, such plays have a direct propaganda function similar to that of the *agitki*. Indeed, some of the more primitive examples are little more than extended *agitki*. For instance, Pavel Arsky's one-act play *For the Red Soviets* ('Za krasnyye sovety') sacrifices all trace of psychological profundity for the sake of its agitational appeal. Like many other examples of the genre, it concerns the plight of peasants caught up in the Civil War when the Whites take over their village. The White troops enter the home of Nikifor Rusanov, a Bolshevik serving with the Red Army, and torture and kill his wife, children and sister, escaping just before Rusanov's division re-takes the village. The sole point of the play is to persuade the audience that the cruelty of the Whites is barbarous. When the White commander can get no information from Rusanov's wife he says to his subordinate, 'Put the glasses on her, Mukhranov', and Mukhranov returns a moment or two later and announces with a wicked grin, 'I put them on'. When Rusanov reaches his home he finds that his wife had been blinded before being put to death, and that his children have been mutilated (mercifully, the gruesome discovery takes place offstage!). His response, however, is not a wave of grief but a direct, strong appeal to the audience for vengeance:

Comrades, we will have revenge on them for all their atrocities. We will have revenge for all the suffering and torment of our near ones, our brothers who have perished in this terrible, unequal struggle with the enemies of the Revolution. We will have revenge for the blood of the many thousands of innocent victims. No pity, no mercy for the vicious enemy. Before the shadow of all those executed and tortured we will swear not to lay down arms until we have crushed the enemies of Soviet power, until we have smashed the enemies of labour, the enemies of freedom. Let us swear on oath, comrades!

The other Red Army soldiers shout out 'Long live Soviet power! Long live Comrade Lenin!', and the final curtain comes down.[54]

Perhaps the clearest indication of the out-and-out agitational function of *For the Red Soviets* lies in the claim made in an article in *Vestnik teatra* that when it was performed in the transit department of the Commission for the Struggle against Desertion five hundred deserters from the Red Army, sentenced to work in punishment divisions in the rear, requested permission to return to the front.[55] In the circumstances, of course, other factors than a play probably influenced their decision, but it is noteworthy that the journalist concerned should emphasise the positive agitational role of *For the Red Soviets*.

I. Kozlov's *The Underground* ('Podpol'e', 1920), which bears a dedication to the Bolshevik supporters in Kharkov who had fought as underground resistance workers in 1919, resembles *For the Red Soviets* in its use of violence; both in the descriptions of the torture of captured Red partisans and in on-stage scenes of violent death, the play sets out to shock the audience into the view that the Whites deal barbarously with all who cross their path.[56]

Other realistic dramas tend to be longer and, in varying degrees, more sophisticated than Arsky's. One of the subcategories of the genre is the dramatic chronicle, which recreates on stage the near-contemporary events of a Civil War incident or battle, mythologising them in the process. S. K. Minin's *The Ringed Town* ('Gorod v kol'tse', 1919–20) deals with the battle for an unnamed besieged town 'on the periphery of Soviet Russia' in the autumn of 1918.[57] Some degree of dramatic interest is provided by one of the story lines, which concerns the betrayal of the Reds by the wife of one of their senior military commanders, but the main focus of the work is on events on the battlefield and in the respective headquarters of the Reds and the White supporters in the town who are plotting a rebellion. The dramatic chronicle is perhaps closer to cinema than to theatre, where the natural limitations of the stage conflict with the attempt to portray events on a wide front, although some of the features of the genre, such as the huge cast and the identification of morality with political allegiance, are carried forward into socialist realist plays like Trenev's *Lyubov' Yarovaya*.

Among realistic dramas of the Civil War period the most successful, both in terms of popular acclaim and in artistic terms, were *Mar'yana* by Aleksandr Serafimovich and Vermishev's *Red Truth*.[58] Both deal with the growing political consciousness of the peasantry through a central character (the eponymous heroine of *Mar'yana* and the old peasant Ipat in *Red Truth*) whose sense of loyalty to the traditional social structure is shaken in the course of the play. The plot of *Mar'yana* anticipates that of *Lyubov' Yarovaya*: a young woman, left alone when her husband fails to return from the First World War, falls in love with a Bolshevik, only to discover that her husband is not dead. When he returns to the village she is unable to resume her previous subservient role and she comes to reject both him and the old society which he represents. Almost uniquely among plays in this category, *Mar'yana* has a believable central character whose behaviour is adequately motivated by a combination of emotional and ideological factors. Mar'yana's growing dissatisfaction with her way of life is indicated initially through her withdrawn, taciturn behaviour. Gradually it becomes clear that her dissatisfaction stems from the values of her father-in-law's home as well as from her presumed status as widow, and she is able to meet her need for both political and personal fulfilment when the Red Army officer Pavel comes to the village. Not all the Reds are above reproach in their dealings with the villagers (a certain Sergeyev abuses his position when he is billeted in the home of Mar'yana's father-in-law), but Pavel has the qualities which Mar'yana is seeking, and under his influence her passive discontent within the money-orientated household turns to active revolt. She tells Stepan, her husband:

> I loved you, oh how I loved you. I would have allowed myself to be cut to pieces for your sake, but now you are a stranger to me, as if you had just come in off the street.[59]

She does not leave Stepan because she has fallen in love with another man (Pavel has, in any case, already moved out of the village by this time), but because she is now ideologically incapable of living with him.

The artistic value of Serafimovich's play should not be exaggerated; Mar'yana herself is convincingly drawn, and her support for the Bolsheviks is well motivated, yet some of the other characters, including the priest and the kulak who are executed in Act Three, seem to belong to another genre, such as the *agitka* or the ROSTA Windows cartoon, and the dramatist seems uncertain of the balance between psychological realism and the openly agitational devices characteristic of the period.

*Mar'yana* was staged early in 1920 by the Second Frontline Troupe of Proletkult under the direction of V. Smyshlyayev. In an enthusiastic note, an anonymous reviewer for *Vestnik teatra* described the production, which was still at a very early stage, as the most interesting theatrical work currently being done by Proletkult. Smyshlyayev's method of 'preliminary improvisations', learned during his years at the Moscow Art Theatre, gave 'brilliant results'.[60] Three months later, however, the dress rehearsal was seen by leading Proletkultists and, in the discussion which followed, subjected to severe criticism. Arvatov drew attention to the deeply traditional nature of the play, particularly to its similarity to the works of Ostrovsky, describing Mar'yana as a second Katerina (from Ostrovsky's *The Thunderstorm*; 'Groza') but without the same depth of character development. Another critic objected to the similarity between the mass scenes and those which were traditional in productions at the Moscow Art Theatre. Kerzhentsev doubted whether the work had any propaganda value, since the audience were more likely to feel sorry for the pathetic priest and kulak than to feel that revolutionary justice was being meted out. In reply, both Serafimovich and Smyshlyayev admitted that the work was a failure (the former even going so far as to describe himself and his plays as 'criminal'), and offered to remove it from the repertoire.[61]

The criticism of *Mar'yana* by Proletkult is not entirely without foundation (particularly in regard to the mixture of Ostrovskian and *agitprop* elements), yet the intensity of the attacks seems excessive, and can perhaps be explained by the danger which *Mar'yana* represented to Proletkult theatrical theory. The return to the model of Ostrovsky appeared wholly regressive to Arvatov and Kerzhentsev, yet the resulting character is one of the most convincing figures in any play of the Civil War period. Three years later Lunacharsky was to signal an important shift away from the dramatic innovations of the early Soviet years with his slogan 'Back to Ostrovsky', and a play such as *Mar'yana* which anticipates that shift could hardly be acceptable to the leaders of Proletkult.

The third category of Civil War play consists of works with a historical, foreign or imaginary setting which may appear, superficially, to have little relevance to the ideological and military struggle, but which provide an oblique and sometimes powerful comment on the Revolution and Civil War. Prominent in this category is the work of Yevgeny Zamyatin and his pupil, the leading theorist of the Serapion Brothers, Lev Lunts. Zamyatin's *The Fires of St Dominic* ('Ogni svyatogo Dominika', 1919–20) is set in Spain during the Inquisition and deals with one of the author's central preoccupations: the opposition between stultifying dogma and the constant questioning of a heretic. The hero, Ruy de Santa Cruz, is eventually burned at the stake because he refuses to renounce views contrary to those of fanatical members of the Inquisition, including his brother, Baltasar. With characteristic irony, Zamyatin exposes to ridicule the unwavering certainty of the Inquisitors, which undoubtedly had its parallels among the Bolsheviks during the Civil War. One of them remarks:

> If the Church told me I had only one eye I would agree even with that, I would believe even that. Because, although I know firmly that I have two eyes, I know even more firmly that the Church can not be mistaken.[62]

*The Fires of St Dominic* can perhaps best be described as a philosophical tragedy, lightened by the humour which is typical of Zamyatin. In terms of language, characterisation and seriousness of purpose it more than meets the requirements of the new Soviet drama; indeed, it was written for the programme of the Historical Pageant Section of the Petrograd Department of Theatres and Spectacles, organised by Gorky. However, the play's political implications run directly counter to those envisaged by the promoters of the programme, and, though published, it was never performed in Soviet Russia.[63]

Like Zamyatin, Lev Lunts used a Spanish setting for *Outside the Law* ('Vne zakona', 1919–20), in which he examines the corrupting nature of political power and the relationship between freedom and tyranny. As in the case of *The Fires of St Dominic*, Lunts's play meets all but one of the criteria for the new Soviet drama; but that one criterion – an acceptable political message – was essential if a play was to reach the stage in the early Soviet period. Despite Gorky's enthusiastic support, *Outside the Law* was banned by the censorship committee, *Glavrepertkom*, and Lunacharsky took great exception to the parallels which he thought Lunts was drawing between the increasingly tyrannical behaviour of the play's hero and the development of the Bolsheviks since the October Revolution. In a letter to Aleksandr Yuzhin, who was considering staging *Outside the Law* at the Maly Theatre in Moscow in 1923, Lunacharsky declared that 'it will be seen in our communist circles and in circles sympathetic to us as openly counter-revolutionary'.[64]

*The Fires of St Dominic* and *Outside the Law* are among the best plays of the Civil War years, yet because of censorship they exerted no direct influence in the development of a specifically Soviet dramatic repertoire, in which political acceptability was from the very beginning a central, defining criterion.

In several respects Mayakovsky's *Mystery-Bouffe* can be regarded as the quintessential play of the Civil War era, and it is for this reason, and because it has no real equivalents, that in the typology proposed in this article it alone occupies the fourth and final category. *Mystery-Bouffe* shares some important features with the mass-revolutionary festivals and other examples of 'people's theatre' (*narodnyy teatr*). The contrast between the satirically portrayed former rulers ('the clean'), who are individualised by costume, speech and gesture, and the undifferentiated mass of workers ('the unclean'), who have a certain monumental quality, can also be found in other Civil War art forms such as the propaganda poster and the mass festival. Just as the poster draws on a popular genre (the *lubok*) for the purposes of propaganda, so *Mystery-Bouffe*, with its clear echoes of the mediaeval mystery play, makes use of an ancient tradition of people's theatre in order to present a schematic and vigorous revolutionary parable which, in tune with the spirit of the age, is romantic and Utopian.[65]

The dramatic works of the Civil War reflect many of the contemporary assumptions about culture. They have an overtly agitational function which generally results in a romantic presentation of revolution in clearly delineated, black-and-white terms which is the scenic equivalent of the poster art of the period. The traditions of people's theatre combined with the influence of such literary movements as Symbolism, Expressionism and Futurism ensure that many plays of the period represent a rejection of realistic drama and theatre epitomised by, for example, Ostrovsky and Stanislavsky. In this respect there are close links between the plays and the mass revolutionary festivals which are, perhaps, the most characteristic artistic genre of the age.

As the social conditions in Russia changed at the end of the Civil War, so did some of the assumptions about the role and nature of art in a revolutionary society and, indeed, the predominant artistic genres themselves. The propaganda poster and the mass festival did not disappear entirely (there was an *instsenirovka* in 1927 to mark the tenth anniversary of the Revolution, for example), but they were more appropriate art forms for a society celebrating fundamental change and fighting against immediate extinction than for one undergoing the various processes of reconciliation of the NEP period. Similarly, in drama the cosmism, god-building and mythological aspects of the first Soviet plays soon disappeared, giving way to the greater psychological realism and social observation of mid-1920s dramatists such as Bulgakov, Erdman and many others. Some of the characteristics of the first Soviet plays re-emerged, however, in the 'monumentalism' of playwrights such as Vsevolod Vishnevsky, whose *First Cavalry* ('Pervaya Konnaya') and *Optimistic Tragedy* ('Optimisticheskaya tragediya') can, perhaps, be seen as the successors to the Proletkult plays of 1918–20, particularly Kerzhentsev's *Amid the Flames*.

The nature of the first Soviet plays was determined by the fact of the Civil War and by contemporary romantic and Utopian views of the Revolution. Very few such plays survived in production beyond the end of the war itself, yet their significance is greater than this fact would suggest, for they reveal much about the art of the new Soviet state, and although their poster-like propaganda and romantic Utopianism were diluted in later plays, these features did not disappear but remained important components of Soviet drama long after the age of Revolution and Civil War had passed.

### Notes

1. *KPSS v rezolyutsiyakh i resheniyakh s'ezdov, konferentsiy, i plenumov TsK,* Part I (Moscow, 1954) p. 420.
2. Central State Historical Archive (hereafter TsGIA), f. 794, op. 1, yed. khr. 25, l. 1.
3. TsGIA, f. 794, op. 1, yed. khr. 25, l. 2.
4. A letter of 8 June 1918 from the Executive Committee of the Petrograd Soviet to the Automobile Section demands the return of Shalyapin's car. See the Leningrad branch of the State Archive of the October Revolution (TsGAORSSL) f. 143, op. 1, yed. khr. 156, l. 3. On 11 November 1918 Zinov'ev and Lunacharsky signed the decree awarding the title of People's Artist to Shalyapin, TsGAORSSL, f. 143, op. 1, yed. khr. 156, l. 4.
5. The article about Shalypin appeared in *Vecherneye Vremya*, 1919, no. 312; the Balmont story appeared under the headline 'Prodazhnoye tvorchestvo' in *Zhizn'*, 26 July 1919. See 'Iz belogvardeyskikh gazet' in *Vestnik teatra*, no. 50 (29 January–4 February 1920) p. 9.
6. *Izvestiya*, 25 October 1918, cited in A. Yufit (ed.), *Sovetskiy teatr: dokumenty i materialy*, vol. 1, *Russkiy sovetskiy teatr, 1917–1921* (Leningrad, 1968) p. 295. (Hereafter *Sovetskiy teatr*.)
7. M. Andrianova, 'K istorii teatra na fronte v period grazhdanskoy

voyny' in *Trudy gosudarstvennogo tsentral'nogo teatral'nogo muzeya im. A. A. Bakhrushina* (Moscow and Leningrad, 1941) pp. 75–112. Among the works containing relevant memoir material are Yu. Smolich, *Teatr neizvestnogo aktera* (Moscow, 1957); and L. Granat, 'Artisty-chapayevtsy', in L. Granat and N. Varzin, *Aktery-agitatory, boytsy* (Moscow, 1970) pp. 9–108.

8. 'Teatral'naya zhizn' osazhdennogo Peterburga', *Vestnik teatra*, no. 41 (11–16 November 1919) pp. 14–15.
9. TsGAORSSL, f. 143, op. 1, yed. khr. 124, l. 64.
10. L. Tamashin, *Sovetskaya dramaturgiya v gody grazhdanskoy voyny* (Moscow, 1961) p. 6.
11. Kerzhentsev's views are expressed in his many newspaper and journal articles and in his influential book *Tvorcheskiy teatr*, 4th edn (Petrograd, 1920). On 'Theatrical October' see K. Rudnitsky, *Meyerhold the Director*, trs. G. Petrov (Ann Arbor, Mich., 1981) pp. 247–81.
12. V. E. Meyerkhol'd, *Stat'i, pis'ma, rechi, besedy*, vol. 2 (Moscow, 1968) p. 514.
13. A. V. Lunacharskiy, 'Revolyutsionnyy teatr. (Otvet tov. Bukharinu)', *Vestnik teatra*, no. 47 (23–8 December 1919) p. 3.
14. V. Filippov, 'Repertuar Oktyabr'skoy desyatiletiya', in *Teatry Moskvy 1917–1921: stat'i i materialy* (*Trudy gos. Akademii Khudozhestvennykh nauk. Teatral'naya sektsiya*, vyp. 4) (Moscow, 1928) pp. 41–2, 49.
15. N. Misheyev, 'Bol'shoy Dramaticheskiy Teatr (k istorii vozniknoveniya)', in *Dela i dni Bol'shogo Dramaticheskogo Teatra* (Petrograd, 1919) p. 35.
16. M. Gor'kiy, 'Trudnyy vopros', ibid., p. 7.
17. A. Piotrovskiy (ed.), *Krasnoarmeyskiy teatr* (*Instruktsiya k teatral'noy rabote v Krasnoy Armii*) (Petrograd, 1921) pp. 23, 3.
18. TsGAORSSL, f. 2551, op. 17, yed. khr. 4, l. 77.
19. See Tamashin, pp. 104–33.
20. *Teatral'naya prodagitatsiya*, vyp. 1 (Moscow, 1920) p. 3.
21. *Kak oni poumneli*, in ibid., pp. 17, 20.
22. It is claimed in a report on the activities of the 'agit-trains' that between December 1918 and December 1920 a total of 2 216 000 people had attended film shows and theatrical concerts mounted from the five special trains and one river steamer used for agitation and propaganda. See V. Karpinskiy (ed.), *Agitparpoezda VTsIK: ikh istoriya, apparat, metody i formy raboty* (*sb. statey*) (Moscow, 1920) p. 18. See also Richard Taylor, 'A Medium for the Masses: Agitation in the Soviet Civil War', *Soviet Studies*, vol. XXII (1970–1) pp. 562–74.
23. R. Russell, 'People's Theatre and the October Revolution', *Irish Slavonic Studies*, vol. VII (1986) pp. 65–84.
24. For details of the competitions see Tamashin, pp. 271–80; and *Sovetskiy teatr*, pp. 358–69.
25. Note in *Zhizn' iskusstva*, 1919, no. 88; cited in Tamashin, p. 271.
26. *Gor'kiy ob iskusstve* (Moscow, 1940) pp. 169–72.
27. A. V. Lunacharskiy, 'Revolyutsionnyy repertuar', *Izvestiya*, 14 September 1919, p. 3.
28. V. (=P. M.) Kerzhentsev, 'O professionalizme', *Gorn*, 1919, no. 2–3,

p. 70; V. Tikhonovich, 'Samootritsaniye ili samoopredeleniye', *Vestnik teatra*, no. 61 (20–5 April 1920) pp. 2–3.

29. See *Sovetskiy teatr*, p. 338.
30. V. Ignatov, *Zori Proletkul'ta* (Rostov-on-Don, 1921). This work was conceived as a Proletkult retort to Meyerhold's production of Verhaeren's *Dawns* to which it bears a superficial resemblance.
31. The 'libretto' of this mass festival is published in *Sovetskiy teatr*, pp. 263–4.
32. P. M. Kerzhentsev, *Sredi plameni* (St Petersburg, 1921) p. 43.
33. Ibid.
34. Ibid.
35. On Expressionist elements in *Sredi plameni* see N. Zelentsova, *Narodnyy revolyutsionnyy teatr v Rossii epokhi grazhdanskoy voyny i nachala 20-kh godov* (Moscow, 1973) pp. 73–9.
36. Kerzhentsev, *Sredi plameni*, p. 13.
37. Ibid., p. 44.
38. For the text of Gastev's poem see Z. Papernyy and R. Shatseva (eds), *Proletarskiye poety pervykh let sovetskoy epokhi* (Leningrad, 1959) pp. 151–4.
39. P. Bessal'ko, *Kamenshchik* (Petrograd, 1918) p. 7.
40. Ibid., p. 16.
41. Ibid., p. 19.
42. I. S., 'Nash teatr', *Gryadushcheye*, 1918, no. 10, pp. 22–3, cited in D. Zolotnitskiy, *Zori teatral'nogo Oktyabrya* (Leningrad, 1976) p. 311.
43. S. Garin, 'Geroicheskiy teatr (P. Bessal'ko – "Kamenshchik")', *Zhizn' iskusstva*, no. 417–18 (3–4 April 1920) p. 1.
44. P. Kozlov, *Legenda o kommunare* (Archangel, 1923) pp. 7–8.
45. Ibid., p. 16.
46. Ibid., p. 23.
47. Ye. Vakhtangov, *Materialy i stat'i* (Moscow, 1959) pp. 105–6, cited in Zolotnitskiy, p. 100.
48. F. Groshikov, 'Teatralizatsiya zhizni', *Zhizn' iskusstva*, no. 430 (22 April 1920) p. 1.
49. V. Rappoport, 'Epizod ili simvol (Bibleyskiye syuzhety v opere)', *Zhizn' iskusstva*, no. 718–19 (16–19 April 1921) p. 1.
50. Kozlov, *Legenda o kommunare*, p. 30.
51. Lunacharsky's remarks are quoted in *Vestnik teatra*, no. 51 (5–8 February 1920) p. 7.
52. Ibid.
53. *Vestnik teatra*, no. 61 (20–5 April 1920) p. 7.
54. P. Arskiy, *Za krasnyye sovety*, in V. Pimenov (ed.), *Pervyye sovetskiye p'esy* (Moscow, 1958) p. 498.
55. Ye. Kuznetsov, 'Teatral'naya zhizn' osazhdennogo Peterburga', *Vestnik teatra*, no. 41 (11–16 November 1919) pp. 14–15.
56. I. Kozlov, *Podpol'e*, in *Pervyye sovetskiye p'esy*, pp. 201–51.
57. S. Minin, *Gorod v kol'tse*, ibid., pp. 123–99.
58. A. Serafimovich, *Mar'yana*, ibid., pp. 7–63; A. Vermishev, *Krasnaya pravda*, ibid., pp. 65–122. For a discussion of *Red Truth* see R. Russell,

*Russian Drama of the Revolutionary Period* (Basingstoke and London, 1988) pp. 34–7.
59. Serafimovich, *Mar'yana*, p. 62.
60. 'V Proletkul'te. *Mar'yana*', *Vestnik teatra*, no. 48 (13–19 January 1920) p. 4.
61. N. L'vov, '*Mar'yana* v Moskovskom Proletkul'te', *Vestnik teatra*, no. 59 (30 March–4 April 1920) pp. 3–4.
62. Ye. Zamyatin, *Ogni svyatogo Dominika. Obshchestvo pochetnykh zvonarey*, (Würzburg, 1973) pp. 48–9.
63. See A. Shane, *The Life and Works of Evgenij Zamjatin* (Berkeley, Calif. and Los Angeles, 1968).
64. V. G. Bazanov *et al.* (eds), *A. V. Lunacharskiy: neizdannyye materialy. Literaturnoye nasledstvo*, vol. LXXXII (Moscow, 1970) p. 375. For a more detailed discussion of *Outside the Law* and Lunts's other plays see R. Russell, 'The Dramatic Works of Lev Lunts', *Slavonic and East European Review*, vol. LXVI, no. 2 (April 1988) pp. 210–23.
65. For an extensive discussion of *Mystery-Bouffe* see A. Fevral'skiy, *Pervaya sovetskaya p'esa* (Moscow, 1971).

# 8

# The Nature of the Soviet Audience: Theatrical Ideology and Audience Research in the 1920s[1]

## LARS KLEBERG

With a degree of simplification the period from the turn of the century to the 1920s in Russian theatre can – in terms of semiotics – be described as a quick successive shift from the dominance of semantics (the relation sign/reality) through the dominance of syntactics (the relation sign/sign) to the dominance of pragmatics (the relation sign/recipient). In the naturalist productions of the Moscow Art Theatre of Stanislavsky as well as the early Symbolist performances of Meyerhold, semantics (referential or ideological) were foregrounded. In the theatricalism of Meyerhold of the 1910s and of Nikolay Yevreinov the problem of syntactics, of the combination of elements (for example, the grotesque) became dominant. Finally, in the constructivist experiments of the early 1920s – not independently of the socio-political context – pragmatics, that is, the relation between sign and recipient, between performer and spectator, came to the fore. Of course, these three aspects — semantics, syntactics and pragmatics – can be singled out in any theatrical system, or indeed any sign system whatsoever. But the shift in dominance that took place in the extremely intense evolution of Russian theatre during the first decades of the century only seems to make the three different aspects more distinguishable. Of course, in the 1910s Stanislavsky as well as Meyerhold already had their conceptions of the ideal relation between sign and recipient, between performer and spectator, between stage and audience. But the problem was not of the first importance for either of them, and their conceptions were rather implied than articulated. Only in the early 1920s did the question of the audience and how its responses could be organised become a matter of conscious theoretical reflection and practical experiment.

## PEOPLE'S THEATRE AND AUDIENCE RESEARCH

Theatre is unique among art forms in its close interrelation between artist, performance and spectator. Even when everything on the stage is planned and rehearsed in detail – as in contemporary director-dominated theatre – there is no real performance until it is all perceived by a live audience, whose attitudes in turn influence the course of the performance. Although such observations are traditional and commonplace, very little actual knowledge exists about the dynamics of the theatre performance and how the audience functions within it.[2] Instead, this has long remained the domain of lofty theoretical declarations or hypotheses which advocate some ideal concept of the interrelation between stage and audience either as existing in actual reality or – more often – as a goal to be reached.

One of the most important modern theatrical programmes, based more on hypothesis than on firm scientific knowledge, was that of a 'people's theatre'. It manifested itself in different forms in Germany, Russia, France and Scandinavia from the end of the nineteenth century to the interwar period.[3] Essential to this socio-politically orientated programme was the idea that theatre was communication between stage and audience, and, moreover, that the audience was – or should be – representative of the collective as a whole. The concept of a 'people's theatre' had its roots in German Romanticism and in the ideas of the young revolutionary Richard Wagner. It was a Utopian programme for a theatre that would regain its moral and political authority by addressing the entire collective – the nation, the people – which was gathered, or at least represented, in the audience, as it once had been in ancient Greece. When the stage spoke, the collective as a whole was thought to listen.

In Russia, after the October Revolution of 1917, the Utopian concept of the people's theatre became very influential, both for the revolutionary mass pageants (sometimes assembling ten thousand or more spectators) and for the professional revolutionary theatre. Before the opening of the RSFSR Theatre No. 1 in Moscow in 1920, the director Vsevolod Meyerhold declared that the foundation of all theatrical art – the relationship between the stage and the audience – had been altered radically by the Revolution, and now 'every spectator is, as it were, a model of Soviet Russia'.[4] The artist's power to influence and intervene in society thus seemed to have increased tremendously. If every spectator was 'a model of Soviet Russia', the theatre could speak with a new feeling of authority and significance. But the problem was, of course, that the 'representativeness' of the audience was pure hypothesis, and that the Utopian programme of an all-uniting 'people's theatre' was soon to be confronted with the change in Soviet reality from radical War Communism to the pragmatic and pluralist New Economic Policy. This confrontation led to basic re-evaluations and changes in Russian theatrical practice and theory. The topic of this article, the discussion about theatre audience responses and scientific audience research of the mid-1920s, can be said to lie at the point where practice and theory meet.[5]

Today, more than sixty years later, the Soviet discussion of the problem of the audience in the mid-1920s is interesting from two points of view. First, it has a general significance as an early attempt to define the object and methods of scientific audience research. In fact, those Soviet theatre specialists who participated in the debate identified and formulated problems (albeit without solving them) which theatre scholars in the West have only recently touched upon. The discussion was, however, not initiated for purely theoretical reasons but because theatre workers themselves had the feeling (no doubt correct) that the concept of the political people's theatre did not work under the conditions of NEP (New Economic Policy). Thus, the second aspect of the topic is the discussion as a symptom of the crisis in people's theatre and the need for new approaches to the audience.[6]

## THE AUDIENCE AS MATERIAL

Meyerhold's theatre, with its central position in Soviet theatrical life and its outspoken political ambitions, was, naturally, to find itself at the centre of the discussion about the audience. It was, however, in a smaller theatre, the First Workers' Theatre of the Moscow Proletkult, headed in 1923–4 by a former disciple of Meyerhold, Sergey Eisenstein, that the problem of the audience, its responses and its social representativeness, was first put under the scrutiny of conscious theoretical consideration.

In his manifesto 'Montage of Attractions' (1923), the young Eisenstein declared that in the new theatre of Proletkult 'the spectator is made the basic material of the theatre; the task of every utilitarian theatre (agit, poster, health education) is the moulding of the spectator in the desired direction and frame of mind'.[7] Eisenstein proposed to 'mould the spectator' not by making him identify emotionally with a revolutionary hero on stage but rather by exposing him to strong theatrical effects, 'attractions', that would cause 'definite emotional shocks' leading to the 'ultimate ideological conclusion'.[8]

The theoretical framework of the First Workers' Theatre of the Moscow Proletkult, developed by Eisenstein in collaboration with the critic Boris Arvatov and the playwright Sergey Tret'yakov, was a rather odd but consistent synthesis of Futurist-Constructivist aesthetics and behaviourism. The constructivist artists had developed the concept of art as the rational organisation of material, and Eisenstein was trained in this tradition. At the same time, wishing to ensure that art activated ideology, the leaders of the First Workers' Theatre adopted the theory of collective reflex psychology for this purpose. Given that a social class had certain collective reflexes – as was implied by the Russian psychologist Bekhterev – any theatre performance, Eisenstein and his colleagues argued, would provoke certain reactions in the spectators according to their class background.[9] Having a purely proletarian audience, as a Proletkult group should, the theatre could turn into an ideological power station for the working class. Or as Sergey Tret'yakov said in a typically forthright way, 'the theatre show is to be replaced by the theatre blow, by the direct processing of the audience'.[10] The image of the audience's class consciousness was that of the column of mercury in a thermometer; if 'heated up' with sufficiently strong and well-directed stimuli, it would rise automatically.

Thus, the constructivist idea of 'the rational organisation of the material' was widened to include *the audience* as material; in Eisenstein's manifesto it was 'the basic material of the theatre'. This meant that the class composition of the theatre audience came to be of the utmost importance. The precondition for 'correct' responses to the stimuli of the Futurist attractions in the Proletkult theatre lay in the correct collective reflexes of the audience, for which it had to have a pure (if only potential) proletarian class-consciousness. Tret'yakov said that 'attractions had to be checked in relation to a certain audience (otherwise the effect will be false and disparate)'.[11] The fact that the productions of the First Workers' Theatre, although generally acclaimed as interesting theatrical experiments by a young director, were not successful as political agitation was consequently ascribed by Tret'yakov to the failure to ensure that the audience was purely proletarian. Tret'yakov's *Gas Masks* ('Protivogazy', 1924) was even staged several times in a real factory in order to guarantee the right audience; this experiment, however, was a failure, both artistically and in terms of its agitational value.[12]

## AUDIENCE RESPONSES: HOW? – WHO? – WHY?

The radical but short-lived experiments of the First Workers' Theatre in 1923–4 had moved the problem of the audience from the shadows of implied theatrical theory to the glare of practice and debate. But there was still no empirical knowledge available. The time had come for a large-scale general discussion on the status of the audience and the possibilities for concrete audience research.

In 1924, in *LEF*, the journal of left-wing art – where a year earlier Eisenstein had published his 'Montage of Attractions' – the critic Mikhail Zagorsky pointed out the need for concrete information about the Soviet theatre audience:

As a matter of fact. Who has studied the Soviet audience during these years of revolution? Who makes up this audience? Of which class groups does it consist? What are the reactions not of this or that spectator but of these different groups to this or that performance? To the play, the staging, the theatre, the movement? To academic or 'left-wing' performances? How do a homogeneous auditorium and an auditorium with a mixed audience react to the same performance? How does this audience become differentiated in terms of class position by a revolutionary show and how does it become emotionally unified by an academic show? What is 'comprehensible' to some and 'incomprehensible' to others? What is it in a play and a performance that lowers or wakens the activity of the audience? Or what has a subduing effect on some and a vitalising effect on others?[13]

These questions had to be raised, Zagorsky made clear, not because of the development of academic scholarship but because Soviet theatre workers talked and argued so much about the audience even though, in fact, they knew almost nothing about it:

> Not to know the answers to these questions means to operate in the dark in the field of theatre work. And it seems to me that all our theatrical 'misunderstandings' spring from the fact that we do not know these answers.[14]

As an example of audience studies that would lead to answers to the questions he had raised, Zagorsky referred to his own experiments in Meyerhold's RSFSR Theatre No. 1 in the 1920–1 season. He found the widespread habit of organising discussions with the audience after the performance useless from a sociological point of view. Instead, he had organised the distribution of questionnaires, which the spectators were asked to fill in before leaving the theatre. Zagorsky regretted the fact that Meyerhold, who during the 1920–1 season had used the information given in the questionnaires for his 'orientation towards the audience', had since abandoned the method.[15]

Presenting his conclusions from the experiment of 1920–1 in his article in *LEF*, Zagorsky focused on the questionnaires he had saved from the RSFSR Theatre No. 1 about Mayakovsky's *Mystery-Bouffe*.[16] Although he had only 186 questionnaires available, Zagorsky contended that this was enough to show at least one thing: in reality the audience could not be viewed as an undifferentiated whole. Different class background had been essential to differences in the spectators' evaluation of *Mystery-Bouffe*. It was not only a matter of approving or disliking, Zagorsky asserted; workers, peasants and intellectuals had reacted positively or negatively to the performance for quite different reasons. He concluded:

> *There is no single spectator, neither is there a single performance.* The revolutionary current turned on from the stage splits up the auditorium, organises and differentiates its positive and negative elements. And the current that is fed back from the auditorium

in its turn splits up the performance, letting each group of people see on the stage what its social preconditioning allows it to see.[17]

This almost phenomenological approach to the theatre performance as an object, concretised in the interplay between the actively perceiving spectator and the stage, seems very far ahead of its time. This becomes all the clearer in the light of the discussion that was soon to be initiated by a report on the new audience research conducted at the Meyerhold Theatre.

In the journal *Zhizn' iskusstva* in the spring of 1925, Vasily Fedorov, an assistant to the great director, presented the results of a wide survey of audience responses in Meyerhold's theatre during the 1924–5 season.[18] The basis for the experiment was strictly utilitarian: the problem of the audience's reactions ought to be studied so that the theatre might reach its audience more effectively. To influence man in the new society, to give him new habits, a new way of thinking, yes, even 'to organise the subconsciousness of man' – all this was, according to Fedorov, a grandiose task which the theatre could solve better than any other art form. Thanks to the research project, Fedorov claimed, objective knowledge about the functioning of the theatrical performance was now available, 'with the help of which we, with evidence, with documents in our hands, can disclose the total emptiness, superficiality and irresponsibility of our theatre criticism'.[19]

The surveys were strictly behaviourist in spirit, the following method being employed. For every performance of a production to be studied, the theatre research group prepared a special chart on which the reactions in the auditorium during the evening could be noted. The chart had a vertical column in which was noted the concrete 'stimulus' (line, gesture, and so on) and a horizontal axis, divided into separate time units or segments of the performance (*epizody*). During the performance the assistant on duty was supposed to fill in a code number in the relevant square on the chart, thereby noting what kind of audience reaction was called forth by what 'stimulus' in which episode. For practical reasons the standard types of reaction had been reduced to twenty in number, ranging from 'silence' through 'laughter' or 'applause' to the extremes, 'leaving the auditorium' or 'climbing on to the stage'. The assistant was also supposed to note down on the chart general comments about the duration of the show, the audience attending (students, workers, and so on, if this was known), and whether or not there was a full house.[20]

In the material presented by Fedorov in the *Zhizn' iskusstva* article, 'laughter' and 'silence' were by far the most frequent reactions and he focused on them. Comparing the sum of reactions per hour in the average performance of the productions in repertoire – Erdman's *Mandate* ('Mandat'), Ostrovsky's *The Forest* ('Les'), Fayko's *Bubus the Teacher* ('Uchitel' Bubus'), the montage *D. E.* (based on Ehrenburg's novel), and Tret'yakov's *The Earth Rampant* ('Zemlya dybom', after Martinet's *La Nuit*) – the research group had arrived at what Fedorov called 'the specific gravity' of each production. Thereafter, the relative distribution of the standard reactions in the different productions were compared. Although several statistical charts were presented, Fedorov did not formulate any more far-reaching conclusions on the basis of the experiment than the 'rule of thumb' that in any comedy 'laughter should make up no less than seventy percent of the audience reactions (otherwise the performance will be boring)'.[21]

The radically objective method of investigating the audience responses put forward by Fedorov had the benefit of being relatively verifiable: in the spirit of the prevailing empiric psychology, one was measuring behaviour, not experience. The theoretical conclusions drawn from the experiment were, however, very modest. The main purpose was evidently to study the audience in order to gain (by changes in the productions if necessary) the maximum degree of control over its responses.

Fedorov's article provoked an immediate response from Mikhail Zagorsky.[22] Referring to his earlier work in the field and his article in *LEF* the year before, Zagorsky contended that the precondition for serious audience research was a more differentiated concept of the audience than that presented by the Meyerhold Theatre's research team. In his view, more important than noting a greater volume of laughter in one production than in another was:

> investigating from *which social groups and layers* the audience was drawn, *the way in which* each group reacted, and *what* it really reacted *to* in a given performance. Who reacts *when*, *how* and *to what* – this is what we want to know when we talk about audience surveys today.[23]

Zagorsky contended that, because the single, unified auditorium was a fiction, the registration of responses of the audience *en bloc* as made by the Meyerhold team had no information value; instead, he supported the questionnaire method.

Soon after the appearance of Zagorsky's article, Professor Aleksey Gvozdev, head of the Theatre Department of the State Institute for the History of the Arts in Leningrad and a close ally of Meyerhold, entered the debate on the side of Fedorov and the audience research experiments he had reported on.[24] Gvozdev argued that Zagorsky was mistaken in his contention that of the questions *who*, *when*, *how* and *to what*, only the third (*how*) had been studied at the Meyerhold Theatre. To answer the questions *when* and *to what*, however, the complete scripts of the plays had to be published and, of course, this was not possible in a journal like *Zhizn' iskusstva*. As for the question *who*, Gvozdev denied that 'the audience' was merely a fiction. The theatre scholar had no other material at his disposal than the spontaneously gathered, 'mixed' audience. The regular audiences of the professional theatres were the only ones that could be studied *systematically* and in a long series of *repeated experiments* – two conditions that had to be met by any research method with pretensions to being scientific.

Gvozdev dismissed Zagorsky's own single experiment in 1920–1 with audience questionnaires (filled in by only 186 of an unknown number of spectators actually present) as amateurish. The scientifically correct way to answer the four questions posed by Zagorsky, he said, was through a *comparison* between the general picture of audience responses already at hand and the responses of an audience whose homogeneous social background could be verified. In practice, however, the task of gathering a 'socially homogeneous audience' – for example, of 'workers from the workbench' – was not so simple. Here too, objective, empirical criteria had to be applied. The importance of the work done by the Meyerhold Theatre research group, Gvozdev said, was that it had laid 'a concrete foundation for scientific audience research'. If in the future one could introduce changes into a production as an experiment, in order to test the change in audience reactions, Gvozdev concluded, then new perspectives opened up for detailed empirical studies.

Vasily Fedorov himself replied to Zagorsky's attacks in the following issue of *Zhizn' iskusstva*, elaborating his criticism of the questionnaire method as totally non-viable.[25] It was not the subjective impressions of the spectators themselves, jotted down spontaneously – or, even worse, 'at home in the evening over tea'! – but only the objective recording of the reactions in the auditorium that could lead to firm knowledge about the fuctioning of the performance.

In order to pinpoint the interrelation between the reactions of the audience and the actual performance, the research team at the Meyerhold Theatre also recorded a vast number of other facts every night. In addition to the responses of the audience, the other facts recorded included which actors were on duty (Russian theatres often work with changes in cast), a time-and-motion study (*khronometrazh*)[26] including the length of pauses and intervals, the performance of the actors, the work of the stage hands, box-office receipts and finally comments by the director or assistants. Fedorov therefore argued that changes in the intended reactions of the audience could be immediately traced to changes in the work of the staff and the latter could be corrected.[27] As for questionnaires, he could only accept them as a means of refining the objective methods applied, not as a method in itself.[28]

Before the discussion on the pages of *Zhizn' iskusstva* ended with a further pair of rejoinders from Zagorsky and Fedorov, repeating their criticism of the behaviourist and questionnaire methods respectively, a third point of view on audience research was introduced.[29] The director A. Bardovsky, who had used questionnaires as early as 1917,[30] reported that his theatre, the Leningrad Youth Theatre, had experimented with audience response research during the past 1924–5 season independently of the Meyerhold Theatre. Bardovsky argued the usefulness of questionnaires for both directors and actors. The weakness of the method was, however, that the questionnaires only recorded the final reactions of the spectator, not those experienced *during* the actual performance. In order to register the latter the Leningrad Youth Theatre had used what Bardovsky called an individual method. Instead of recording 'the common denominator' of the audience, as proposed by Fedorov and the Meyerhold Theatre, Bardovsky's assistants had scrupulously registered 'the reactions of single, outstandingly typical children' and then summed them up in a 'general survey'. This type of 'individual objective' method had in fact been introduced very early in Russian children's theatre and was used at least throughout the 1920s.

The interest of the Meyerhold Theatre and the Leningrad Youth Theatre was clearly practical: they were seeking methods to check the responses provoked by the stimuli emitted from the stage. By 'responses' they thought only of the *empirically measurable* reactions of the spectators in the auditorium. How the stimuli on stage were interpreted by the spectators and what the reactions of the audience in turn really meant was never asked by the research teams. In fact, no one participating in the discussion in *Zhizn' iskusstva* had posed the question of the *experiences* of the theatre spectator and how to find methods to describe them. In other words, no one had complemented Zagorsky's four questions – who, when, how and to what – with the essential fifth one: *why*?

This important addition was made by Mikhail Zagorsky himself in a kind of postscript to the discussion in *Zhizn' iskusstva*, published in another theatre journal, *Novyy zritel'*.[31] Zagorsky criticised Professor Gvozdev's proposal of confronting the responses of 'the mixed audience' with an objectively checked audience of 'workers from the workbench' as an effort to correct one abstraction with the help of another.

> Who laughed at a certain line in 'the mixed audience'? A Komsomol member, a bourgeois, an intellectual? – I don't know, answers Gvozdev, it was 'the audience' that laughed. And who were these 'workers from the workbench'? Proletarians brought up in the city or newly urbanised peasants who have only just begun to be recast in the big melting pot of the factory? Were they young or old, literate or illiterate? Why did they remain silent at a moment where the mixed audience laughed, and what was the meaning of this silence?'

By asking *why* the spectators would respond in this way or that way, Zagorsky had undoubtedly moved the whole discussion on to a new level. His summing-up of the empiricist limitations of Gvozdev's – and, essentially, the Meyerhold Theatre research team's – project was devastating:

> To all these questions, Gvozdev has no answer, because they do not fit into the 'scientific method' he recommends. He operates with the fictions of 'the audience' or 'the workers from the workbench' and their outward behaviour without trying to explain the concrete nature of the given spectator and the inner meaning of his emotions.

Zagorsky has no real alternative proposals for future audience research, apart from further developing the sociological aspect of the questionnaire method. Nevertheless, his criticism of the Meyerhold Theatre research project was important in two ways. First, it pointed out the downfall of the myth of the audience as a homogeneous entity, representative of the collective as a whole. Each of the participants in the discussion in *Zhizn' iskusstva* agreed that the audience had to be studied closely, that is, that its character could no longer be regarded as self-evident; the days when the spectator could be called 'a model of Soviet Russia' without anyone protesting seemed to be long past. Secondly, Zagorsky's opposition to the 'objective' methods of Meyerhold's research assistants had led him to a critique of the behaviourist approach to aesthetics which was perhaps more far-reaching than he himself realised.

Zagorsky's thesis as formulated in the article in *LEF* in 1924 – *'there is no single spectator, nor is there a single performance'* – seemed even more convincing after the discussion in *Zhizn' iskusstva*. This state of affairs had consequences in two interrelated spheres, namely, theatre research and artistic production. Whereas the research project at the Meyerhold Theatre soon seemed to have come to a halt, other experiments in empirical audience research were to continue elsewhere for the next few years. Statistical surveys of Moscow audiences and their social background, theatre-going habits and attitudes were organised by a special commission within the cultural section of the Moscow *Glavpolitprosvet*.[32] Such experiments were, however, not to last long; indeed, they disappeared entirely until empirical sociology was 'rehabilitated' in the Soviet Union in the 1960s.[33] As a kind of compromise between the questionnaire and the 'objective' method, V. Filippov of the Moscow City Department for People's Education (*MONO*) introduced another approach. This was the so-called 'excursion', originally a cultural educational enterprise, in which a limited and homogeneous group of spectators was organised and prepared in advance for the performance through preliminary lectures; they then watched the performance as a group and afterwards discussed the experience, the whole process taking place under the guidance of a cultural or theatre worker. For a while after its launch this scheme was regarded as a new way to observe the theatre audience's reactions and at the same time take into account the spectators' social background as well as their subjective experiences.[34] Although well established for cultural and educational purposes, this 'method' was never applied systematically in a scientific context.[35]

## THE CASE OF CHILDREN'S THEATRES

In one branch of Soviet Russian theatrical life, audience research was more firmly established and continued unbroken for longer than elsewhere, namely in children's and youth theatre. In fact, it seems that all the methods of audience research tried and discussed in 1925 were first used in the *TYuZs* (*Teatr Yunogo Zritelya*, 'Young Spectator's Theatre') and only later in the professional theatre for adults.

Before the Revolution, in 1910, the theatre historian N. V. Drizen had prepared questionnaires as the basis for a report to the International Congress on Education in Brussels. But it was only after 1917 that audience research in children's theatre was introduced systematically. From the first production of the new Moscow Children's Theatre, founded by the well-known directors and pedagogues Sergey Rozanov and Natalya Sats in 1921, audience research was considered an integral part of the life of the theatre. The Soviet children's theatre was supposed to fulfil several tasks. Besides satisfying general aesthetic needs (common to all theatres), the children's theatre should prepare future generations of theatregoers as well as contribute to the general ethical and political education of the young.[36]

Rozanov and Sats summarised their experience with what, after only a few years, had established itself as the leading Soviet theatre for children and youth, in their book *Theatre for Children* ('Teatr dlya detey', 1925).[37] Significantly, questions of audience research, its methods and practical results, occupy a prominent place in the book. The Moscow directors did not exclude any method that might help to elicit the reactions of the young audiences, in order – if necessary – to change the production so as to make it serve its purpose better. Three kinds of sources were particularly favoured: (a) letters and drawings (sent to the theatre by the children's teachers) which spontaneously reflected the reception and understanding of a given performance by the young spectator; (b) questionnaires, filled in not by the children themselves but by their parents or teachers; (c) observation of the reactions of the audience during the performance, registered by members of the theatre staff.

The children's letters, drawings and essays enabled Rozanov and Sats to make a rough qualitative analysis of the reception of the performance according to the level of understanding (from the more primitive to the more profound). Not surprisingly, the authors were able to observe 'a picture of a gradually more complicated understanding of the play according to age'. On this basis the theatre could draw practical conclusions from letters and drawings about any specific production that deviated from the expected pattern of understanding:

> The lack of recurring references to basic moments in the play, the incorrect description or interpretation of individual scenes – these make it necessary to reconsider those parts of the production, to introduce changes in order to simplify or clarify the course of events.[38]

The information received through questionnaires seems to have been insignificant in comparison with the material provided, on the one hand, by the children themselves and, on the other, by the pedagogical staff of the theatre; in practice, the Moscow Children's Theatre soon gave up asking parents and teachers to send in the blanks distributed after the performances.[39]

The third type of audience research initiated by Rozanov and Sats was a kind of direct observation of the reactions of the spectators, classified according to a scheme of twelve basic types of reaction which were registered on charts similar to those used in 1925 in the Meyerhold Theatre. Obviously, the method of direct observation was introduced at the Moscow Children's Theatre one or two seasons before it was launched by Fedorov and the other assistants at *GosTIM* (as Meyerhold's theatre was known). One may even speculate as to whether the inspiration for the Meyerhold team's attempts came from an interview with Rozanov and Sats in a theatre journal in the spring of 1924.[40] What is more interesting, however, is the way in which the methods of the Moscow *TYuZ* and the Meyerhold Theatre actually differed. Based on the common principle of objective description of the reactions of the audience as a whole, the two research programmes used different lists of basic reactions to be registered. Rozanov and Sats constructed a scale of twelve standard types of reaction, ordered according to the intensity of attention and ranging from 'involuntary intrusion into the action' to 'longing for the end of the performance'.[41] With the help of the charts provided by several observers in the auditorium, a general chart of the 'curve of intensity (effectiveness)' of the day's performance was constructed, and then several of these were used as the basis for a general standard curve for the audience response to the performance. This general standard curve was then used for the analysis of further individual performances with special spectator categories.[42]

From a methodological point of view, this 'objective method' is open to the same criticism as the audience research practised at the Meyerhold Theatre: the concept of the audience as a homogeneous entity, the uncertainty of observations, the behaviourist approach to 'responses'. But the differences are significant. First, the Moscow Children's Theatre's twelve standard types of reaction already imply a certain degree of involvement on the part of the observer (contrary to behaviourist principles); thus there are several types of 'conversation', and when laughter is recorded this is done in conjunction with the supposed stimulus. Secondly, the charts of registered responses were never regarded by Rozanov and Sats as sufficient source material for the 'control' of the audience. With its strong involvement in pedagogical work, the Moscow Children's Theatre (as well as its Leningrad counterpart) was more interested in 'soft' information about the audience reactions – so long as it proved to be useful – than were Meyerhold's ideologically strict assistants.

In the discussion in *Zhizn' iskusstva* in 1925 following Vasily Fedorov's report on the experimental audience research in the Meyerhold Theatre, a spokesman for the Leningrad Children's Theatre underlined the importance of the achievements in this field made by the *TYuZs* in both Leningrad and Moscow. The author, N. Bakhtin, pointed out that methods for registering responses had been tried out by the staffs of both theatres; at the same time he stressed that the value of charts and curves should not be exaggerated: after all, they only registered the intensity of responses, not the contents. As a necessary complement to the response charts on the one hand, and the free essays or letters (which the Leningrad pedagogues, unlike their Moscow counterparts, did not use systematically) on the other, Bakhtin emphasised the significance of regular consultations with chosen groups of spectators, so-called 'delegate meetings'. Nowadays, the term 'reference group' would perhaps be used for such a channel of feed-back information from the audience to the theatre; such groups have become a normal institution in the Soviet Union as well as in the West as audience researchers still struggle with many of the same methodological problems faced by their predecessors in the 1920s. [43]

## TWO CONCEPTS OF THE AUDIENCE

The discussion about the principles of audience research was, as we have seen, not an 'academic' or purely scientific one. It involved, or was a symptom of, a critical re-evaluation of the audience as an element of the theatrical performance. At the time of the debate in *Zhizn' iskusstva* the old concept of the people's theatre with its 'representative' audience was no longer feasible. Two possible trends of development were already to be seen: on the one hand, a series of efforts to save the idea of the 'total' theatre, using biology, depth psychology, ritual or any other discipline which might assist in the search for a common, firm basis for the unification of the audience; on the other, a more modest and more realistic concept in which the spectator was no longer to be viewed as an object for the director's skills, but as an independent, reflective and productive subject.

The first trend had already been pursued in Meyerhold's constructivist productions in 1922–4, an odd kind of 'rational' theatre where – at least in theory – rationality was completely preserved for the director and the actors, whereas the role of the audience was completely 'ideologised' and its feelings and reactions were controlled by the will of the director. [44] Eisenstein's and his collaborators' idea of the 'theatre of attractions' at the First Workers' Theatre of the Moscow Proletkult represented a further step in the direction of behaviourist or 'physiological' aesthetics. In spite of the attempts to control the class structure of the audience at the First Workers' Theatre, the reactions of the audience had remained unpredictable. Leaving the theatre for the cinema in 1924, Eisenstein pursued his search for forms that would be able to 'organise the material of the audience' in a more reliable way than by the stimuli and responses of the theatre of attractions: forms that in a *universal* way produced images and concepts in the minds of the spectators, forcing them to feel the intended feelings and think the intended thoughts. In a word, he was searching for symbols. In his first films (*Strike* and *Battleship Potemkin*), Eisenstein considered that he was not using symbols universal to all men but working within the framework of a strict class psychology. But the road lay open. Parallel with the development of Soviet ideology during the 1930s from that of class struggle to that of national unity, the landscapes, faces and movements in Eisenstein's films would become more and more universal in their symbolism (*Bezhin Meadow, Alexander Nevsky*).

Meyerhold probably never had the same high ideological ambitions as his disciple. But his ambitions to keep the audience in a firm grip, exposing it to the total power of his own art, were no less far-reaching. The purpose of the behaviourist audience surveys that he launched in his theatre in 1924–5 was to confirm that the director had the maximum degree of control over the effects of his productions. Although Meyerhold himself did not take part in the press discussion of 1925, one can be sure that he did not approve of Mikhail Zagorsky's insistence that 'there is no single spectator, nor is there a single production', because this implied nothing less than the end of the dream of the total theatre. On the other hand, Meyerhold soon seems to have given up the idea of being able to control the reactions of the audience by means of scientific studies in the spirit of behaviourism; the chart method seems to have been used only occasionally after 1926.[45] In fact, the director's only guiding principle was that in the theatre 'all means are good if they lead to the necessary result!'.[46] For example, in 1931, in a production of Vsevolod Vishnevsky's *The Final Battle* ('Posledniy, reshitel'nyy'), Meyerhold planted a 'weeper' in one of the front rows of the auditorium with the task of sobbing when the play came to its tragic finale. And of course, the audience wept. Later Meyerhold added an extra concluding scene; the commander of the Soviet naval vessel, whose crew had been killed in 'the final battle', went to the front of the stage and challenged everyone in the audience who was ready to take up arms and defend the Fatherland to stand up. No one remained seated![47]

Meyerhold probably never gave up the Wagnerian ideal of the grandiose, unifying spectacle performed before the 'representative' audience. But in the final analysis the original ethical and social unity, which in the ideology of the people's theatre at least was understood as the goal to be pursued, was replaced in his theatre by the total domination of the audience by a director who was prepared to use any means to that end. This tendency was not unique to Meyerhold or the Soviet Union, as Helen Krich Chinoy has pointed out (although one might wonder whether Meyerhold was not always more of a Wagnerian than a Marxist):

> The personal distillation of the director was the modern substitute for the whole complex of social and theatrical factors that had once made theater the great collective art. Reinhardt illustrates this process in its baroque, Wagnerian aspect. Vsevolod Meyerhold illustrates it in its constructivist, Marxian aspect.[48]

The alternative trend, which can be discerned in the 1925 discussion, leads radically away from the dream of rediscovering the social importance of theatre by basing it on 'collective reflexes', archetypal symbolism or any other universal category. This alternative approach, non-Utopian in essence, also considers the spectator 'the basic material of the theatre', however no longer as an object to be 'emotionally organised' or 'processed' – as in the theatre of attractions – but as a subject. Outside Russia, the foremost exponent of this concept of the active, critically participating spectator is, of course, Bertolt Brecht. It would, however, be a gross exaggeration to claim that this approach, even today, sixty years later, has eclipsed or even managed to balance the post-Wagnerian concept of 'total' theatre in Europe in general and in the Soviet Union in particular.[49]

The specialist discussion of 1925 can thus be interpreted as a symptom of a transitional age. It signalled the heavy downfall of the classical model of a people's theatre, based on the myth of the representative and united audience. The reason why this crisis in theatrical ideology came so early and sharply to the fore in the Soviet Union was undoubtedly that the problem of the interrelation between the theatre and its audience had been posed with such emphasis in Russian theatrical practice for two decades or so.[50] The discussion of 1925 gave no indication, however, of what was to come. Soviet ideology of the 1930s was to be extremely suspicious of empirical research in the field of sociology as well as aesthetics. Instead, it postulated the unity and homogeneity of society ('enemies of the people' excepted, of course). Socialist Realism in the theatre can then, in the light of our analysis, be understood as a revival of the old model of 'total' and unifying people's theatre, based on the new collective ideology and the famous slogan 'engineering the minds of men' as a sombre transformation of the 1920s concept of 'emotional organisation' or 'processing' of the audience.[51]

### Notes

1. This article is based on research summarised in my Ph.D. thesis, published in Swedish as *Teatern som handling. Sovjetisk avantgardeestetik 1917–1927* (Stockholm, 1977; 2nd edn, Stockholm 1980; revised English version forthcoming). Earlier, significantly shorter versions of the article were published in *Russian History/Histoire Russe*, vol. IX (1982) pp. 227–41; and *Il Dramma* (Rome), no. 7–8 (1982) pp. 45–55. The special research for the article was made possible by a short-term grant at the George Kennan Institute for Advanced Studies, Washington, D.C.

2. H. Kindermann and M. Dietrich (eds), *Das Theater und sein Publikum. Referate der Internationalen theaterwissenschaftlichen Dozentenkonferenzen in Venedig 1975 und Wien 1976* (Vienna, 1977) gives an overview of current approaches and the still elementary level of research in the field. See also the contributions to the special issue 'Le rôle du spectateur' of the French journal *Le Théâtre Public*, vol. LV (1984).

3. For a general historical survey see D. Bradby and J. McCormick, *People's Theatre* (London, 1979). On the 'Utopian' aspect of people's theatre in Russia see Lars Kleberg, '"People's Theater" and the Revolution', in N. Å. Nilsson (ed.), *Art, Society, Revolution: Russia, 1917–1921* (Stockholm, 1979) pp. 179–97; and Robert Russell, 'People's Theatre and the October Revolution', *Irish Slavonic Studies*, vol. VII (1986) pp. 65–84.

4. V. E. Meyerkhol'd, *Stat'i. Pis'ma. Rechi. Besedy*, vol. II (Moscow, 1968) p. 13.

5. A similar discussion about Soviet film and its audience in the same years is well summarised by N. Khrenov, 'K probleme sotsiologii i psikhologii kino 20-kh godov', in *Voprosy kinoiskusstva* (Moscow, 1976) pp. 163–84.

6. The only researchers who, to my knowledge, have dealt with this topic approach it exclusively from the point of view of the development of Soviet theatrical sociology, leaving unconsidered the question of the relationship between theatrical practice and research methods. See V. Dmitriyevskiy, 'O konkretno-sotsiologicheskom izuchenii teatral'nogo zritelya', in *Teatr i dramaturgiya*, vol. II (Leningrad, 1967) pp. 146–69, and 'Nekotoryye voprosy metodiki izucheniya interesov i reaktsii teatral'nogo zritelya', in *Khudozhestvennoye vospriyatiye. Sbornik I* (Leningrad, 1971) pp. 366–85; also L. I. Novozhilova and I. L. Nosova, 'Teatr i zritel'' in *Nauka o teatre. Mezhvuzovskiy sbornik* (Leningrad, 1975) pp. 418–34; and N. A. Khrenov, 'Sotsiologicheskiye i sotsial'no-psikhologicheskiye mekhanizmy formirovaniya publiki', in *Voprosy sotsiologii iskusstva* (Leningrad, 1980) pp. 59–75.

7. S. M. Eyzenshteyn, *Izbrannyye proizvedeniya v shesti tomakh*, vol. ii (Moscow, 1964) p. 270.
8. Ibid.
9. On Eisenstein and 'reflexology' see T. F. Selezneva, *Kinomysl' 1920–kh godov* (Leningrad, 1972) pp. 106ff.
10. S. Tret'yakov, 'Teatr attraktsionov', *Oktyabr' mysli* (1924) no. 1, p. 54.
11. Ibid., p. 55.
12. *Gas Masks* only had seven performances, four of which were held in the gasworks and three on the stage. This compared badly with over fifty performances of Eisenstein's other productions at the First Workers' Theatre of the Moscow Proletkult. Ten years later Eisenstein commented on the failure of *Gas Masks*, explaining that the enormous gasworks had 'swallowed' the tiny play. See Eyzenshteyn, vol. iv, p. 62.
13. M. Zagorskiy, 'Kak reagiruyet zritel'?', *LEF* (1924) no. 2(6) pp. 141–51. Quotation on pp. 141–2.
14. Ibid., p. 142.
15. In fact, this was not the first time questionnaires were used in the Russian theatre. In September and early October 1917 the so-called Mobile Public Theatre from Petrograd, led by P. P. Gaydeburov and N. F. Skarskaya, toured the front and had their soldier-audiences fill in questionnaires which were interestingly described in A. A. Bardovskiy, *Teatral'nyy zritel' na fronte v kanun Oktyabrya* (Leningrad, 1928). Zagorsky first presented his audience studies from 1920–1 in the article 'Teatr i zritel' epokhi revolyutsii' in *O teatre* (Tver', 1922) pp. 102–12.
16. Questionnaires from the other famous production of the RSFSR Theatre No. 1, *Dawns* ('Zori', based on the Belgian Symbolist Verhaeren's *Les Aubes*), are preserved in the archive of the Meyerhold Theatre in the Central State Archive of Literature and Art, Moscow, TsGALI, f. 963, op. 1, yed. khr. 9.
17. Zagorskiy, p. 151.
18. V. Fedorov, 'Opyty izucheniya zritel'nogo zala', *Zhizn' iskusstva* (hereafter referred to as *ZhI*) (1925) no. 18, pp. 14–15.
19. Ibid., p. 14.
20. Copies of pre-printed charts with the heading *List VII. Uchet reaktsii zritel'nogo zala* ('Chart VII. Account of reactions of the audience'), which are double folio in size, are preserved in the Meyerhold Theatre archive in TsGALI, f. 963, op. 1, yed. khr. 1048. The complete list of standard reactions with code numbers reads as follows: '1. Silence. 2. Noise. 3. Great noise. 4. Reading in chorus [probably the audience following the text by reading aloud – L. K.] 5. Singing. 6. Coughing. 7. Stamping. 8. Clearing throats. 9. Exclamations. 10. Weeping. 11. Laughter. 12. Sighs. 13. Commotion. 14. Applause. 15. Whistling. 16. Hushing. 17. Leaving the auditorium. 18. Rising from seats. 19. Throwing objects on to the stage. 20. Climbing on to the stage.'
21. Fedorov, p. 15.
22. M. Zagorskiy, 'Eshche ob izuchenii zritelya', *ZhI* (1925) no. 20, pp. 5–6.

23. Ibid., p. 5.
24. A. Gvozdev, 'Zritel' i ego issledovateli', *ZhI* (1925) no. 22, p. 6.
25. V. Fedorov, 'Opyty izucheniya zritel'nogo zala. II', *ZhI* (1925) no. 23, pp. 10–11.
26. This concept was introduced on the analogy of the Taylor system in industry, which was strongly propagated in the Soviet Union in the early 1920s.
27. It is doubtful whether such total records of the performances at the Meyerhold Theatre were ever kept as systematically as Fedorov implied. The documentation available in the archive of the theatre in TsGALI is, in fact, scanty. There exist, for example, twenty-one charts of the type mentioned in Note 20 from the performances of *Bubus the Teacher* in the spring season of 1925, some of them covering the same performance, filled in by two different assistants (f. 963, op. 1, yed. khr. 1048). The charts often have only a few notes on them or have been left incomplete; the most detailed charts are, not surprisingly, those countersigned by the future chronicler of the theatre and editor of Meyerhold's writings – the infallibly accurate Aleksandr Fevral'sky. Only three of these twenty-one charts contain any information about the composition of the audience (*sostav zritel'nogo zala*): in one case all the tickets had been taken by a group of Young Pioneers, in the other two there is a note saying that the auditorium was only half full or one-third full. In TsGALI there are charts of the same type relating to. at least two more productions: 131 charts with very few notes from Erdman's *Mandate*, May–December 1925 (f. 963, op. 1, yed. khr. 1049) and from the dress rehearsals and opening night of the famous production of Gogol's *Government Inspector* ('Revizor'), December 7–9, 1926 (f. 963, op. 1, yed. khr. 1050). These 'Accounts of the Reactions of the Audience', made on the large form No. VII, were in principle to be accompanied by six other smaller and less detailed charts, copies of which are also preserved: 'I.   Account of the Staff', 'II.   *Khronometrazh*', 'III.   Account of the Intermissions', 'IV.   Account of the Actors' Work', 'V.   Account of the Stage Hands' Work', 'VI.   Box-Office and Administration Account'. As far as I can judge from the material made available to me in TsGALI, these other charts were only used sporadically to supplement the large chart No. VII.
28. As a matter of fact, questionnaires *were* used by the Meyerhold Theatre at this time parallel to the 'objective' research project. In TsGALI (f. 963, op. 1, yed. khr. 918) there are 188 questionnaires from the theatre's guest performance of Ostrovsky's *The Forest* in Ivanovo-Voznesensk in March, 1925. Under the heading 'What do you think about "The Forest"? Question Form' the following questions were asked: '1. Have you seen "The Forest" in other theatres? 2. Where do you think "The Forest" was best staged? 3. What was the difference? 4. Was "The Forest" as we staged it an agitational play? 5. Did you find the performance exhausting? (If yes, state why.) 6. Do you have any further comments?' In addition, the respondent was asked to state sex, age, profession, trade union and party affiliation. The purpose of this questionnaire, as well as that of another one from

1928 (f. 963, op. 1, yed. khr. 919), was evidently to help the theatre evaluate its guest performances in towns outside Moscow. The questionnaires from *Dawns* in 1920 mentioned in Note 16, as well as the later ones, await further research.

29. A. Bardovskiy, 'Izucheniye zritelya', *ZhI* (1925) no. 23, p. 16; M. Zagorskiy, 'Diskussiya o zritele prodolzhayetsya', *ZhI* (1925) no. 26, pp. 12–13; V. Fedorov, 'Diskussiya o zritele', *ZhI* (1925) no. 27, p. 9.
30. See Note 15.
31. M. Zagorskiy, 'Kak izuchat' zritelya', *Novyy zritel'* (1925) no. 28, p. 8.
32. 'Zritel' moskovskikh teatrov', pt. I, *ZhI* (1926) no. 27, pp. 11–12; pt. II, *ZhI* (1926) no. 28, pp. 13–14; 'Koordinatsiya raboty po izucheniyu rabochego zritelya', *ZhI* (1926) no. 32, pp. 16–17. Statistics were also used by A. I. Mogilevskiy, 'Moskovskiye teatry v tsifrakh', in *Teatry Moskvy 1917–1927* (Moscow, 1928) pp. 5–34.
33. The revived interest in the discussions of the 1920s is, of course, a result of this 'revival' of sociology; hence the fact that the authors mentioned in Note 6 have turned to the past in search of viable methods for today. See V. Dmitriyevskiy, 'Nekotoryye itogi obsledovaniya teatral'nykh zriteley', in *Teatr i dramaturgiya*, vol. III (Leningrad, 1971) pp. 333–52.
34. Vl. Filippov, 'Teatral'nyye ekskursii kak metod izucheniya zritelya', *Sovetskoye iskusstvo* (1926) no. 1, pp. 55–62.
35. A comparison of the three approaches mentioned was made by A. P. Borodin, 'O razlichnykh priyemakh izucheniya teatral'nogo zritelya', *Sovetskoye iskusstvo* (1925) no. 9, pp. 30–7, and by N. Izvekov, 'Zritel' v teatre', in *Teatral'nyy Oktyabr'. Sbornik I* (Leningrad and Moscow, 1926) pp. 79–88. A contemporary bibliographical survey of the discussion can be found in A. I. Beletskiy, N. L. Brodskiy, L. P. Grossman, I. N. Kubikov and V. L. L'vov-Rogachevskiy (eds), *Noveyshaya russkaya literatura: Kritika – Teatr – Metodologiya* (Ivanovo–Voznesensk, 1927) pp. 245–7.
36. Valuable information about audience research in children's theatres is provided in V. Dmitriyevskiy, 'O konkretno-sotsiologicheskom izuchenii teatral'nogo zritelya', in *Teatr i dramaturgiya*, vol. II (Leningrad, 1967) pp. 148–53. For a general history of Soviet children's theatre see L. G. Shpet, *Sovetskiy teatr dlya detey. Stranitsy istorii 1918–1945* (Moscow, 1971). Natalya Sats's own impressionistic memoirs, *Novelly moyey zhizni* (Moscow, 1979), have recently been translated into English as *Sketches from My Life* (Moscow, 1985).
37. S. Rozanov and N. Sats, *Teatr dlya detey* (Leningrad, 1925).
38. Ibid., p. 100. The source materials (letters and essays) were classified according to the following levels of understanding: '1. Letters reflecting a general attitude to the performance (liked it, did not like it). 2. Letters containing references to the characters. 3. Description of events in the play involving several characters. 4. Exposition and dénouement of the plays. 5. Consecutive description of the plot. 6. Description of events including the motives of various characters. 7. Essay analysing the idea of the play'. The many examples of children's comments given by Rozanov and Sats are interesting and sometimes extremely

entertaining. The material contained in *Teatr dlya detey*, together with the other sources available on early Soviet children's theatre, certainly merits a special study.

39. The basic questions put to parents and teachers were the following: 'The notes [of the interview with the child after the performance – L. K.] should be made approximately in accordance with the following plan: 1. title of play and date of attendance at performance; 2. characteristics of the child: age, sex, social background (in family, in orphans' home), school, interests, peculiarities; 3. behaviour of the child during the performance; 4. opinions of the child about the performance, conversations, questions; 5. did the child recount the content of the performance and in what form?; 6. the children's general impressions of the visit to the theatre: expectation, the exterior of the entrance, auditorium, seats; 7. opinions of the pedagogues and the parents about the performance' (ibid., p. 95–6).

40. 'Nauchnoye issledovaniye spektaklya. Iz besedy s Nat. Sats i S. Rozanovym', *Novyy zritel'* (1924) no. 12.

41. The complete list of standard types of reaction used by Rozanov and Sats reads as follows: '1. Involuntary intrusion into the action. Expression of empathy with the actor, warning him. 2. Visible intense attention (stretched necks, open mouths). 3. Laughter in connection with inherent comical character of the situation. 4. Silence. Conversations concerning the action. 5. Conversations with the actor about his role unconnected with the action. 6. Laughter at external situation, at "tricks". 7. Conversations about the events on the stage. 8. Laughter in inappropriate places (misunderstanding). 9. Guesses about what is coming next. 10. Yawning. 11. Irrelevant conversations. 12. Longing for the end of the performance' (Rozanov and Sats, p. 111).

42. In the book by Rozanov and Sats detailed descriptions of audience responses to four productions of the Moscow Children's Theatre are to be found, namely *Hiawatha, Chief of the Iroquois*; *A Thousand and One Nights*; *Pinocchio*; and *Adalmina's Pearl*. See ibid., pp. 112–28.

43. N. Bakhtin, 'Uchet teatral'nogo vospriyatiya v Teatre Yunykh Zriteley', *ZhI* (1925) no. 34, pp. 14–15. See also N. Bakhtin, 'Pedagogicheskaya rabota', in *Teatr yunykh zriteley 1922–1927* (Leningrad, 1927) pp. 109–21; N. Bakhtin, 'Bibliografiya', ibid., pp. 122–7; A. Avdeyev, 'Opyt izucheniya spektaklya dlya detey', in *Teatr yunykh zriteley 1922–1932* (Leningrad, 1932) pp. 75–86.

44. Christian Mailand-Hansen argues that Meyerhold's approach to the audience, his 'Rezeptionsästhetik', was based equally on intellect and emotion; but he also concludes that the homogeneous audience presupposed by this aesthetic did not exist during NEP. See *Mejerchol'ds Theaterästhetik in den 1920er Jahren* (Copenhagen, 1980) pp. 195–208.

45. A chart with recorded audience responses from as late as 18 March 1934 – the dress rehearsal of *Camille* by Dumas fils – is preserved in TsGALI (f. 963, op. 1, yed. khr. 1060).

46. 'Meyerhold Speaks', in Andrew Field (ed.), *Pages from Tarusa* (London, 1963) p. 320.

47. A. Fevral'skiy, *Zapiski rovesnika veka* (Moscow, 1976) pp. 306–7.

48. Helen Krich Chinoy, 'The Emergence of the Director', in T. Cole and H. Krich Chinoy (eds), *Directors on Directing* (Indianapolis and New York, 1963) p. 53.

49. Sergey Tret'yakov, once Eisenstein's collaborator in the First Workers' Theatre, did come close to some of the notions of Brecht's 'rational' theatre in the late 1920s, but the influence of his ideas then – as well as those of Brecht, whom Tret'yakov translated – was only marginal in the Soviet theatre. See Marjorie L. Hoover, 'Brecht's Soviet Connection Tretiakov', in *Brecht Heute/Brecht Today, Brecht Jahrbuch*, vol. III (Frankfurt am Main, 1973) pp. 39–56; also Katherine Bliss Eaton, *The Theater of Meyerhold and Brecht* (Westport and London, 1985); and Lars Kleberg, 'In the Sign of Aquarius', in Lars Kleberg and Håkan Lövgren (eds), *Eisenstein Revisited* (Stockholm, 1987) pp. 39–63.

50. See Lars Kleberg, 'Sootnosheniye stseny i zritel'nogo zala. K tipologii russkogo teatra nachala XX veka', *Scando-Slavica*, vol. XX (1974) pp. 27–38.

51. The fact that Meyerhold, Tret'yakov and many other members of the avant-garde themselves fell victim to Stalinism does not prevent us from drawing this conclusion; in a way they fell victim to a machine which they had assisted in constructing – though certainly with other intentions than the Master Builder, Comrade Stalin.

# 9

# German Expressionism and Early Soviet Drama

## HAROLD B. SEGEL

In the long history of Russo-German cultural relations there is one period in particular in which relations intensify to the point of meaningful interaction. That is the period approximately from 1910 to 1925, coinciding with the emergence and development of literary Expressionism. It is to the Russian aspect of that interaction that the present essay is devoted.

Expressionism began as a revolutionary aesthetic movement which sought no less than a transformation of art and ultimately society itself. With turn-of-the-century neo-Romanticism, to which it owed its genesis in part, it shared a profound contempt for virtually every aspect of bourgeois culture. But Expressionism was more dynamic and activist. The neo-Romantic fled a world of ugliness, banality and materialism and sought refuge in the remote past, in the exotic, in legend, in myth, in fantasy and, finally, in the occult. The Expressionists chose instead to achieve the transformation they sought from within society by overturning its conventions and values, by shocking its consciousness into new perceptions. Spirit was no less a concern to the Expressionists than it was to the neo-Romantics, but the spiritual was not an alternative realm to them, a greater reality; it was instead a vision of man at last triumphant over his own baseness and meanness. To the Expressionists, Nietzsche's *Übermensch* was above all a spiritual concept.

The Expressionists' impatience with fashionable turn-of-the-century otherworldliness was paralleled by their repudiation of naturalistic representationalism. To be sure, they recognised the service the Naturalists had rendered by revealing more of society than art had dared to do previously. They acknowledged the Naturalist achievement in laying bare the rot of bourgeois civilisation. But they faulted Naturalism for its passivity, for its failure to go beyond mere portrayal. Moreover, the passivity of Naturalism was rooted in its determinism – man is what he is because of his primordial animal nature which reveals itself as much in the class conflict as in relations between the sexes. Vehemently opposed to this determinism, as Schopenhauerian as it was Darwinian, the Expressionists insisted on a view of man utterly free to become whatever he wished, free from restraints, limitations and inhibitions of origin or class. In order to convey this vision, they stressed the need to clear away all the cobwebs of the past; everything had to be stripped down to essences and this could be accomplished only if traditional, conventional and even conscious patterns of thought and expression were challenged and, finally, overthrown. Language especially needed regeneration. As the Expressionists saw man yoked by the prevailing modalities of bourgeois society and culture, so did they see the word weighted down by the cultural baggage of the past. The liberation of the word was thus an integral part of man's total liberation.

Broadly viewed, Expressionism was one manifestation of the whole so-called modernist movement of the early twentieth century nourished by Marx, Freud and Einstein. It shares features with Cubism, Futurism and, in the theatre, theatricalism, or theatricality (what was known in Russian as *uslovnost'*), but it also acquired certain distinctly German contours which cannot be ignored.[1]

Socially, much of the distaste for the bourgeois among the Germans was a reaction to the smugness resulting from the victory over France in the Franco-Prussian War of 1870–1 and the new pride of empire. Compare with this the widespread feelings of frustration and embarrassment in Russia following the war with Japan in 1904–5. In both cases a need for social renovation was felt, but the need proceeded from quite different circumstances. Where bourgeois complacency existed on one side, aristocratic indifference reigned on the other. The Italian Futurists' enthusiasm over the machine was bound to have less appeal in a much more industrialised and technologically advanced Germany where as early as 1910 and 1911, when programmatic Expressionism began, the machine could already be viewed as a link in the chain of society binding man. Where the Futurists worshipped at the altar of technology – in their view it was principally through the machine that the transformation of society would be effected – the Expressionists made man their god and sought out the spirit to which technology often seemed to bar the way.

In the arts, the Expressionists shared with other avant-garde movements the same impulse toward media synthesis as the means to create the entirely new total work of art. But the base on which the German Expressionists had to build was firmer – Wagner, after all, had formulated his ideas on the *Gesamtkunstwerk* and had pointed the way to its practical realisation as early as the 1850s.[2] And finally – probably because these were the areas in which the *Gesamtkunstwerk* had the greatest possibility of coming to life – drama and theatre came to enjoy a special relationship with Expressionism in Germany which they did not acquire elsewhere in the avant-garde, neither with Futurism in Italy and Russia nor with Surrealism in France. From the outset, in fact even a few years before the appearance of programmatic Expressionism, drama became a fertile field for the experimentation designed to realise the then crystallising Expressionist vision. On the stylistic and structural levels, the abstraction and compression, the new equality of gesture and word identified with later Expressionist drama were powerfully anticipated in the first plays of the painter-dramatist Oskar Kokoschka – *Mörder, Hoffnung der Frauen* ('Murderer, Hope of Women', 1907) and *Sphinx und Strohmann* ('Sphinx and Strawman', 1907). Like a number of Expressionist plays, the works are short, no more than playlets. Conflict, which is portrayed rather than dramatically evolved – in a further anticipation of later Expressionism and Brechtian epic theatre – has not yet become generational (son vs. father) or social, as it appears in much Expressionist literature. Closer to Strindberg and Wedekind in this respect than to the dramatists who followed him, Kokoschka pits man against woman. Conflict is, therefore, sexual; what gives it the special Expressionist aura in Kokoschka is the sense of the world moving toward the inevitable apocalyptic upheaval conveyed by the plays' symbolic and dreamlike sexual confrontation and the ultimate triumph of man transformed arising phoenix-like from the ashes of a dead civilisation.

This early period of German Expressionism typified by Kokoschka's first dramatic works has distinct parallels in Russia. Aleksandr Blok's *The Puppet Show* ('Balaganchik'), mixes the arts on stage and achieves striking visual effects. In this respect, as well as in its obvious aim of breaking with specific conventions of world view and play technique, it is compatible with early Expressionist drama. But Blok's play is a very personal statement by the poet-dramatist who proclaims not only his break with

Symbolist metaphysicality but also with the archetypal expression of this metaphysicality in the drama, the early programmatic plays of Maurice Maeterlinck. In the final analysis, *The Puppet Show* is best seen as theatricalist rather than Expressionist, though it does share features with Expressionism.

More representative of a kind of pre-Expressionism in Russian drama is the work of Leonid Andreyev (1871–1919) and Nikolay Yevreinov (1879–1953). Although frequently dismissed on grounds of philosophical pretentiousness and shallowness, several of Andreyev's major plays – above all, *The Life of Man* ('Zhizn' cheloveka', 1907), *King Hunger* ('Tsar' Golod', 1907), *The Black Masks* ('Chernyye maski', 1908), and *Anathema* ('Anatema', 1909) – deserve a fresh reading in the context of the emergence of an Expressionist art in Russia.[3] The first two plays have in common the abstraction, schematisation, generic character names, absence of individual psychological development, puppet motifs, epic structure, use of space and exclamatory style of much dramatic Expressionism.[4] Both convey a sense of loathing for bourgeois society. *The Black Masks* makes effective use of such common Expressionist devices as the mask, the double, the externalisation of a character's inner states and a dramatic opposition of light and darkness. The third play introduces the theme of the quest for the absolute (in this instance, for the answers to cosmic mysteries on the part of Anathema, a figure combining elements of Mephistopheles and Faust)[5] and biblical stylistic elements and allusions (above all, to Jesus) characteristic especially of early Expressionist drama.

Although Andreyev eventually became an implacable foe of the new Soviet state, at the time he wrote *The Life of Man* and *King Hunger* he shared with the modernist movement in general both a hatred for bourgeois society and a sense of frustration over the perceived ineffectuality of the intelligentsia. These feelings are clearly reflected in his plays. Rebellion – on which much Expressionist drama turns – figures in each of the above-mentioned plays, most obviously in *King Hunger*. 'Haves' and 'have nots' (factory workers and the hungry) in *King Hunger* are pitted against each other, but the outcome is the same foregone conclusion that it is in other Expressionist drama. So long as the moneyed class dominates the means of production and can command superior forces, its triumph is assured. But its victory is pyrrhic, since the conflict is destined to be repeated again and again, from one generation to the next, so long as society remains the same. Where

Andreyev and the Expressionists part company is in the area of vision. Much influenced by Schopenhauer, Andreyev had a bleak, essentially pessimistic view of man hopelessly ensnared by the foredoomed strivings of the will. A symbol of bourgeois culture, the central character of *The Life of Man*, an architect, is brought by his ambition to the pinnacle of success only to be toppled from it and reduced at the end to a wretched death. The antagonists in *King Hunger* act out a terrifying drama of predestination which concludes with the grim forecast of an inevitable resumption of struggle.

The extreme subjectivity of some earlier Expressionist writing also characterises Yevreinov's theory of monodrama as exemplified in such plays as *The Performance of Love* ('Predstavleniye lyubvi', published 1910, never produced) and *Backstage at the Soul* ('V kulisakh dushi', which had its première in 1912).[6] In the latter play, the three selves of the clerk which appear as stage characters – the Rational Self, the Emotional Self and the Eternal Self, and the respective concepts of Wife and Café Singer introduced later as projections of the clerk's inner being – bring to mind the masked players representing the Russian revolutionary student's Ego, Super Ego and Id in the major dramatic work, *Methusalem*, by the German Expressionist Ivan Goll. Now Goll's play is later than Yevreinov's – it was staged for the first time in Berlin in 1922 – but the similarities of structure and satire ought to be thought of in relation to common sources in Expressionist technique, in this instance Expressionist anti-psychologism. The evidence for such an assumption seems even stronger in the case of *The Performance of Love*. Accompanying the changes of mood of the play's central character identified simply as 'I' and the shifts of attitude of 'I' toward 'She', are corresponding changes in the colour and brightness of the stage lighting as well as in the stage scenery itself. These were *Gesamtkunstwerk* innovations used by two exceptionally interesting figures in the early history of Expressionist art – the more interesting since their reputations are as much European as Russian: the composer Aleksandr Skryabin, and the painter, poet and dramatist Vassily Kandinsky. Skryabin's famous *Prometheus, Poem of Fire*, which was composed between 1909 and 1910, featured a full orchestra, a so-called colour organ which integrated sound and pre-coded visual colour projections, and perfume. Kandinsky's *Der gelbe Klang* ('The Yellow Chord'), also dating from 1909 but written apparently after Skryabin's work, presents a symbolic, ultra-abstract, virtually non-verbal performance in which coloured light, music and form are completely integrated with the movements of dancers and the singing of an offstage choir.[7] That Kandinsky knew and in fact was influenced by Skryabin's *Prometheus* is clearly indicated by an article on the work which appeared in the well-known Expressionist *Der Blaue Reiter* ('Blue Rider') almanac. Tracing the possible links between Kandinsky and Yevreinov presents problems, but the direct Skryabin–Yevreinov association can be substantiated.

When the First World War finally came the Expressionists greeted it with enthusiasm. Here at last was the fulfilment of their visions of the Apocalypse, the embodiment of the vague pre-war sense of impending doom. Many of the leading Expressionist writers took part in the war and several died in it, among them Ernst Stadler, Reinhard Sorge and the Austrian Georg Trakl. But the early enthusiasm soon gave way to horror. Prophesying the Apocalypse was one thing; experiencing it, another. Expressionism was profoundly shaken and changed by the war. The prewar disdain for technology and machine culture now became a violent hatred for the machine as an instrument of mass dehumanisation and mass destruction. Shaping and intensifying the Expressionist social philosophy was the widely held view that the true victim of the war was the common man and that the machines of destruction were built by Capital and directed by professional military officers whose goals were the same – the preservation of an unjust and privileged social structure.

While appalled at the human losses in the war, the Expressionists found some comfort in the collapse of Imperial Germany. They also followed the events in Russia closely both because of the Russo-German adversarial relationship during the conflict and because of the impact on Russian and German policy of the February and October Revolutions. The collapse of the Romanov dynasty in Russia followed by that of Wilhelminian Germany and Hapsburg Austria-Hungary confirmed the Expressionists' earlier belief in the imminent disintegration of the old order and the birth of a new one. War, therefore, was finally looked upon as the suffering that had to be experienced if the much heralded regeneration of the spirit was to occur.

After the war, Expressionism entered a new phase which was to last until the movement virtually expired with the amelioration of German economic and political life in late 1923 and early 1924.

This new phase was marked by a heightened social awareness often expressed in social activism, a political left inclination strongly attracted to Marxism, and a Utopian universalist belief in a new world community of brotherhood and love. The post-war Expressionists were imbued with a profound sense of mission. This, together with their passionate belief in the unity in brotherhood and love of all men, brought them close to essential Christian thought; to a considerable extent this explains the prevalent Christian motifs in Expressionism.

In view of the proletarian and socialist ideology of post-First World War Expressionism in Germany, the quickening interest in Russian society and culture follows logically. It reinforced the earlier interest in Russia focused on the Russian presence in Expressionist art (above all, Kandinsky) and on the discovery of Dostoyevsky whose appeal to the Expressionists as a writer and thinker can only be described as considerable. The success of the Bolsheviks in 1917, the support of the Revolution by such artists as Blok, Gorky and Mayakovsky – who were already known in a limited way in Germany – and the Bolsheviks' call for world revolution were heady stimulants to the German Expressionists.

As postwar Germany plunged into chaos, economically, politically and socially, the aspirations of the Expressionists found very real outlets, notably the attempt by the Spartakists led by Karl Liebknecht and Rosa Luxemburg to establish a Marxist regime in Berlin from November 1918 to January 1919 and the short-lived Soviet Republic (*Rätterrepublik*) of Bavaria of 1919. The entire complex of Expressionist social and spiritual messianism found full voice in literary almanacs and anthologies with such characteristic titles as *Kamaraden der Menschen* ('Comrades of Men', 1919), *Die Erhebung* ('The Revolt', 1919/1920), *Die Gemeinschaft* ('The Community', 1920), *Menschheitsdämmerung* ('The Twilight of Mankind', 1920), and *Verkündigung* ('Proclamation', 1921), and in such outstanding plays of the period as Ernst Toller's *Masse-Mensch* ('Masses-Man', 1920) and *Die Maschinenstürmer* ('The Machine Wreckers', 1922) and Georg Kaiser's famous trilogy *Die Koralle* ('The Coral', 1917), *Gas* (1918), and *Gas: Zweiter Teil* ('Gas II', 1920).

The enthusiasm of many of the German Expressionists for the Russian Revolution was matched by the Russian interest in the political drama unfolding in Germany between 1918 and 1924. This interest represented, I believe, the first general experience of German Expressionism by the Russians and was by no means limited to manifestations of friendly curiosity. Artistic creativity in the early years of the Soviet state was notable for its variegated experimental character. Artists searched for new ways to express themselves, for new forms compatible with the end of the old order in Russia and the beginnings of a socialism which to the Russian artist of the time and his Expressionist counterpart in Germany seemed to hold out the promise of universal brotherhood and love.

That Expressionism was one of the creative options explored by Russian art in the first years of the Soviet regime becomes apparent on closer scrutiny of early Soviet painting, theatre and drama. Since the drama has been less investigated in this respect than the other arts, this will be the focus of the present discussion.

The period of greatest receptivity toward German Expressionist drama in the Soviet Union was from 1918 to about 1925, although a few of the plays considered here slightly post-date this time frame. The way had been partially prepared by Yevreinov's monodramas of 1910 and 1912 and by certain works of Meyerhold and Mayakovsky. The combined nos 6–7 issue for 1914 of Meyerhold's journal *Love for Three Oranges*, which appeared only in February 1915, contained an eight-scene-plus-apotheosis scenario of a work called *Fire* ('Ogon''') by Meyerhold, Yury Bondi and Vladimir Solov'ev. Anti-militarist in theme and designed as a vehicle primarily for *commedia dell'arte*-derived improvisation and pantomime, the play had a definite Expressionist character.[8] The same may be argued for Mayakovsky's first dramatic work, *Vladimir Mayakovsky: A Tragedy* ('Vladimir Mayakovskiy: tragediya', 1913), in which the visionary prophetic concept of the poet developed in the play recalls that of Reinhard Sorge's *Der Bettler* ('The Beggar', 1912), now generally regarded as the first full-fledged Expressionist drama. Even more striking are the Expressionist features in *Mystery-Bouffe* ('Misteriya-Buff'), which Mayakovsky actually began not long before the October Revolution. In its use of mediaeval mystery play formulae to preach the gospel of proletarian revolution, *Mystery-Bouffe* is distinctly compatible with the Expressionist integration of progressive social philosophy and Christian symbolism. Kaiser made a similar use of mystery play technique in his fine drama *Von morgens bis mitternachts* ('From Morn till Midnight', written 1912, published 1916) and Toller was to do the same in his *Masses-Man* of 1921. We know also that the episodic structure of a number of German plays is not only a testimony to the rediscovery of Georg Büchner's drama *Woyzeck*, which Berg made the subject of an opera in 1925, but also a derivation of the Stations of the Cross, hence the designation of these plays in German as *Stationendramen*. The stations here are stages in the hero's spiritual evolution. Like several German Expressionist plays, *Mystery-Bouffe* portrays the coming of the Apocalypse in the form of the biblical flood and the discovery of a proletarian Utopia – the promised land – where brotherhood, love and justice reign supreme at the end of the play. The diction of *Mystery-Bouffe* may not exactly correspond to the highly compressed so-called telegraph style of German Expressionism, but it derives more from Expressionism and Futurism than from any primitive *agit* literature to which Soviet scholars have often likened it.

Soviet interest in revolutionary Germany ran so high between 1918 and 1925 that a fair number of Expressionist plays were translated into Russian and published in the Soviet Union. Ideology was no obstacle, at least in the early years. So many of the German plays either champion the proletarian revolution or portray the evils of capitalist society that there was much from which to choose. By the late 1920s enough of Hasenclever, Kaiser, Sternheim and Toller was available in Russian to permit a respectable acquaintance with German Expressionist drama. Productions were also mounted. Meyerhold attracted much favourable attention with his staging of *The Machine Wreckers* at the Theatre of the Revolution in November 1921 and of *Masses-Man* at the same theatre in January 1923; Walter Hasenclever's *Antigone* was produced by Tairov in 1927. When we consider that the first public performance of an Expressionist drama took place only in 1916 – that of Hasenclever's *Der Sohn* ('The Son') in the German National Theatre in Prague – and that public performances of Expressionist plays in Germany itself came only in 1917 and at that slowly, then the Russians were not very far behind.

Something of the importance with which the Russians regarded the entire German Expressionist movement can be gleaned from their publications on the subject in the 1920s.[9] Apart from translations of German studies there were several outstanding original essays. The first issue of the journal *Zhizn'* in 1922, for example, carried the article 'A Few Words about German Expressionism' ('Neskol'ko slov o nemetskom ekspressionizme') by the first Soviet Commissar of Education, Anatoly Lunacharsky, who also happened to be a prolific dramatist keenly interest in all matters relating to theatre. Lunacharsky's article was, in fact, part of a longer piece on German Expressionism and on the plays of Georg Kaiser in particular. (It was used as the introduction to a Russian edition of six of Kaiser's plays published in Moscow and Petrograd in 1923.) It was also in 1923 that the first number of *Iskusstvo*, the prestigious journal of the Russian Academy of Arts, included two extensive and by-and-large objective articles on Expressionism. The first, by P. Markov, was entitled 'Contemporary Expressionist Drama in Germany' ('Sovremennaya ekspressionisticheskaya drama v Germanii'); the second, by M. Fabrikant, was addressed to 'Expressionism and its Theorists' ('Ekspressionizm i yego teoretiki').

Buttressing the ideological interest in German Expressionism was the situation in Russian drama at the time. Because of the unsettled and unprecedented conditions both socially and artistically in the early post-revolutionary years, dramatists found it difficult to write plays about Soviet life. The theatre, on the other hand, was badly in need of a post-bourgeois repertoire by contemporary writers to counterbalance the fare of world classics then filling Soviet stages. Soviet dramatists began to assemble such a repertoire by writing plays with foreign settings. In order to make such plays ideologically respectable, they concentrated on depicting a capitalist society either irretrievably in decline or already in the throes of a proletarian revolution. Since it was precisely such subjects to which many German Expressionist plays were devoted, it was natural that the contemporary German drama would serve as a model. This accounts for the many early Soviet plays with foreign, and in particular German, settings and the Expressionist elements not just in these plays but in early Soviet drama in general.

Perhaps the best examples of this kind of interaction are plays by two popular Soviet dramatists of the 1920s: Sergey Tret'yakov (1892–1939) and Aleksey Fayko (1893–1978). The play that established Tret'yakov's international reputation was *Roar, China!* ('Rychi, Kitay!', 1925). Based on an actual occurrence in China, where Tret'yakov spent a year as a visiting lecturer on Russian literature, the play is noteworthy primarily as an example of the so-called literature of fact (*faktografiya*, in Russian) then becoming fashionable in Soviet literature and paralleling, in some respects, the *Neue Sachlichkeit* ('New Realism') that supplanted Expressionism in Germany around 1924.[10]

Tret'yakov's first two plays – *Are You Listening, Moscow?!* ('Slysh-ish', Moskva?!, 1923), subtitled an 'agit-guignol' in four acts, and *Gas Masks* ('Protivogazy'), a three-act melodrama dating from 1924 – leave little doubt as to their Expressionist genesis despite Soviet insistence on seeing them only as outgrowths of the *agit* and mass-spectacle productions of the immediate post-revolutionary period. Both plays are relatively short, notwithstanding their division into acts, and are written in a very spare, compressed, at times exclamatory style reminiscent of the telegraph technique of the Germans. The simultaneous shouting of several voices at a number of points in the action heightens the emotional aspect of the situation and creates the sense of urgency often experienced in Expressionist drama.

*Are You Listening, Moscow?!*, about a communist-led workers' revolt somewhere in Germany, is structurally the more interesting of the two plays. Film techniques, screen projections, split stage, different lighting effects, pantomime, dance and dramatised dream sequences were often woven into the texts of Expressionist plays and represent ultimately a legacy of the *Gesamtkunstwerk* idea. Tret'yakov's artistic collaboration with Mayakovsky, Meyerhold and Sergey Eisenstein placed him very near the centre of avant-garde experimentation, traces of which can be seen in his playwriting. *Are You Listening, Moscow?!* illustrates this. Count Stahl, the governor of a province, is arranging a pantomime in the town square to celebrate the unveiling of a monument to an illustrious ancestor. The pantomime will re-enact the victory of the ancestor and his followers over the aboriginal inhabitants of the area. At a certain point, the group playing the savages intercross in such a way as to form the pattern of a hammer and sickle. This is a signal for both groups to merge and, using the real ammunition they smuggled into the ceremony, to begin their revolt. When the bas-relief of Count Stahl's ancestor is unveiled, a huge portrait of Lenin stands in its place. The partisan crowd massed to watch the pantomime becomes wild with excitement and rushes to join the insurrectionaries. The outcome of the revolt is assured. This little play-within-a-play in the form especially of an outdoor pantomime pageant becomes the focus of interest in Tret'yakov's play and proceeds directly from the strong visual orientation of Expressionist drama and theatre. There is something much like this structurally in Georg Kaiser's *Der Protagonist* ('The Protagonist') of 1921, although the German play deals with sublimated incest rather than with political upheaval. At the end of Tret'yakov's play, in a parting theatricalist–Expressionist shot, the character Hugo, one of the revolutionaries, addresses the audience with the question, 'Moscow! Are you listening, Moscow?!', to which the reply 'I am listening!' is presumably shouted back by the audience.[11] The stage direction reads 'general reply from the auditorium'.

Tret'yakov's second play, *Gas Masks*, is set in the Soviet Union, although no place of action is specified except for the interior of a gas factory. That we are, in fact, dealing with a Russian milieu is established when Russian names are mentioned shortly after the curtain goes up and, later on, when Komsomol youths put in an appearance. A few of the characters are assigned names in the dramatis personae; most, however, are the types, the abstractions and generic figures usually encountered in German Expressionism: Director of the Factory, Secretary, Engineer and so on. The schematic plot of the play exposes the negligence of the factory director when a gas pipe bursts and the workers have to repair it at considerable risk because they lack gas masks which were supposed to have been ordered. Instead of the masks, the factory director had wine shipped in the gas mask cartons. The gas-factory setting, the indifference and callousness of the director who easily fits the shoes of the capitalist-factory owner in German Expressionist literature, the heroism of the workers, and especially the director and his son, are all familiar motifs in literary Expressionism. Reinforced by its style and easy transferability, the play could just as well have come out of the German tradition. Although a drama of greater depth and significance, Georg Kaiser's 'gas' trilogy anticipates Tret'yakov's work in some respects – above all, thematically – and probably served as its immediate inspiration.

Aleksey Fayko's *Lake Lyul* ('Ozero Lyul'') and *Bubus the Teacher* ('Uchitel' Bubus'), the first a five-act melodrama, the second a three-act comedy, were written about the same time as Tret'yakov's plays: *Lake Lyul* in 1923 and *Bubus* in 1924. Apart from their Expressionist elements, the plays are lightweight. The reputation they enjoyed in their own day owed considerably more to the popularity of Expressionism and Meyerhold's flamboyant productions of them than to their intrinsic worth as dramatic literature.[12]

In order to portray the universal decline of capitalism, Fayko again employs the typical Expressionist device of the vague transferable setting in *Lake Lyul* – 'somewhere in the far West or, perhaps, in the extreme East. A large island, the centre of civilisation and cosmopolitanism'.[13] There is much complicated intrigue in the play, but the plot basically recounts a successful popular uprising against the 'island'. It is directed by a revolutionary organisation located on a certain Lake Lyul. The play's central character is the duplicitous adventurer and opportunist Anton Prim, who is slain at the end by his girlfriend Maisie for trying to betray the revolution to which she is passionately devoted.

What attracted audiences and critics alike when *Lake Lyul* was staged was the frenetic pace of the characters representing the twilight of capitalist society, reminiscent in ways of Kaiser's *From Morn till Midnight*. But more than the nervous, frenzied rhythms of a dying capitalism, *Lake Lyul* glitters with the resplendent colours and costumes of a Western decadence which must have been a sheer visual delight to Russian audiences at the time. Even accentuating the play's terse Expressionist dialogue and episodic structure, Meyerhold's production on 7 November 1923 in the Theatre of the Revolution made the play's visual potential its principal source of appeal. Illuminated titles and advertisements were used as well as back-lit silvered screens. The costumes conveyed the greatest visual effect – brilliant, marvellously variegated and hinting at the fantastic. The kaleidoscope-like movement of the action was enhanced by area lighting which enabled Meyerhold to switch the action constantly from one level to another and sometimes to play two scenes simultaneously in different places.

Soviet drama critics and theorists, above all Lunacharsky, were at first sympathetic to the use of Expressionist techniques by Russian dramatists in the early 1920s – especially in works with Western settings depicting the collapse of capitalism and philistinism. But they had reservations about certain aspects of the Expressionist *Weltanschauung* and about the overall dramatic style. As time went on and Expressionist techniques became more widely used in Soviet drama and theatre these reservations hardened into outright condemnation, so that by the end of the period of the New Economic Policy (NEP) in 1928 a markedly Expressionist play had no place any more in the Soviet repertoire. Ideologically, the critics faulted German Expressionism for its frequent Christian symbolism and for the vague Utopian philosophy of the typical Expressionist 'hero'. It was in this spirit that K. V. Dryagin, in his 1928 study of the plays of Andreyev as Expressionist drama,

characterised the Expressionist movement in general in the following terms:

> Expressionism is the feeble shout of the petty bourgeois *intelligent*
> pressed down by the heel of the imperialistic bourgeoisie, a
> shout full of anger and hopelessness, full of helplessness. Such
> a shout against the strong and powerful can really be made only
> in union with the proletariat, with the proletarian socialist
> revolution before which the petty bourgeois feels only a panic
> dread.[14]

Stylistically, the more extreme manifestations of Expressionist play
technique were cautioned against, lest the play become little more
than a cultist exercise in a certain modish formalism.

Sensitive to such admonishment, dramatists tended to become
more conservative in their handling of Expressionism. On occasion,
they appear to be trying to offset the use of elements of the
Expressionist style with satire of the Expressionist 'hero'. This is
evident, I believe, in Fayko's *Bubus the Teacher*. The titular character
himself – the secondary schoolteacher Bubus – is little more than a
comic reduction of the well-intentioned but ineffectual bourgeois
liberal. The play, which has a Germanic, possibly Dutch setting
(though not specified as such by Fayko) relates the adventures of
Bubus who takes refuge in an aristocrat's mansion during a great
demonstration of unemployed workers. There are a number of
amusing incidents mostly built around the stock comic device of
mistaken identity. Bubus, however, is the main attraction of the
play; in his figure Fayko tries to show the bumbling and stumbling
of the Western humanitarian when confronted with a real revolution. Bubus identifies himself with the cause of the unemployed
workers and even refers to himself as a 'representative of the
masses'. But when the jobless take to the streets to demonstrate,
he is so frightened by the tumult around him that he runs away
and hides in the garden of the aristocrat Van Kamperdaff. Even at
the end of the play when the revolution is in full progress and
Van Kamperdaff's estate is seized, Bubus cannot control his fear
and conceals himself behind a piece of furniture. His cowardice is
but one sign of his Expressionist origins. Fayko also has Bubus
voice a number of statements intended to establish the unreal
Utopian outlook of the Expressionist 'hero'. The following are
typical:

Citizens, comrades, friends. Life is full of paradoxes and terrors –
that is completely evident. But mankind is moving along the
path of progress and in brotherly effort will reach the shores of
good fortune and happiness. I believe in this and I know that
you, too, believe. Let us forget dissension and discord and let
us join together in a mighty creative outburst of life . . . I see
before the eyes of my soul valleys of prosperity and love. There
will be neither oppressors nor oppressed. A smile will not leave
a person's face from the day he is born to the day he dies. I see
fragrant green lawns and children playing on them. I see great
illuminated halls through which young boys and girls, husbands
and wives, and stately elderly people walk arm in arm. They
engage in quiet, wise conversation and solve one after the other
all the riddles of the universe. I weep, citizens, I weep and
through the shroud of my tears I clearly behold the future
beautiful life.[15]

At the end of the play when he is 'liberated' in Van Kamperdaff's
mansion, Bubus offers his services to the revolutionaries in these
words: 'Now I have reached my goal. Take me into your ranks
and I shall conduct a merciless struggle with tyranny and falsehood'.[16] The response is predictable. Bubus is told to come back a
week later when things have quietened down and perhaps a lower
school assignment in the capital district can be found for him.

A more original and provocative use of Expressionist technique
appears in two later manifestations of the mode in Russian drama
of the 1920s: Yury Olesha's *The Conspiracy of Feelings* ('Zagovor
chuvstv'), staged by the Vakhtangov Theatre in Moscow in March
1929 but absent from Soviet theatres after 1931, and Mikhail
Bulgakov's *Flight* ('Beg'), written between 1926 and 1928 and staged
in the Soviet Union for the first time in 1957 at the Gorky Theatre
in Volgograd.

References are occasionally made to Olesha's Expressionism in
*The Conspiracy of Feelings*,[17] but what this Expressionism consists of
seems to go largely undefined.[18] The more obvious Expressionist
aspect of the play is its theme: the individual against the mass.
The conflict, to be sure, is often depicted in unmistakably ambivalent terms in German Expressionism. In earlier Expressionist
literature, the hero is frequently presented as struggling to break
free from the patterns and restraints of bourgeois society, to
discover his authentic identity by thrusting himself away from the

conformist pressures of the mass. In the later more socially committed and politically activist literature, the hero often identifies with the mass, with the struggle and aspirations of the multitude, entering into a kind of spiritual and even mystic union with it. The Expressionist vision of the future is of a Utopian brotherhood of mankind united in love. The concept presupposes the dissolution of the individual identity. Man ultimately becomes one with all humanity, the theme suggested, for example, by Hasenclever's extreme Expressionist play of 1918 *Die Menschen* ('Humanity'). As the comedies of Carl Sternheim demonstrate, however, this fine Utopian vision is sometimes mocked within the central tradition of Expressionism itself.

Much of the railing of the Expressionists against capitalism was rooted in a hatred and fear of modern technology. Because of the machine, they believed, man faced a twin danger: that of physical annihilation as exemplified by the use of the machine as a horrible instrument of war between 1914 and 1918, and that of spiritual annihilation inevitable in the subordination to and eventual dehumanisation of man by the machine.

As Soviet society developed in the 1920s, the unfolding vision of a technology-dominated future of faceless automata gave rise to a substantial anti-Utopian literature, among the monuments of which are Yevgeny Zamyatin's justly famous novel *We* ('My') and Mayakovsky's satirical comedy *The Bedbug* ('Klop'). This Soviet anti-Utopianism became another bridge between Russian literature of the 1920s and German Expressionism. In the field of drama, Olesha's *The Conspiracy of Feelings* – a stage version of his short novel *Envy* ('Zavist", 1927) – offers convincing evidence of it.

Written in 1928, both Mayakovsky's *The Bedbug* and Olesha's *The Conspiracy of Feelings* plead for the rights of the individual and of the individual identity threatened by a machine-dominated collective. Probably for political reasons, both plays treat the central characters in a sufficiently ambivalent way to make different interpretations possible. This is true of what Prisypkin signifies in Mayakovsky's play and of what Ivan Babichev and Kavalerov signify in Olesha's. However, despite their similar concerns, the plays are different in style, with many of the essential differences stemming from Olesha's use of Expressionist techniques shunned by Mayakovsky in *The Bedbug*.

Apart from the subject itself – the counter-revolution of Ivan Babichev and Kavalerov in the name of the individual against a technological society embodied in the figure of the Soviet sausage king Andrey Babichev – Olesha's Expressionism manifests itself in several other key areas. The polarities represented by Andrey, on the one hand, and Ivan, on the other, and the conflict they symbolise between individual and collective, offer a modification of the familiar pattern of father vs. son conflict in German Expressionism. Here, instead of son against father, Olesha pits brother against brother like the biblical Cain and Abel. Kavalerov, Ivan's most ardent disciple who eventually betrays him, also is the focus of the play's erotic subplot. This culminates in the unmistakably Expressionist dream of Kavalerov in the fifth scene in which his erotic anxieties concerning Valya (Ivan's daughter) and Andrey Babichev are played out before the audience as dramatised projection. The erotic nature of the dream and the enormous, erotically suggestive bed as both the point of departure for the dream and the central environment of the dream experience itself directly relate to the use of dream and erotic subject matter in Expressionist drama. Enhancing the expressionistic ambience of Kavalerov's dream are Olesha's stage directions: 'the stage seems to vibrate. All at once the shadows shift position as if an invisible source of light had sprung up somewhere from within the depths of the furniture. An unpleasant yellowish light.'[19]

Of greater importance in the play's overall structure from the viewpoint of Expressionism is Olesha's use of Christian imagery. German Expressionist drama often operates subversively with Christian motifs for non-Christian purposes. Although not an Expressionist play as such, Mayakovsky's *Mystery-Bouffe* effectively demonstrates this process of subversion. In *The Conspiracy of Feelings*, Ivan Babichev is a prophetic Christ-like figure, but in one of several ironic reversals in the play, he is the herald not of a new age but of an old age – the dead nineteenth century, the age of feeling, the age of the individual. The pattern of New Testament parallels and reversals is sustained throughout the play. Ivan Babichev is a new Christ whose teaching leads not to salvation but to destruction; instead of turning one cheek then another when struck, he advocates murder, as in the play's phantasmagoric second scene; re-enacting the miracle of the transformation of water into wine at the wedding at Cana, Olesha's miracle-worker turns wine into water; the nameday party in the sixth scene is a grotesque inversion of the Last Supper with Ivan at the centre of the table; Kavalerov is Ivan's most devoted disciple and at the end of the play not only betrays Ivan but murders him; shortly before the murder, Ivan kisses Kavalerov as Christ kissed Judas. Finally, Ivan's travels from house to house with his symbolic pillow in hand can be viewed as a grotesque repetition of the Stations of the Cross.

Dream and the episodic structure of the *Stationendramen* link Olesha's *The Conspiracy of Feelings* and Bulgakov's *Flight*. The phantasmagoric effect Olesha achieves in Kavalerov's dream assumes a broader dimension in Bulgakov's play.[20] The flight of the title refers to the mass exodus of anti-Bolshevik Whites from Russia during the Civil War. The play's principal division is into eight 'dreams'. Chiaroscuro functions importantly both structurally and atmospherically. Each 'dream' opens and closes in darkness or near darkness. In the first, a church choir is heard singing in the dark before the stage is illuminated, an opening strikingly like that of Ernst Toller's *Masses-Man*. The cinematographic fade-in/fade-out technique establishes the dream context and at the same time indicates a change of scene. Atmospherically, the dream quality of the play lapses into nightmare by means of grotesque episodes usually developed around the cockroach as a metaphor for the wretched existence of the Russians in emigration. Bulgakov's point is abundantly clear, and the play's use of light and elements of the grotesque makes it visually stunning: the life of the Russian who has chosen to flee his country during the Civil War rather than remain in it and try to make a place for himself in the new society is as unreal as a dream and as sinister as a nightmare.

Again, as in Olesha's *The Conspiracy of Feelings* and many of the German Expressionist plays, biblical allusions abound. Since the theme of the play is the unreality of emigration, they cluster around the Exodus. Just as the Expressionist hero in a *Stationendrama* progresses to spiritual redemption, so, too, in Bulgakov's play does the return to Russia of the central characters Serafima and Golubkov assume the analogous significance of spiritual deliverance. In the case of General Khludov, whose hands are stained with the blood of his victims in the Civil War, the return to Russia becomes an act of Christian atonement, of expiation for sin. To view the eight-part dream structure of *Flight* in terms of the German *Stationendrama* seems entirely valid; the dreams represent the stations the characters traverse on their way to the spiritual redemption and rebirth that await them upon their return to Russia. The return marks at the same time a return to reality, hence the end of the nightmare of émigré existence. This is underscored at the end when Serafima says to Golubkov as they prepare to leave Constantinople: 'What was it, Seryozha, what was it this past year and a half? Dreams?'[21] As she speaks, the chorus performing at Artur's cockroach-racing arena can be heard singing 'Let us pray to the Lord and tell the ancient tale!'[22] This infuses the play's last moment with a biblical aura which is reinforced by the voice of a muezzin calling from a minaret.

Other aspects of *Flight* contribute to its Expressionist character. The chiaroscuro of the beginning and end of each dream is not the play's only use of light to create a sense of Expressionist phantasmagoria. In the all-night card game between former General Charnota and Korzukhin, who has abandoned his wife Serafima and established himself comfortably in Paris, light assumes an important role. The game is played at night; the stage is illuminated just by candles on the playing table. Korzukhin, who is portrayed as money-mad, is losing heavily and from time to time has to go to a safe to withdraw money. Each time he opens the safe, light flashes on stage, bells ring and music plays. The card game itself is a component in the elaboration of the play's overall phantasmagoric structure.

The unflattering portrayal of Korzukhin as a greedy bourgeois was definitely inspired by Expressionist drama. This is most apparent in the play's seventh scene when Korzukhin refuses Golubkov's plea for a thousand dollars in order to help the ailing Serafima. Korzukhin tells him:

Ah, my dear young man! Before you talk about a thousand dollars, I'll tell you what a single dollar means. [*Launches into a paean about the dollar, becoming more and more inspired.*] The dollar! That great omnipotent spirit! It is everywhere! Take a look there! There, far away, on a roof, a golden sunray burns, and next to it, high in the air, is a crouching black cat! The dollar is there, too! The chimera is guarding it! [*Points mysteriously to the floor.*] A vague emanation, not a noise, not sound, but, as it were, the very breath of the bulging earth: trains are flying there as swift as arrows, and they carry the dollar. Now shut your eyes and imagine – darkness, and waves as huge as mountains. Darkness and water – the ocean! It is terrifying, it will devour you. But a monster moves through the ocean, with hissing boilers, churning up millions of tons of water. It moves, groaning, carrying lights!

It ploughs up the water, it strains, but in the infernal boiler rooms the naked stokers tend the flames, and in its belly it carries the golden child, its divine heart – the dollar! And suddenly the world is troubled! [*Sounds of military music in the background.*] And now they come! They come! They come in the thousands, and then in the millions! The heads are encased in steel helmets. They walk! Then they run! Then they throw themselves upon barbed wire! Why? Because the sacred dollar was insulted somewhere! But now the world is at peace, and trumpets blare triumphantly in every city! It is avenged! They blow in honour of the dollar! [*Calms down, music recedes.*][23]

Notwithstanding his initial enthusiasm for Expressionism, Commissar Lunacharsky eventually dismissed it as something that would always be felt as alien in Soviet drama. This set the tone for the later Soviet repudiation of Expressionism as the product of a sick society and as a half-way house to full-fledged formalism. For a long time after the 1920s Soviet scholarship piously observed a strict silence about it. When in the post-Stalinist period it again became possible to deal with the subject of the impact of German Expressionism on early Soviet drama, an official view of it had already been formulated. We see this reflected, for example, in the first volume of the *A History of Russian Soviet Drama* ('Ocherki istorii russkoy sovetskoy dramaturgii'), published in 1963 and covering the period 1917 to 1934. Writing about the role played by German Expressionism in the development of Soviet drama in the period 1920–5, S. V. Vladimirov writes:

Expressionism, especially its left wing, as opposed to other bourgeois movements, appeared beneath the flag of rebellion. The Expressionist dramatists declared themselves opponents of the bourgeois system; they renounced imperialism. That is why the Soviet theatre, in its search for a revolutionary repertoire, also turned to the plays of German writers. But the very first productions demonstrated that in the conditions of a country engaged in the practical building of socialism, the plays of the German Expressionists were absolutely meaningless.[24]

Using a production of Georg Kaiser's *Gas* by the Bolshoy Dramatic Theatre of Leningrad as an example, Vladimirov goes on to point out that in view of the inability of the theatre to share the author's enthusiasm for what he terms 'Tolstoyan–Rousseauesque truth-seeking tendencies',[25] it could only concentrate on the plot – the downfall and rehabilitation of a factory. These were the only elements of the play capable of arousing the interest of the Soviet viewer during the years of economic reconstruction. Since the formal properties of a German Expressionist play, such as Kaiser's *Gas*, were a reflection of the author's particular view of contemporary bourgeois society, the attempt by Soviet dramatists and theatres to assimilate German Expressionist play technique could only be limited to external features of this type of drama. This, in turn, would open the way to formalism.

Despite the systematic downplaying by Soviet scholarship of the contribution of German Expressionist drama, the literary and theatrical-historical evidence establishes beyond a doubt, I believe, that in the development of early twentieth-century Russian drama, and particularly of early Soviet drama and theatre, Expressionism deserves to be considered perhaps the most productive of any of the avant-garde movements.

## Notes

1. The literature on German Expressionism and Expressionist drama is vast. Among relatively more recent studies, the following are of particular interest: R. Brinkmann, *Expressionismus: Internationale Forschung zu einem internationalen Phänomen* (Stuttgart, 1980); H. Denkler, *Drama des Expressionismus: Programm, Spieltext, Theater*, 2nd rev. edn (Munich, 1979); M. Durzak, *Das expressionistische Drama: E. Barlach, Ernst Toller, Fritz von Unruh* (Munich, 1979); H. J. Knobloch, *Das Ende des Expressionismus: Von der Tragödie zur Komödie* (Berne and Frankfurt am Main, 1975). Among studies in English, highly recommended are: W. H. Sokel, *The Writer in Extremis: Expressionism in Twentieth-Century German Literature* (Stanford, 1959); W. H. Sokel (ed.), *An Anthology of German Expressionist Drama* (Garden City, N.Y., 1963); P. Raabe (ed.), *The Era of German Expressionism*, trs. J. M. Ritchie, (Woodstock, N.Y., 1974); and J. M. Ritchie, *German Expressionist Drama* (Boston, Mass., 1976).
2. Wagner's concept of the *Gesamtkunstwerk* and the derivative notions of 'total theatre' and 'theatre of the future' are defined in E. T. Kirby (ed.), *Total Theatre: A Critical Anthology* (New York, 1969) pp. xiii–xxxi.
3. For a good general study of Andreyev in English, see J. B. Woodward, *Leonid Andreyev: A Study* (Oxford, 1969). An early analysis of several of Andreyev's plays as pre-Expressionist drama was undertaken by K. V. Dryagin in *Ekspressionizm v Rossii* (Vyatka, 1928).

4. Certain formal properties of Andreyev's pre-Expressionist plays are analysed in M. Cymborska-Leboda, *Dramaturgia Leonida Andriejewa: Technika i styl* (Warsaw, 1982).
5. On the figure of Anathema, see Woodward, p. 214.
6. A translation of *Backstage at the Soul*, under the title *The Theatre of the Soul*, appears in C. Collins (ed. and trs.), *Life as Theater: Five Modern Plays by Nikolai Evreinov* (Ann Arbor, Mich., 1973) pp. 21–31. For a good monograph on Yevreinov, see S. Golub, *Evreinov: The Theatre of Paradox and Transformation* (Ann Arbor, Mich., 1984).
7. A translation of the work, with commentary, appears in Victor H. Miesel (ed.), *Voices of German Expressionism* (Englewood Cliffs, N.J., 1970) pp. 137–45.
8. The work is discussed briefly by Eugene Bristow in his article 'Expressionist Stage Techniques in the Russian Theater', in Ulrich, Weisstein (ed.), *Expressionism as an International Literary Phenomenon* (Paris and Budapest, 1973) p. 217. J. L. Styan's very useful *Modern Drama in Theory and Practice, 3: Expressionism and Epic Theatre* (Cambridge, 1981) pp. 75–97 also discusses Expressionist productions by Meyerhold, Yevreinov and Vakhtangov.
9. There is a good bibliography of the Russian literature on Expressionism in V. Markov, 'Russian Expressionism', in Weisstein (ed.), pp. 315–27.
10. The literature on Tret'yakov is sparse. For an interesting German study, see F. Mierau, *Erfindung und Korrektur: Tretjakows Ästhetik der Operativität* (Berlin, 1976).
11. My translations of the play are based on the 1966 Moscow edition of Tret'yakov's dramatic works: *Slyshish', Moskva?! Protivogazy, Rychi, Kitay!* p. 28.
12. For a brief but informative account of Meyerhold's productions of Fayko's plays, see E. Braun, *The Theatre of Meyerhold: Revolution on the Modern Stage* (New York, 1979) pp. 184–6, 190–3.
13. My translations from the original follow the text as it appears in A. Fayko, *Teatr* (Moscow, 1971) p. 8.
14. Dryagin, p. 3.
15. Fayko, pp. 162–3, 170.
16. Ibid., p. 182.
17. For two English versions of the play, see B. F. Dukore and D. C. Gerould (eds), *Avant-Garde Drama: A Casebook* (New York, 1976) pp. 207–56, and M. Green and J. Katsell (eds and trs.), *Yury Olesha, The Complete Plays* (Ann Arbor, Mich., 1983) pp. 13–67.
18. For example: 'One of Olesha's achievements is his adaptation of expressionistic themes and techniques to the struggle of old and new in Soviet life. . . . Utilizing the techniques of the expressionists, Olesha eschews their passionate, ideological rhetoric and instead mocks both bourgeois man's ineffectual anguish and socialist man's foolish arrogance' (Dukore and Gerould, p. 203).
19. Ibid., p. 240.
20. For English versions of the play, see *Flight: A Play in Eight Dreams and Four Acts*, trs. M. Ginsburg, (New York, 1969), and E. Proffer (ed.),

*The Early Plays of Mikhail Bulgakov*, trs. C. R. Proffer and E. Proffer (Bloomington, Ind., and London, 1972) pp. 159–239.
21. *Flight*, p. 107.
22. Ibid.
23. Ibid., p. 90–1.
24. S. V. Vladimirov and D. I. Zolotnitskiy (eds), *Ocherki istorii russkoy sovetskoy dramaturgii*, vol. I (Leningrad and Moscow, 1963) p. 55.
25. Ibid.

# 10

# Down with the Foxtrot! Concepts of Satire in the Soviet Theatre of the 1920s

## J. A. E. CURTIS

The first anniversary in 1918 of the October Revolution was the occasion for the performance in Petrograd of what is generally held to be the earliest substantial post-Revolutionary satirical work, Mayakovsky's anti-religious pageant *Mystery-Bouffe* ('Misteriya-buff'). But such innovative epic undertakings, like the new outdoor spectacles for mass audiences, were to have little significant impact on theatrical developments during the mid-1920s period of the New Economic Policy (NEP), not least because of the financial and organisational difficulties these productions presented. Instead, smaller-scale events – such as Mayakovsky himself would also contribute to – became the real focus for satirical work during most of the 1920s.

Another town where October/November 1918 saw distinguished artists contributing to the celebrations was Vitebsk. In September 1918 the local newspaper had reported that the painter Marc Chagall had been made Commissar with powers to 'organise art schools, museums, lectures on art, and all other artistic ventures in the city and region of Vitebsk', and that he was also empowered to intervene in theatrical matters.[1] Judging by a letter Chagall wrote in December 1918, he tackled his most immediate task with great enthusiasm: 'To celebrate the anniversary of the October Revolution the Vitebsk region was decorated with around 450 large posters, numerous flags for workers' organizations, tribunes and arches. . . . the evening of 6 November burned with an unforgettable fire. It was a celebration of our art as well.'[2] Chagall's final comment here is a reminder of the fact that for him aesthetic considerations were always ultimately more important than sober ideological requirements; and he later recalled that, although the workers appeared amused by his contributions, 'the leaders, the Communists, seemed less gratified. Why is the cow green and why is the horse flying through the sky, why? What's the connection with Marx and Lenin?'[3] Over the next eighteen months or so, Chagall made Vitebsk an extraordinary centre for artistic activity, especially through his Academy of Fine Art where he worked and taught alongside El Lissitzky and Malevich, among others, until the Academy broke up in the spring of 1920 amid bitter recriminations. But what is less well known is that during his time in Vitebsk Chagall also put his talents at the disposal of a small theatre group which provided the nucleus from which a great deal of theatrical satire in Moscow was to grow during the 1920s.

The group, known as the Terevsat ('Theatre of Revolutionary Satire'), was set up in Vitebsk in January 1919 by the poet M. Ya. Pustynin (1884–1966).[4] His initial idea was to bring the influential ROSTA propaganda posters to life by turning them into staged sketches, and his first show on 7 February 1919 was indeed based almost entirely on ROSTA materials (the *tantomoresk* or animated poster sketch included in Terevsat shows was a genre later much used by the 'Blue Shirt' ('Sinyaya Bluza') *agitprop* groups). The first item on the programme, however, was the specially written *March of the Terevsat*, which began 'May our Terevsat be the merriest of troublemakers, may it stigmatise with sparkling satire those who want to turn back. We will defeat grey tedium, we believe fervently in that.'[5] This kind of text is, of course, virtually impossible to translate into English without it appearing ridiculous; but even in Russian it reveals a naïve and curiously humble tone. And yet this sort of material was to make up a considerable proportion of what went under the name of satire in the 1920s. One of the reasons for this, of course, was that the materials were designed to reach the least educated of audiences. During the first year of its activity Terevsat toured up and down the front lines, giving over 300 performances to a total of some 200 000 spectators. These performances were invariably preceded by an 'agitator's report' on the current political situation, which was considered an integral part of the show. One participant recalled that 'the reports greatly helped the spectators to understand the show correctly, for they saw amongst the characters those opponents of Soviet power about whom the agitator had just been speaking'.[6] Just as the ROSTA posters drew extensively on the folk traditions of tree-bark printing (*lubok*), so the repertoire of Terevsat relied heavily in the first year of its work on variations of popular theatrical forms: the names of items on the programme frequently invoked fairground forms such as the *balagan* streetshows, the character of Petrushka, the peepshow (*rayok*) and so on. And for as long as the theatre was based in Vitebsk, the only artist mentioned as stage designer was, strikingly, Marc Chagall; we can only regret that nothing seems to have survived of his designs.

In the early spring of 1920 the theatre was transferred to Moscow. Neither M. Ya. Pustynin (who went on to work in cabaret and for the 'Blue Shirts', as well as for *Krokodil*) nor Chagall remained closely involved with the theatre in Moscow, although much of the Vitebsk repertoire was reused at first; one direct link with the original group was maintained through M. A. Razumny, who had been involved from the very beginning as an actor and went on to help with writing and directing as well. Terevsat enjoyed popularity in Bolshevik circles, and even before its official Moscow première on 14 May 1920 it was invited to contribute to Lenin's fiftieth birthday festivities,[7] and to the May Day celebrations. Terevsat's principal director in Moscow was David Grigor'yevich Gutman, who in 1918–19 had run a 'Revolutionary Petrushka' theatre on the southern front. During the summer of 1920 Terevsat's activities spread more and more widely as brigades went out to perform in factories, for the troops, or on trams which travelled around the squares of Moscow; and analogous Terevsat groups using much of the same repertoire were established in Petrograd, Tomsk, Kiev, Baku and other Soviet towns. But by the end of 1920 Terevsat was already beginning to feel that its function had to change; a document composed by its artistic committee on 20 December argued that

> Terevsat . . . bore that name . . . inasmuch as its weapon up until the end of 1920 was precisely satire. . . . The reason why this situation must change . . . lies in the change in the conditions of the political life of the Republic. . . . If earlier the basic task of the theatre was merciless criticism of the enemies of the revolution and a call to do battle with them, now, in the context of the victory over Vrangel' . . . the theatre should tackle new tasks, in other words it should conduct agitational work aimed at consolidating the achievements of Soviet power.[8]

Accordingly there was a shift in the repertoire away from sketches towards larger-scale works, and the replacement of Gutman by Vsevolod Meyerhold in the summer of 1922 coincided with the end of Terevsat as such; it provided the nucleus for the new Moscow Theatre of the Revolution, which after further amalgamations would eventually become the Mayakovsky Theatre.

The history of Terevsat is typical of other such theatre groups in Moscow and elsewhere, which underwent a transformation in 1920–1 with the end of the Civil War and the introduction of the New Economic Policy and experienced a need to move on from very small-scale agitational sketches to more extended and considered dramatic writing. But Terevsat was not just typical; it was also central. One is struck time and again when looking at repertoire lists for all the Moscow and Petrograd 'light' theatres of the period by the extent to which the selfsame authors and directors originally associated with Terevsat went on to work for so many others during the early 1920s. Even during its Vitebsk period Terevsat was using material written by D. G. Gutman (under the pseudonym 'Dege'), 'Argo' and N. A. Aduyev as well as M. Ya. Pustynin. In Moscow the repertoire was quickly extended until eventually over a hundred original pieces had been written for Terevsat; the new authors included Razumny, but also more distinguished figures such as Demyan Bedny, Mayakovsky, Ye. D. Zozulya, V. Ya. Shishkov, L. V. Nikulin, Mark Krinitsky (M. K. Samygin) and others. Between 1920 and 1922 the theatre also employed figures such as V. I. Pudovkin and S. V. Obraztsov as directors, while I. O. Dunayevsky became their principal composer.

Another point about Terevsat, which would perhaps bear further investigation, is that it represents an interesting Jewish contribution to the early history of Soviet satirical theatre. Chagall himself, after creating the sets for Terevsat's work during the Vitebsk period, was invited in Moscow to work on the decoration of murals and sets for the opening of A. M. Efros and A. M. Granovsky's Jewish theatre in 1920. He was apparently excited to have an opportunity to explore Jewish themes in this work – it was with some pride, for instance, that he later claimed that 'Ansky' (S. S. Rappaport, himself born in Vitebsk) initially told him he was the only person who could stage his play *The Dibbouk*.[9] It is difficult to evaluate the extent to which Chagall's work in Vitebsk, the work of Pustynin (real name Rozenblat) or of a vital figure such as 'Argo' (real name Abram Markovich Gol'denberg) was formed by their Jewish backgrounds. But undoubtedly the enormous sense of liberation many Jews felt at the lifting of Tsarist restrictions on their movements and activities meant that their enthusiastic participation made an influential contribution to much early Soviet satire.

An essential facet of the explosion of satirical writing in the Soviet Union after 1917 is its interconnection with established 'small forms' (*malyye formy*) such as cabaret, music-hall and variety (*estrada*). The music-hall had attracted Lenin's attention and sympathy when he visited it in London in 1903: 'There is a sort of satirical or sceptical attitude towards received ideas in this. . . . It's intricate, but it is interesting.'[10] Some of the best known cabarets such as 'The Bat' (*Letuchaya mysh'*) and 'The Distorting Mirror' (*Krivoye zerkalo*, more commonly – though less accurately – translated as 'The Crooked Mirror'), both founded in 1908, were permitted to survive after the Revolution. At the end of 1919 some regulations were introduced to control their activities and those of other variety theatres (*estrada* and *teatry miniatyur*),[11] indicating that they were regarded with some nervousness; but they then thrived under NEP before being very firmly restricted in the late 1920s as epitomising – and engendering – all the worst NEP values. And entries in the *Theatrical Encyclopaedia* ('Teatral'naya entsiklopediya') on topics such as 'music-hall' or 'variety' (*estrada*) or 'current affairs sketches' (*obozreniya*) are notable for the fact that the same names reappear all the time: Aduyev, V. E. Ardov, Argo, Bedny, Dunayevsky, Nikolay Erdman, Gutman, V. Mass, Mayakovsky, Nikulin, N. P. Smirnov-Sokol'sky, V. Tipot and M. D. Vol'pin seem to have been indefatigable in creating new works for every 'light' theatre in Moscow. Frequently they worked in assorted collaborations for various theatres; and all the time they were also contributing to associated genres such as the circus (the clown Vitaly Lazarenko using Mayakovsky's texts) as well as, in the case of N. Erdman and Mayakovsky for instance, writing full-length plays for more formal theatres. Several of them (including Aduyev, Ardov, Argo and Tipot, as well as Mikhail Zoshchenko) also wrote for the 'Blue Shirts' *agitprop* group, whose aims were rather more didactic than satirical, and whose impact was enormous. A newspaper story of September 1929 reported that the 'Blue Shirts' had given 17 500 performances in Moscow alone since their foundation in 1923, reaching well over fourteen million spectators. It also boasted that the 'Blue Shirts' had participated in every major campaign of 1928: pre-election, anti-Christmas, anti-Easter, for literacy, for the Five-Year Plan, for 'socialist emulation', against militarism and against alcohol.[12] By then, however, their somewhat schematic methods (ranging from declamation to gymnastics) had begun to pall on an increasingly sophisticated audience, and the 'Blue Shirts' rapidly lost popularity in the early 1930s. It is important, nevertheless, to bear in mind the extent to which those figures whom we associate most closely with satirical writing in the 1920s (and this extends to writers of prose fiction such as Ilf and Petrov as well) were deeply rooted in agitational work, popular entertainment and light comedy.

All this, however, might seem rather far removed from any concept of satire as it is understood in the West; and before going on to consider the role played by a number of key figures involved in the debate, I should like to look at the kinds of meanings which seem to have been attached to the idea of satire by those in the 1920s who were most concerned about whether satire should be allowed to survive at all, and if so, in what guises.

There is a curious vacuum at the centre of much of the discussion in Soviet writing about the actual nature of satire and how it should be defined. It may be significant in this respect that the otherwise admirably detailed *Theatrical Encyclopaedia* lacks a substantial entry on the subject: the entry for 'satire' (briefer even than the one for 'music-hall') refers only to the classical Greek variety, thereby making it appear remote and of little relevance to the late 1960s reader for whom the encyclopaedia is intended. This may be because of a desire to gloss over the political implications of what satire is generally held to be concerned with in Western European culture; but the consequence is that any discussion of satire in the Soviet Union appears to operate with a large number of unspoken assumptions, whose nature can only be guessed at in relation to the narrow and highly encoded language of what is actually said. The fact that discussion of the subject is compressed so tightly is perhaps indicative of the great importance it was felt in reality to have for the developing of a specifically Soviet literature; and, as is sometimes the case with similarly delicate topics, a literary-historical approach is often adopted by Soviet scholars as a substitute for any discussion of topical problems.

The pre-eminence of satire as the most successful genre in nineteenth-century Russian drama – from Fonvizin through Griboyedov and Gogol to Sukhovo-Kobylin and Ostrovsky and on to Chekhov – lends these pre-Revolutionary dramatists a particularly high value in the eyes of many Soviet literary commentators. Satire

is viewed as a major progressive force against the Tsarist regime,
a weapon for social and political reform; and of course, its influence
on the development of radical thought is indeed difficult to
calculate. This function was one which could appropriately be
pursued during the Civil War period, as an effective means of
propagandising the Bolshevik cause. But the crucial question was
whether – and how – this could be allowed to continue after 1921.
My concern here will not be to attempt definitions of satire; nor
particularly to consider the distinctions between satirical drama
and satirical prose or verse. What I should like to examine are the
vocabulary of the debate and the justifications put forward for the
continued existence of satirical drama in the 1920s.

As early as 1920 Lunacharsky was beginning to point out that
he had observed workers getting bored at 'revolutionary' plays,
and that he had even read a petition from workers and sailors
asking for them to be stopped and for Gogol and Ostrovsky to be
put on instead.[13] He was evidently concerned not just that better
writing should be made available to the masses, but also that the
benefits of laughter should not be denied to the workers. This dual
goal – a rediscovery of quality as well as of comedy – was doubtless
equally implied in his well-known 1923 call to theatres to go
'Back to Ostrovsky!'.[14] Reflections of this concern to rediscover
nineteenth-century satire are to be found in the views of Meyerhold,
which will be considered below. But they are also indicated by
details such as the delight with which the first decent publication
since 1869 of Sukhovo-Kobylin's trilogy was greeted by one critic
in 1928;[15] or the fact that in 1929 the fortieth anniversary of Saltykov-
Shchedrin's death was seized upon in one journal as an occasion
to deplore the current neglect and ignorance of his work. It was
hoped that this might be remedied by a recent (1926–8) publication
of a six-volume edition of his works.[16] Certainly, the existence of a
large demand for comedy and satire was universally recognised,
although some statistics may help to indicate just how popular it
was: a review in 1928 by S. Okhitovich pointed out that during
the month of September 1927 alone nearly a million volumes of
writing in humorous genres had been produced; and that a
comparable number of volumes (947 160) of Zoshchenko's works
had been published during 1926–7.[17] But while there was a general
recognition of the fact that comedy and nineteenth-century satire
were desirable, the fate of contemporary Soviet satire was still
a matter of considerable dispute. The debate was effectively

inaugurated by the critic V. Blyum in 1924–5; but before examining that, there are questions of terminology which I should like to address.

As I suggested above, the vocabulary of the debate was extremely restricted. A common assumption amongst commentators of the day was that the way satire achieved its effects was through universalisation (*obobshcheniye*), which was what raised it above the level of lampoon (*paskvil'*) and enabled it to become a weapon (*oruzhiye*) in the progressive struggle for social and political reform. Truly effective satire was 'lashing' (*bichuyushchaya*) and merciless (*besposhchadnaya*) rather than merely 'smiling' (*ulybayushchayasya*), a term apparently used to designate a sort of fond and brotherly awareness of the occasional failings of a comrade. The sort of reproach regularly levelled at the satirical shows of the variety theatres was that they were mere 'baring of the teeth' (*zuboskal'stvo*) – a kind of blend of sneering and mocking for its own sake, with no legitimate purpose. A recurrent term to indicate the decadence of cabaret theatres derived from the popularity of the foxtrot — as in a critique by M. Zagorsky of a 1929 show called *Have Your Tickets Ready* ('Prigotov'te bilety'), which, he claimed, was guilty of 'all sorts of entertaining, foxtrotting situations and scenes' (*vsyacheskikh uveselitel'nykh, fokstrotiruyushchikh polozheniy i stsenok*).[18] Indeed, in 1931 Glavrepertkom issued a document in which it proposed to 'conduct a decisive campaign against pseudo-Gypsy songs, "harsh" boulevard romances, and against the foxtrot, which has spread widely through gramophone records, the music-hall and variety theatres, and more recently through the talking cinema and the radio, and which is patently the product of West European *thés dansants*, music-hall and *cafés chantants*'.[19] Hence perhaps the horror of Pavel Korchagin in *How the Steel was Tempered* ('Kak zakalyalas' stal'') when the foxtrot is performed at a sanatorium concert he attends; the shameless foxtrotting sparrow which so terrifies poor Professor Kuz'min in Bulgakov's *The Master and Margarita*;[20] or the girl and the couple corrupted by Prisypkin who dance the foxtrot in Scene VII of Mayakovsky's *The Bedbug* ('Klop').

As to the more serious political targets regarded as appropriate for satire, pre-eminent were, of course, all survivals of capitalist vices (*perezhitki*) – which was how anti-Bolshevik activities could conveniently be categorised. The introduction of NEP in a sense prolonged the life of satire, since it enabled it to find further acceptable targets in the form of *grimasy NEP-a* (distortions and divergences from pure Bolshevism, here literally the 'grimaces' of NEP), and in particular the resurgence of all sorts of greedy, middle-class consumerist behaviour which could be lumped under the heading of 'bourgeois vulgarity' (*meshchanstvo* – yet another of the terms rendered virtually untranslatable by the density of meanings, however unstable, with which it has been invested). As NEP wore on, however, satire's function came to be justified in terms of another crucial notion promulgated by Stalin around 1928 – that of 'self-criticism' (*samokritika*). Satire was accorded this further burst of legitimisation as part of the attempt to counter those extremists of the 'proletarian' camp who were endeavouring to proscribe all negative comment in literature. It remains the case, however, that even the defence of satire was only discussed by the middle of the 1920s in terms of the interests of the State; and that in an extensive range of materials I have not encountered a single commentator within the Soviet Union who has felt able to propose satire as a healthy gingering-up force which might criticise the Party, the leadership and its policies, the Revolution, Stalin or Lenin himself. Most of these remain the great literary taboos even now, in the era of Gorbachev's *glasnost'*.

From about 1925 onwards the drama and music critic V. Blyum had begun a personal campaign in the press to persuade his audience that satire had no viable future in the Soviet Union. This finally attracted wide attention during 1929, in a debate which raged during that year and into 1930 in the pages of *Literaturnaya gazeta*. In the very first number of the newspaper A. Lezhnev, reviewing a novel by A. Novikov, deplored the lack of good current satirical prose; he suggested that the old kind of allegorical, 'Aesopian' satire of Saltykov-Shchedrin's day was no longer appropriate since it was now possible to denounce evils more frankly – but that in consequence literary satire had rather lost ground to journalistic satire. Novikov's novel, he felt, offered some hope of a revival in satire's fortunes.[21] Blyum replied with a notorious article entitled 'Will Satire Revive?' ('Vozroditsya li satira?') in which he pointed to the lack of good satirical writing despite all the clamouring for it, and argued that this was scarcely surprising because its function had never been redemptive, but always to serve as a weapon in the class struggle. Now that in the Soviet Union the interests of the people were identical with those of the State, he suggested, that function had become redundant: 'The tradition of satire has abruptly broken off.' Nor was there any need to revive it, for survivals of the past (*perezhitki*) were more effectively dealt with by other means.[22] July's *Literaturnaya gazeta* saw firstly G. Yakubovsky, and then an unsigned front-page leader arguing that Blyum was misguided; satire could be a useful contribution to 'self-criticism' and a useful weapon against 'bourgeois vulgarity' (*meshchanstvo*), so long as it avoided the Aesopian mode and pursued the goal of realism without lapsing into naturalism. Soviet satire 'must cleanse the consciousness in order to prepare it for a reconstruction [*perestroyka*] unexampled in the whole world'. This was followed by an even more exhortatory piece by M. Rogi calling on satirists to show up wreckers and saboteurs – although that was no reason for it not to point up at the same time the constructive role of the party and the unions.[23] By this point the discussion had begun to run out of steam; but the subject under discussion had also begun to lose any resemblance to any recognisable concept of satire. In any case, it was soon swept from the pages of the press by the virulent controversy over Zamyatin and Pilnyak which occupied the energies of most critics for the remainder of 1929.

In a sense, the issue was left hanging in the air, not least because those who defended satire in the official press were only capable of doing so by exercising remarkable skills of doublethink and defining satire's functions in an entirely abstract manner. For Blyum was, of course, quite correct in his argument that satire was effectively impossible in Soviet conditions. Certainly it was true that, in the conditions of what was increasingly being required of Soviet literature by those who controlled it, satire could have no meaningful place; as Bulgakov was to comment in 1933:

> I am convinced that all attempts to create satire are doomed to utter failure. It is impossible to create satire. It creates itself, quite suddenly. And it will create itself when a writer appears who considers that modern life is not perfect, and who will indignantly undertake an artistic denunciation of it. I imagine that the path of such a writer will be extremely hard.[24]

As far as the theatre in Moscow was concerned, after the flurry of satirical writing in minor genres which characterised the period between 1918 and 1925, the attempts which many theatres made to establish contemporary satire as a major new tradition for the most part foundered. In 1924 the Satire Theatre (*Teatr Satiry*) opened under V. Tipot's direction with a show by Nikolay Erdman, Gutman, Mass and Tipot called *Moscow from a Point of View . . .* ('Moskva s tochki zreniya . . .'). The Satire Theatre was based on a theatre company which, as seems to have been the case with a number of influential theatres, had in fact begun its existence outside Moscow. This was the 'Crooked Jimmy' (*Krivoy Dzhimmi*) theatre from Kiev. Up until 1929 the 'current affairs sketch' (*obozreniye*) predominated in the repertoire of the Satire Theatre; and it is no surprise to find that it was run between 1926 and 1929 by D. G. Gutman, formerly of Terevsat, who along with Ardov, Argo, Erdman, Mass, Nikulin, Tipot and Vol'pin also contributed to the writing of sketches. One of its few larger-scale successes was Katayev's *The Squaring of the Circle* ('Kvadratura kruga'); and after the autumn of 1929, when the theatre underwent a major reorganisation, this was one of only two or three shows to be retained in the repertoire. During the 1930s, with the advent as director of Nikolay Gorchakov, the repertoire developed in the direction of 'everyday' (*bytovaya* – a kind of Soviet 'kitchen-sink'?) comedy; this was epitomised by Shkvarkin's 1933 *Another's Child* ('Chuzhoy rebenok'), a feeble and laboured play about a young girl discovering the inadequacy of her parents' and friends' reactions when they imagine, through a misunderstanding, that she is pregnant.[25] This play provoked scathing comments from Meyerhold, who deplored the poverty and vulgarity of its language and its horrifyingly corrupting laughter'.[26] He also regretted the theatre's weak-willed move – possibly under the influence of Blyum – away from satire towards comedy, and recommended that the Satire Theatre should endeavour to regain its health by an urgent study of Molière, Gogol and Saltykov-Shchedrin.[27]

Most other theatres either complained of an acute repertoire crisis – or, when they found a satirical drama of good enough quality, found that they paid an intolerable price politically for putting it on. Apart from obvious figures such as Erdman and Mayakovsky, we should not forget that the 1920s and the early 1930s were the era of the satirical drama of Bulgakov, Zamyatin, Babel and Platonov, as well as of lesser figures such as Fayko and Romashov. The fact that the works of the more distinguished of these authors were banned with such regularity in a sense gives the lie to the view that there really was a repertoire crisis; it was rather that it became increasingly difficult to find a satire which would both live up to its claims as a genre as well as satisfying the criteria of the arbiters of theatrical repertoire. Typical in this respect was the experience of Tairov at the Kamerny Theatre in 1928, when he put on Bulgakov's satirical play *The Crimson Island* ('Bagrovyy ostrov'), a disrespectful allegory of the Revolution which simultaneously mocks the crassness of theatrical censorship in the figure of the censor Savva Lukich – who was made up to look like Blyum.[28] The play aroused a furore of protest and had to be taken off early in 1929; and as Bulgakov pointed out in his letter to the Soviet government a year later, this precisely confirmed the point that he was making in the play, which was that Glavrepertkom was strangling drama in the Soviet Union.[29]

Almost the only figure on the theatrical scene who appeared to succeed, at least for a time, in reconciling the conflicting demands of satire and of political orthodoxy was Meyerhold. This he achieved by blending his concept of a revolutionary 'Theatrical October' (which he had proclaimed in 1920) with Lunacharsky's call to go 'back to Ostrovsky!'. It is interesting to reflect whether there is something in the nature of satire which lent itself particularly aptly to the kind of experimentation he wanted to explore in his theatrical work, or whether it was the satirical content of the plays that so attracted his attention. But the fact remains that the repertoire which Meyerhold staged during the 1920s consisted to an overwhelming extent of satirical works, either by foreign writers or by Russian authors of the pre- and post-Revolutionary era. Meyerhold was absolutely convinced that good satire was a much more effective medium for propaganda purposes than explicitly agitational writing. As he put it in 1921 in relation to Ostrovsky, 'he knows the secret of the rules of theatre! He didn't choose to bring on a "raisonneur", or his own kind of Chatsky, or some student-liberal. Above all he took into account the power of theatrical laughter.'[30] Meyerhold repeatedly expressed his distaste for agitational theatre as a genre, suggesting that audiences took no pleasure in it and were more likely to be moved by buffoons than by positive heroes – hence the need to draw more on popular traditions and create a Red *balagan* ('fairground theatre'), as long as this Red *balagan* did not degenerate into a Red cabaret.[31]

In 1924 Meyerhold found what he was looking for in *The Mandate* ('Mandat'), the first substantial piece by the young Nikolay Erdman, who had contributed so extensively to the 'lesser genres' of Soviet satirical comedy since 1917. Meyerhold may have been being a little disingenuous when he insisted that the play's only satirical targets were the middle class, who now either yearned for the old Tsarist regime or relished the prospect of exploiting NEP – rather than, say, the political environment which provoked such responses. The production received a mixture of admiring and carping reviews, but ran untroubled for some 350 performances before dying what appears to have been a more or less natural death in the early 1930s. This represented the real high point of Soviet satire in the 1920s, an almost unique instance of a sharply satirical text winning official toleration as well as widespread acclaim as an artistic achievement. But Meyerhold found it difficult to follow up that single triumph, and increasingly turned to the pre-Revolutionary repertoire to sustain the satirical impetus of his theatre. In 1926 he extended Lunacharsky's 1923 slogan by proclaiming his own – 'Back to Ostrovsky, back to Gogol!';[32] by 1927 this had become: 'Back to Ostrovsky, back to Griboyedov, back to Gogol!'[33] as he followed *The Government Inspector* ('Revizor', 1926) with *Woe from Wit* ('Gore ot uma', 1928). He justified this return to the past with the argument that the conditions of pre-Revolutionary Russia had made it impossible for the plays to be staged during the nineteenth century in a way that would fulfil their true satirical potential in exposing the iniquities of Tsarism, so that he was effectively releasing them from the constraints of the past.[34] In 1933 he still deployed much the same arguments as a justification for putting on Sukhovo-Kobylin's *Krechinsky's Wedding* ('Svad'ba Krechinskogo'), although he did cautiously indicate that the play might have a contemporary relevance as well by demonstrating to any Soviet citizen still obsessed with money the corrupting power it could have on the individual. There is no doubt that Meyerhold would have been delighted to stage further contemporary satires if he had been able to find some which would meet his criteria, particularly in terms of skilful and poetic handling of the verbal material. But in any case, the negative reactions which greeted his productions of Mayakovsky's *The Bedbug* ('Klop', 1929) and *The Bath-house* ('Banya', 1930) indicated that the problem of staging good modern satire no longer derived so much from the dearth of adequate writing – Maykovsky's plays were arguably no less accomplished than Erdman's – but rather from a political climate which would no longer brook satirical approaches of any kind.

In other words, Blyum's epitaph on satire pronounced in 1929–30 was a realistic appraisal of the actual state of affairs; and nothing occurred in the years running up to the First All-Union Congress of Soviet writers in 1934, despite the curbing of RAPP in April 1932, to alter that situation. The speeches made by delegates to the Congress demonstrated that the terms in which the subject could be discussed had congealed at the inconclusive stage they had reached by the beginning of 1930. Thus, in the only really substantial speech to address the subject, Mikhail Kol'tsov averred that even since 1932 the view still prevailed that satire had no role to play once the working class had come to hold power together with the Bolshevik Party. Boldly he countered this view by suggesting, not just that 'survivals' of capitalism remained to be eradicated in the Soviet Union, but also that they might need to be sought out within the Party itself; and that to deny the need for satire was to deny the need for 'self-criticism'. He proposed on behalf of his colleagues that 'we, the satirical writers in Soviet literature, aspire to and will achieve a situation where in our future literary life the contradiction between the real position of satire in our country and the attitude taken up towards it by editors and critics should be eliminated'. Kol'tsov maintained that satirical writers, through their skills of 'universalisation' (*obobshcheniye*), often came closer to true Socialist Realism than the most painstaking realists. He pointed out that Party orators were fond of quoting from the classics of satire, and expressed the hope that by the next Congress it would be Soviet satirists that they quoted. And finally he commented on the way satire tended to become marginalised by being published – as it is to this day – in the back pages of journals and newspapers.[35] While this speech represented a brave attempt to defend the position of satire, it should be noted how much Kol'tsov is obliged to rely on notions of the tasks officially required of literature in the Soviet context. And while the speech was welcomed by subsequent speakers, their comments in reality indicated that satire was no longer to survive as an independent genre. As part of the general move towards the blurring of genre distinctions that resulted from the proclamation of socialist realism as the official method of Soviet literature, satire would henceforth only be evaluated in terms of its utilitarian and inspirational effects.

Hence the claim of another speaker at the Congress, Panteleymon Romanov, that it was time to discard the assumption that satirists are incapable of describing 'positive' characters and situations.[36] This was echoed in his keynote speech on the state of Soviet drama by Vladimir Kirshon, who declared that 'A new type of comedy is being created in the Soviet state — a comedy of positive heroes.'[37]

Romanov had also expressed the wish that Soviet writers should prove such effective 'engineers of the human soul' that by the end of the third Five-Year Plan the necessity for satire as such would fall away, leaving only a vigorous demand for humour and for merry, optimistic laughter. This suggestion was met by the delegates with applause.[38] In other words, satire could be tolerated for a while longer as a 'lashing' weapon against any 'survivals' of bourgeois habits, but it was anticipated that in due course it would naturally wither away. For, as Kirshon put it, 'the laughter of victors, a laughter as refreshing as morning gymnastics, a laughter inspired not by mockery of the hero, but rather by joy on his behalf, is ringing out more and more loudly on the stages of our theatres'.[39] And Boris Romashov, author of a successful if wordy satirical comedy called *The Meringue Pie* ('Vozdushnyy pirog') sustained the health theme by looking forward to 'cheerful comedy which would have the same effect as lemonade in hot weather'.[40] Only rare voices such as those of Nikolay Nikitin were left to express doubts about the 'cloudless skies of Soviet comedy' which were indeed to reign in the theatre over the next decades.[41]

The 1930s saw the decimation of the ranks of the outstanding dramatic satirists who had endeavoured to integrate their work into the new state during the 1920s. Emigration was not to prove an option for Bulgakov as it was for Zamyatin, yet his attempts to get his work staged within the Soviet Union met with repeated rebuffs; Erdman's *The Suicide* ('Samoubiytsa') also failed to pass the censors, and he was perhaps lucky to find himself already in internal exile by the end of the 1930s, when his mentor Meyerhold was arrested and shot. Erdman's capitulation to official views of satire is particularly poignant in view of the bright hopes he had seemed to hold out in the mid-1920s; for after his wartime writing for the NKVD Song and Dance Ensemble (*ansambl' pesni i plyaski*) he reverted with great circumspection to the 'lesser forms' of his early career. And the outstanding allegorical satirist Yevgeny Shvarts had to wait until after the death of Stalin to find an audience for much of his writing of the 1930s. The tradition of satire on the Soviet stage had indeed come to an end as Blyum had recognised, and satirical drama for many years afterwards was written either for the desk drawer or in emigration.

After Stalin's death some literary critics emerged to discuss the question of Soviet satirical theatre as though they had simply been existing in suspended animation since 1930. Yury Dmitriyev, writing in 1954, reiterated in just the same terms as Blyum and his contemporaries points about satire's innate capacity for universalisation and its function as an aspect of 'self-criticism' or as a weapon in the battle against 'bourgeois vulgarity'. He dismissed almost all the notable achievements of 1920s satire by complaining that 'Representatives of bourgeois-formalist tendencies, making capital out of the Soviet people's interest in comedy, attempted to drag on to the stages of our theatres under the guise of comedy plays which were in fact vulgar lampoons on Soviet life and on Soviet people.'[42] Instead, he dated the beginnings of genuine Soviet satire from the Satire Theatre's 1933 production of the Shkvarkin play which had so dismayed Meyerhold, *Another's Child*. This play Dmitriyev saw as initiating the Soviet theatre's crucial battle for 'the affirmation of the traditions of Soviet satire, the traditions of realism'.[43] The fact that Dmitriyev went on to play an important role in theatrical criticism during the 1960s contributed to the way in which discussion of satire after its comprehensive defeat in the 1930s ossified in the post-Stalin period. And in the late 1980s attempts to liberate it from the vocabulary, preconceptions and expectations of the past are only just beginning to be undertaken.

## Notes

I wish to record my gratitude to the British Academy for its support during the period when this article was written.

1. S. Compton, *Chagall* (London, 1985) p. 40.
2. From a letter of 22 December 1918 published in *Iskusstvo kommuny*, quoted in M. Frost, 'Marc Chagall and the Jewish State Chamber Theatre', *Russian History*, vol. VIII, nos 1–2 (1981) p. 93.
3. M. Chagall, *My Life*, 2nd edn (London, 1965) p. 137.
4. Much of my information on Terevsat has been drawn from A. N. Manteyfel', 'Teatr revolyutsionnoy satiry (Terevsat)', in *Sovetskiy teatr – dokumenty i materialy 1917–67*, (*Russkiy sovetskiy teatr 1917–21*) (Leningrad, 1968) pp. 181–90.
5. 'Pust' razveseloy zadiroy / Budet nash Terevsat, / Pust' iskrometnoy satiroy / Kleymit on tekh, kto khochet nazad. / My pobedim skuku seruyu, / Veruyem v to goryacho' (ibid., pp. 185–6).
6. S. V. Kozlovskiy in ibid., p. 187.
7. Yu. Dmitriyev, 'Teatry komedii i satiry', in *Ocherki istorii russkogo sovetskogo dramaticheskogo teatra*, vol. I: *1917–34* (Moscow, 1954) p. 380.
8. Manteyfel', p. 190.
9. Chagall, p. 164.

10. Quoted in Yu. Dmitriyev, 'Myuzik-kholl', in *Teatral'naya entsiklopediya*, vol. III (Moscow, 1964).
11. *Sovetskiy teatr – dokumenty i materialy, 1917–67 (Russkiy sovetskiy teatr 1917–21)* (Leningrad, 1968) p. 60.
12. *Literaturnaya gazeta*, 30 September 1929.
13. *Sovetskiy teatr – dokumenty i materialy, 1917–67 (Russkiy sovetskiy teatr 1917–21)* p. 17.
14. See note 10 (pp. 563–4) to the article 'Ob Aleksandre Nikolayeviche Ostrovskom i po povodu ego' (1923), in A. Lunacharskiy, *Sobraniye sochineniy*, vol. I (Moscow, 1963) pp. 200–10.
15. *Na literaturnom postu* (1928) nos 11–12.
16. Ibid. (1928) no. 19 and (1929) no. 9.
17. Ibid. (1928) no. 4.
18. *Literaturnaya gazeta*, 25 November 1929.
19. *Sovetskiy teatr – dokumenty i materialy 1917–67, (Russkiy sovetskiy teatr 1926–32. Chast' pervaya)* (Leningrad, 1982) p. 81.
20. N. Ostrovskiy, *Kak zakalyalas' stal'* (Moscow, 1973) pp. 341–2; M. Bulgakov, *Romany* (Moscow, 1973) p. 631.
21. *Literaturnaya gazeta*, 22 April 1929.
22. Ibid., 27 May 1929.
23. Ibid., 8, 15 and 22 July 1929.
24. See my *Bulgakov's Last Decade – The Writer as Hero* (Cambridge, 1987) pp. 17, 18.
25. V. Shkvarkin, *Chuzhoy rebenok*, in *P'esy sovetskikh pisateley*, vol. IV (Moscow, 1954).
26. V. Meyerkhol'd, *Stat'i, pis'ma, rechi, besedy*, vol. II (Moscow, 1968) p. 319.
27. Ibid., pp. 355–6.
28. L. Ye. Belozerskaya-Bulgakova, *O, med vospominaniy* (Ann Arbor, Mich., 1979) p. 59.
29. From a letter of 28 March 1930, published in 'Pis'ma-protesty M. Bulgakova, A. Solzhenitsyna i A. Voznesenskogo', *Grani*, vol. LXVI (1967) p. 157.
30. Meyerkhol'd, p. 26.
31. Ibid., pp. 27 and 489–90.
32. Ibid., p. 105.
33. Ibid., p. 137.
34. Ibid.
35. *Pervyy vsesoyuznyy s"ezd sovetskikh pisateley — 1934. Stenograficheskiy otchet* (Moscow, 1934) pp. 221–3.
36. Ibid., p. 247.
37. Ibid., p. 403.
38. Ibid., p. 248.
39. Ibid., p. 403.
40. Ibid., p. 428.
41. Ibid., p. 453.
42. Dmitriyev, p. 381.
43. Ibid., p. 682.

# 11

# Mikhail Bulgakov: the Status of the Dramatist and the Status of the Text

## LESLEY MILNE

The theatrical authority of a play or dramatist is based on the accumulated experience of major productions, which start in the country of origin in the dramatist's lifetime and spread, geographically and historically. This creates the cultural context in which each subsequent major production utters its own 'new word' for its own place and time. History has robbed Mikhail Bulgakov's plays of this theatrical authority.

In the decade between 1925 and 1935 Bulgakov wrote nine original dramatic works, of which only four were produced in his lifetime. Two others were rehearsed but not produced; three more never passed the read-through stage. These bare facts alone make the case for Bulgakov as one who has qualified for the status of an 'undeservedly neglected' playwright. But this is a defensive, apologetic category. Before Mikhail Bulgakov can be assessed properly as a dramatist, the 'undeservedly neglected' stereotype needs to be abandoned and replaced by a contextual space which will enable his true authority to be appreciated.

Between 1925 and 1930 Bulgakov wrote no fewer than five plays for three outstanding theatres at a time of a unique flowering of Russian theatrical culture. *The Days of the Turbins* ('Dni Turbinykh', translated under the play's original title *The White Guard*; 'Belaya gvardiya') was written under commission in 1925–6 for the Moscow Art Theatre, for which Bulgakov also wrote the play *Flight* ('Beg') in 1926–8. In 1925 the Vakhtangov Theatre in Moscow also commissioned from Bulgakov a play, *Zoyka's Apartment* ('Zoykina kvartira'), which was completed in 1926. The next commission, in January 1926, was from the Moscow Kamerny Theatre and resulted in *Crimson Island* ('Bagrovyy ostrov'), completed in 1927.[1]

This period of Bulgakov's dramatic creativity culminated in 1929–30 with the play *Molière* (the original Russian title, *The Cabal of Hypocrites* ('Kabala svyatosh'), had *Molière* as its subtitle). Written between April 1925 and January 1930,[2] these five plays represent a single creative sweep that must be grasped in its entirety. Due to external circumstances, however, this perspective on Bulgakov's work has proved difficult to achieve. *The Days of the Turbins* (première: 5 October 1926) was passed for performance in the Moscow Art Theatre only: no other theatre in the Soviet Union could stage it. *Zoyka's Apartment* (première: 28 October 1926) was performed in theatres outside the capital;[3] but it was obliterated from the repertoire in 1929 when the press campaign against Bulgakov's plays, which had begun in October 1926 following the première of *The Days of the Turbins*, achieved its object of forcing the removal of all his plays from the repertory stock. *Crimson Island*, which had opened at the Kamerny on 11 December 1928, closed at the end of that theatrical season, as did *The Days of the Turbins*.[4] Rehearsals of *Flight* had begun in the Art Theatre on 10 October 1928, but ceased on 25 January 1929.[5] And in the following March the organ of theatrical censorship, the Main Repertory Committee (Glavrepertkom), banned *Molière*. These events of 1929–30 destroyed Bulgakov's status as a dramatist and, even in the Soviet Union, it has still been restored only partially.

Plays written in a single dramatic breath within a five-year period trickled back on to the stage over the following sixty years. The production of *The Days of the Turbins* was restored to the Art Theatre (but the Art Theatre only) in 1932 and ran there until 1941, becoming an object of theatrical pilgrimage.[6] *Molière*, finally produced at the Art Theatre in 1936, was immediately taken off after a critical attack in *Pravda* and had to wait until the mid-1960s for its next production.[7] *Flight* had its première only in 1957. The attempts to restore Bulgakov to the Soviet stage, which began in the mid-1950s with new productions of *The Days of the Turbins*, came up against bureaucratic apathy and the ill-will of old enemies (or such of them as had survived the purges). Bulgakov had died in 1940; they had kept him off the stage in his lifetime and saw no reason to change their minds about him a decade and a half after his death.[8] Only gradually did the climate change to one of acceptance and enthusiasm for Bulgakov's plays, but even then *Zoyka's Apartment* and *Crimson Island* had to wait until the 1980s for publication in the Soviet Union and restoration to the repertory stock.[9]

This dismal account of the history of Bulgakov's plays on the Soviet stage can be set against a theoretical model that outlines the true contours of his theatrical authority. Imagine, if you will, a non-existent year 1930, when *The Days of the Turbins* and *Flight* are alternating at the Moscow Art Theatre, *Zoyka's Apartment* is running at the Vakhtangov, *Crimson Island* is playing at the Kamerny, *Molière* is in rehearsal, and Meyerhold, who has been seeking to enlist Bulgakov as a writer for his theatre ever since 1927, is persisting in his attempts to woo this dramatist who is playing hard-to-get, claiming that he 'feels quite ill' at the thought of any type of theatre other than the box-stage with the proscenium arch and the magic raising of the curtain.[10] Between 1925 and 1930 Bulgakov reached his dramatic zenith at the peak of Russian theatrical culture. His five plays of this period exemplify the psychological subtlety of the Art Theatre, the artistic grotesque of the Vakhtangov, the aesthetic theatricality of Tairov and the restless lighting of the revolutionary theatre of Meyerhold.[11] Bulgakov could have become the dramatist who, with his great rival Mayakovsky, expressed the period's theatrical bloom. The ideological blast that withered this bloom helped to kill Mayakovsky, but he had been a major literary figure for eighteen years before his suicide in 1930, and his status was thus easily grasped, easily restored. Bulgakov was only in the process of creating his status when it was destroyed. The five plays that would have created it – the conditional mood here says all – never achieved the simultaneous or closely sequential performance necessary to establish theatrical authority. Hence the need to resort to an abstract model to set against the historical reality.

In order to make the model work for today, however, the plays have to be cleared of a crust that has formed in the intervening years. It is around *The Days of the Turbins* and *Zoyka's Apartment* that this crust has set hardest, since they ran long enough (1926–9) to figure in the theatrical histories of the period. Both offended against a vociferously zealous literary grouping which had control of the theatrical press and the organs of censorship in the year in which they had their première, 1926. In the case of *Zoyka's Apartment* this resulted in a distorted reception of the play. In the case of *The Turbins* the result was a distortion of the play itself, and the task here is the truly fundamental one of establishing a text. Only when both plays are cleared of the accumulated layers of misrepresentation can their true shape be seen.

*Zoyka's Apartment* is set in the period of NEP – the New Economic Policy – which restored a measure of private trade and market forces to the Soviet economy. NEP was suddenly, although never formally, abandoned at the end of 1928.[12] Replaced by Stalin's programme of rapid industrialisation and collectivisation, NEP was until recently always viewed in the Soviet Union through the prism of one artistic image. There had been many heroes of the revolutionary struggle for whom NEP represented a betrayal of revolutionary ideals, a response which was articulated by the poet Nikolay Aseyev in his aphoristic description of NEP as 'coloured not red, but ginger'.[13] This became the master-image of a falsehood that was felt to inhere in the epoch. For the bourgeois intelligentsia of Russia's two capitals, however, NEP had brought, after the starvation years of War Communism, food, light, work and, for a writer like Bulgakov, somewhere to publish, because during NEP there was a proliferation of private publishing enterprises. Bulgakov had his own, different, aphorism on NEP: 'Every NEP has a silver lining' (*Net NEPa bez dobra*), an expression of relief that Moscow was again 'beginning to live'.[14] In this context it should be noted that the name Zoyka, the diminutive of Zoya, derives from the Greek word for 'life'.

In 1926 Bulgakov defined the genre of *Zoyka's Apartment* as that of 'tragic buffonade' (*tragicheskaya buffonada*).[15] The stereotyped image of NEP as 'ginger-coloured', however, precludes tragedy and imposes a satirical viewpoint. This disjunction showed in the Vakhtangov Theatre's approach to the play, with the director, Aleksey Popov, heavily emphasising the satire (at least in interviews with the press) and some of the actors undermining the 'satirical' concept by playing up the lyrical-elegaic line in the roles.[16] Only in the late 1980s did one of the leading economic theoreticians of *perestroika*, Nikolay Shmelev, create an intellectual climate in the Soviet Union which has legitimised a more positive view of NEP.[17] In this new climate *Zoyka's Apartment* can at last, without interference, be played as its author actually conceived it – as a 'tragic buffonade'.

After all, what do the characters in Zoyka's entourage want? They want money – not money for its own sake, however, but money to realise a dream, which is to escape with the person they love into their own individual geographical concept of paradise: for Zoya and Alla this is Paris, while for the Chinaman Cherubim it is Shanghai. Only the unfortunate Goose, director of a state trust, is seeking to create his dream of personal happiness in Moscow, but he becomes ensnared in the infinitely seductive meshes of Zoyka's apartment, finds himself deceived by the woman he loves, and is killed – for his money – by Cherubim in pursuit of his dream of Shanghai. There *is* satire in the play, but it is directed very specifically at one of Bulgakov's *bêtes noires*: the chairman of the house committee who, narrow-minded and corrupt, is hoarding money for its own sake. For the other characters, in particular the inspired rogue Ametistov, there is sharply stylish theatrical buffoonery. The lyrical-elegaic shadings turn the play into a tragic buffonade of the 'sweet life', and one that is always recognisable in periods of relative economic prosperity, where semi-artistic bohemian circles, dabbling in drugs and shady financial deals, pursue false dreams with consequences that can be fatal.

Although several variants of *Zoyka's Apartment* exist, they do not present a textual problem. Two texts of 1926, one of which is the play as produced in the Vakhtangov Theatre and the other the play as published in lithograph, presumably for performance in other theatres, reflect the details of the NEP period very vividly. A text prepared by Bulgakov in 1935 for translation into French sheds some of this period detail and tightens the dialogue, but at the price of losing some irreverence, some eccentricity and some lyricism.[18] The 1935 text is the one that is most readily available in publications of *Zoyka's Apartment*.[19] The first scholarly edition of Bulgakov's collected theatrical works, planned in four releases, includes variants where these exist.[20] Thus it will be possible for directors to combine elements from various texts in order to find their own particular balance in the play's mixed genre of 'tragic buffonade'.

In the case of *The Days of the Turbins* the establishment of a text is inhibited by powerful external factors. That play, throughout the 1920s and 1930s, was only ever performed by the Moscow Art Theatre and this production became a theatrical legend. (Because the critics from 1926 to 1929 were far too busy anathematising the production to describe it, a recent study had to turn to the diary of the stage-struck theatre policeman in order to find out something more of how the play had actually been performed.)[21] The extent to which *The Days of the Turbins* dominated the theatrical scene at the time can be seen from the reminiscences of Aleksey Popov, who directed *Zoyka's Apartment* at the Vakhtangov. Writing in the early 1960s, he recalled the latter play as having been produced

'in the season after the resounding success of *The Days of the Turbins*
at the Art Theatre'.[22] In fact, the premières of the two plays were
only three weeks apart, taking place on 5 and 28 October 1926.

The production of *The Days of the Turbins* was very important for
the Moscow Art Theatre's development in that it was the theatre's
first post-revolutionary production on a contemporary theme and
therefore became the pivot on which the theatre turned its repertoire towards the new epoch. More significant for the legend which
grew up around the play, however, was its role in transfusing into
the theatre's main company the young actors from the Second
Studio. Khmelev, Yanshin, Sokolova, the Moscow Art Theatre's
'second generation' of actors, all awoke on the morning after the
première of *The Days of the Turbins* to find themselves famous, and
as their fame grew, so did the legend around the production with
which it had all started. That legend now obscures the textual
history of the play.

It has long been known that the text of *The Days of the Turbins*
underwent considerable revision between September 1925, when
Bulgakov brought the first variant of his play to the Moscow Art
Theatre, and October 1926 when it had its première.[23] The first
fundamental textual revision was carried out between September
1925 and January 1926, when the play went into rehearsal.
Bulgakov's commission from the theatre had been an adaptation
of his own first novel, *The White Guard* ('Belaya gvardiya'), and the
version that he brought to the theatre in September had not freed
itself from the novel's structural patterns. By January, rehearsals
were able to start on a completely new text, in which the dramatic
structure had been created around a new central character, Colonel
Aleksey Turbin. Combining three of the novel's figures, Colonel
Malyshev, Colonel Nay-Turs and Dr Aleksey Turbin, the new role
of Colonel Turbin made the Turbin household the centre of the
defence of the city, and his death at the climax of the battle in Act
Three brings tragedy into the domestic haven. The revised text,
while shaped around this new central role, still retained the novel's
comic scenes with the Turbins' downstairs neighbours, Vasilisa
(the woman's name is used behind its male bearer's back; to his
face he is always called Vasily Lisovich) and his wife Vanda.
Vasilisa is the cowardly double whose subplot shadows the main
action with mock loss and mock disaster, teaching him one of
those moral lessons that Henri Bergson saw as the intention of
comedy: 'to correct our neighbour, if not in his will, at least in his

deed'.[24] The revised text, numerically the play's second variant, also included episodes from the Turbins' family rituals: two games of cards. The first is a comic diversion in Act One, setting up a symmetry with the finale, where another game of cards serves as a metaphor for expressing responses to defeat. Although this defeat is not yet definitive – it is still only mid-way in what the revolutionary song, the 'Internationale', declares to be *'la lutte finale'* – the spectators have the benefit of a hindsight which is denied the characters on the stage, and therefore know who won the 'final struggle'.

The Turbins and their friends have to make their decision without such knowledge. The young enthusiast, eighteen-year-old Nikolka Turbin, in love with war and heroism, will fight on, as will the stoical Captain Studzinsky. The hard-swearing, hard-drinking Captain Myshlayevsky, who is no slouch and no coward, chooses to opt out of any more fighting in this war, of which he has had a bellyful. To the news that the Reds are entering the city he responds: 'Well, let's not prevent them. Bring out the cards, gentlemen. War for some, but a game of "vint" for us.'[25] Vasilisa too is invited to join the game, but Vanda makes it clear that 'Vasya doesn't play for high stakes.' (No more he does. He staked nothing on the defence of the city.) Nikolka is asked to sing his song of the officer cadets 'as a farewell'. Instead, the irrepressible youth strikes up the first chords of the 'Internationale': 'Arise, ta-ta-ta, ta-ta- . . .'. Myshlayevsky's retort is swift and trenchant: 'Arise?' Just when he's settled down comfortably? Not on your life. Nikolka sings his officer cadets' song, which he sang in Act One. Then the city was in the hands of the White Guard, and a military unit had passed by outside, swelling his song:

> Hark, the sound of marching feet,
> Tramping, tramping down the street!
>
> . . .
>
> Hurrah! Hurrah! Hurrah!
> The guards . . . the guards . . . the guards . . .
> For the guards are marching past.[26]

Now, in the finale, there is new music outside. Although still 'indistinct', it is discernible as a band playing the 'Internationale' which 'mingles strangely with Nikolka's guitar'. Vasilisa and Vanda jump up in fright. Yelena and Shervinsky run to the window. At the card table the men hum along with Nikolka as he sings his song of the officer cadets, adapting the words to substitute 'farewells' for 'greetings'. Lariosik, the Turbins' poetically effusive cousin, marks the momentousness of the event: 'Gentlemen, listen, they're coming. You know, this evening is the great prologue to a new historical play.' The scene continues as follows:

MYSHLAYEVSKY.  No, for some a prologue, but for me an epilogue. Comrade audience, this is the end of the White Guard. The non-party Captain Myshlayevsky is leaving the stage. I have drawn a losing hand.
    [*The stage suddenly plunges into darkness. Only Nikolka remains spotlit at the footlights.*]
NIKOLKA [*sings*].  Run to the gate, girls . . .
               Don't you be late, girls!
               Hurrah! Hur . . .
               [*The light goes out and he disappears.*
CURTAIN.[27]

This, still bearing the title *The White Guard*, is the play that was rehearsed in the Moscow Art Theatre from January until June 1926. On 24 June the production was shown to the theatrical censors of the Repertkom, who on 25 July banned the play, but left open the question of whether it could be revised and brought into an acceptable form.

In order to save the production, the author and the theatre revised the play, and on 17 September showed it again to the Repertkom, who once more voted against it, but still left open the possibility of further alterations. This next set of changes having been made, the production was shown at a closed preview on 23 September and passed for public performance, although only in the Moscow Art Theatre.[28]

These events supply the background to Bulgakov's 'pamphlet play' *Crimson Island*, which was written soon after the première of *The Days of the Turbins*. Completed by February 1927, *Crimson Island* was not passed for performance until eighteen months later, which is why the première at the Kamerny could not take place until December 1928.[29] *Crimson Island* is a virtuoso parody of all forms of theatrical cliché, including the clichés of 'revolutionary theatre', which require last-minute alterations to a play's finale. In *Crimson Island* there is an instant switch to a 'variant with international revolution'.[30] In *The Days of the Turbins* the last, conclusive alteration concerned the rendering of the 'Internationale' which, as the rehearsal diary recorded for posterity, 'is not to fade away, but grow louder'.[31]

The finale of *The Days of the Turbins* (a title that avoided the politically problematic reference to the Whites), was thus passed for performance in a form that realigned its ideology. Clear-eyed Nikolka and far-sighted Myshlayevsky have declared themselves sympathetic to Bolshevism. There is no frivolity or symbolism with a card game, and only one dominant musical motif.

> [*Off-stage, far away but coming closer, a military band is heard playing the 'Internationale'.*]
>
> MYSHLAYEVSKY.   Do you hear that, gentlemen? The Reds are coming.
>
> [*All go to the window.*]
>
> NIKOLKA.   Gentlemen, this evening is a great prologue to a new historical play.
>
> STUDZINSKY.   For some a prologue; for others it's the epilogue.
>
> CURTAIN.[32]

This text, trimmed to meet the ideological requirements of the Repertkom in 1926, is the 'final text' of *The Days of the Turbins*, established by performance and publication. But in the era of *glasnost'* in the second half of the 1980s many works banned in the 1920s are being published and performed in the Soviet Union. Bulgakov's novella *Heart of a Dog* ('Sobach'e serdtse'), for example, was regarded in 1925–6 as 'absolutely impermissible';[33] in 1987 it was published, adapted for the stage, and was soon playing in theatres all over the Soviet Union.[34] Thus the tacit admission has been made that not all decisions of the censors in the mid-1920s retain their validity for the 1980s. It is surely time, therefore, to look not only at works which are known to have been banned but also at those which are known to have been 'adjusted' to suit ideological requirements that have been now been recognised as no longer applicable.

In the 1920s themselves the *diktat* of the Repertkom was felt as something akin to a natural disaster. The first People's Commissar for Enlightenment, Anatoly Lunacharsky, said as much at a party conference on questions of the theatre in May 1927:

We hear a constant lament. Even our own theatres, like the Theatre of the Revolution, even they lament. Constant delay, holding up productions, carping objections, one correction here, another there. A play, once passed, is checked again at the last dress rehearsal and is banned, not because the Repertkom sees that the text has been altered, but because it is re-correcting a text that already bears its stamp of permission.[35]

Even the most convinced collectivist would have doubts that such a practice necessarily improves a play.

The text of *The Days of the Turbins* that was passed for performance in the Moscow Art Theatre in October 1926 is a most interesting historical document, showing the extreme limit of the ideologically acceptable at that particular moment. But the legend which grew up around the Art Theatre production has served both to canonise this version and to provide a justification for inertia: why tamper with what has worked so well? However, among Bulgakov scholars in the Soviet Union there is now a growing dissatisfaction with this 'final text'. Marietta Chudakova has found it lacking in resonance for today's audience.[36] Anatoly Smelyansky has warned against quoting the 'ideologically sound' speeches that were patched in to make the text the right colour for the Repertkom.[37] Aleksandr Ninov has called for an awareness of its lack of true status as an established text.[38] Yakov Lur'e has suggested the need to examine the various alternative texts proposed by the theatre *after* the Repertkom had rejected the play in June 1926 but *before* the play had to acquire its crescendoing 'Internationale'.[39] The projected four-volume edition of Bulgakov's drama, containing variants of the text, should enable directors to find what they are seeking: a version of the play that will be maximally effective in the late twentieth century, which prefers its ideological certainties to be seasoned with at least some element of dialogic complexity. A rearguard action is being fought against this mood by the conservative wing of the Soviet literary establishment, which refers to the final text of *The Days of the Turbins* as 'a masterpiece of our dramaturgy' – apparently oblivious to the irony of using the collective 'our', rather than 'Bulgakov's', as a possessive.[40]

For its own time, *The Days of the Turbins* was a high-water mark. No other play of the Soviet period depicted the Whites sympathetically while at the same time refraining from portrayal of the Bolsheviks in a heroic, romantic spirit.[41] To be sure, the 'conversion' of Nikolka and Myshlayevsky to Bolshevism at the end does create a sudden disturbing shift in the finale, but this is something of which audiences at the time were very well aware.[42] What was lost when the production became a legend was precisely this contemporary sense that the text of the play represented a negotiated compromise.

The extent to which *The Days of the Turbins* ran counter to prevailing ideological currents can be seen from the reminiscences of a left-wing foreign intellectual like Walter Benjamin. Unaffiliated to the Communist Party, but seeking to discover whether he could survive as a 'left-wing outsider', Benjamin visited Moscow in December 1926 and was taken to a performance of *The Days of the Turbins*. He immediately detected an ideological and artistic falsehood, finding the 'last act, in which the White Guard "convert" to Bolshevism . . . as dramatically insipid as it is intellectually mendacious. . . . Whether this final act was added on at the request of the censors, . . . or whether it was there all along, has no bearing whatsoever on the assessment of the play.'[43] As Benjamin declared the play to be altogether an 'absolutely revolting provocation' and the 'communist opposition' to it to be 'justified and significant', it seems unlikely that he would have responded differently to the play in any form. A text distinguished by intellectual integrity and dramatic effectiveness would, it seems, have had no hearing if it ran totally counter to ideological commitment, and Benjamin, a cultured Western intellectual with a strong aesthetic response, exemplifies the mood of the time. He did not go to Moscow in order to adjust his attitude to the White Guard. All the same, it would have been interesting to hear the reaction of an aesthetically competent observer like Benjamin to the original finale of Bulgakov's play.

That original finale is much more 'experimental' than the staid platitudes of the final text. There is theatrical irony in Myshlayevsky's address to the 'comrade audience', for the play was at this point still called *The White Guard*. There is a tragic reality implied in the lighting, which suggests the death of Nikolka in some future battle. For although the play *The White Guard* is over for tonight's audience, the White Guard fought on and eighteen-year old Nikolka is a typical victim of the military idealism, enthusiasm and intransigence of the young men of the period who are commemorated in graveyards across Europe.

As is the nature of experiment, the finale was too advanced for some of Bulgakov's contemporaries. Lunacharsky, for example, found the original ending of the play 'an affront in its vagueness and total dramatic ineffectiveness'.[44] With regard to 'vagueness', it could be argued that the original ending conveys no less decisively than the final text the historical message that Stalin saw as the play's saving grace: there is no virtue in conquering a weak enemy, and if even such people as these are defeated by Bolshevism, then Bolshevism must indeed be an all-powerful force.[45] With regard to 'dramatic ineffectiveness', it could be pointed out that the *coup de théâtre* at the end, when a character is swallowed up by darkness in mid-line, is the very same as that used with brilliant effect by Tom Stoppard in the finale of *Rosenkrantz and Guildenstern are Dead*. It is not the original ending of *The Days of the Turbins* that is the 'affront', but the ending of the 'final text', where Nikolka and Myshlayevsky are converted to Bolshevism, and the 'Internationale' does not fade away but 'grows louder'.

Now that this has been recognised among Bulgakov specialists in the Soviet Union, the point at issue in the scholarship on the subject is: at which moment in the evolution of the play's text should the base 'line' be established? The view has already been advanced that the text rehearsed in the Moscow Art Theatre before June 1926 provides such a base.[46] This, the most 'radical' of the solutions, has been rejected by Yakov Lur'e, however, as 'too simple'.[47] But there is an interesting document in the archive of the Moscow Art Theatre which suggests that a director who had before him only the first variant and the third (final) variant spontaneously reinvented the second. The director was V. I. Vershilov, the prototype of K. Ilchin in Bulgakov's 'theatrical romance' *Black Snow* ('Teatral'nyy roman') and the very same Moscow Art Theatre director who had in 1925 invited the author to adapt his novel *The White Guard* for the stage. In 1956 Vershilov asked to see the first variant, which had been brought by Bulgakov to the theatre in September 1925 and in which Malyshev, Nay-Turs and Aleksey Turbin still figured as separate characters. Here is his reaction to a reading, three decades on, of that original text:

How fortunate that it has been preserved and that future readers will be able to penetrate into the creative laboratory of Mikhail Afanas'evich, discover how the dramatist's mind worked! . . .

Of course it was a splendid idea to unite the figures of Aleksey Turbin, Malyshev and Nay-Turs. Splendid too is a whole series of alterations carried out in the final variant. But all the same there are things that one regrets losing. I shall always dream that Vasilisa and Vanda will one day take the stage along with the three desperate bandits. Perhaps too much has been cut from the depiction of the Turbins' family life and from the observations and retorts of Myshlayevsky.

And it will always seem that the superbly written 'return of Tal'berg' is superfluous and rather artificial. The Tal'bergs did not return to Russia, especially not at that time. At the expense of this scene and also at the expense of a certain amount that could be shortened, future directors will restore the magnificent pages of this variant of *The White Guard*.[48]

Vershilov's instinct actually led him to a line that bears a close resemblance to that of the second variant, with Vasilisa and Vanda, the three bandits who rob them, the games of cards at the Turbins', and Myshlayevsky's trenchantly ironic wit. Even the return of Tal'berg in the second version is treated plausibly: that arch-opportunist returns in order to collaborate with the new Soviet power.[49] Vershilov's 'future directors' have in fact had the work of compiling a text done for them by the author himself in his 'second variant'. Since there is a copy of this text in three separate archive repositories, Bulgakov must have regarded it as in some way 'definitive' of a moment in the play's textual evolution. The archives contain, moreover, two translations of this text, one into English, the other into German.[50] Given that the 'second variant' already has such a distinct identity in the author's archive, it seems unnecessary to look elsewhere in order to establish a new 'base text' for *The Days of the Turbins*, which would, of course, have to revert to its original title of *The White Guard* for the ironies in the finale to work to proper effect. All that this text lacks is the theatrical authority that only production in major theatres can confer.

The crumbling of the textual status of *The Days of the Turbins* on its rock of legend raises the question of how many other Bulgakov plays have been published in textual variants of dubious provenance. Bulgakov's next play for the Moscow Art Theatre was *Flight*, which likewise exists in several versions. The first was completed in 1928 and went into rehearsal at the Art Theatre in October of that year, but rehearsals were stopped by the press campaign which culminated in the removal of *The Days of the Turbins*, *Zoyka's Apartment* and *Crimson Island* from the repertoire in 1929. In 1932 the ideological watchdogs of the Russian Association of Proletarian Writers (known by its Russian acronym RAPP), who had made all the running in matters of literary politics in the years from 1928 onwards, were suddenly reined in by Party directive. *The Days of the Turbins* was restored to the Moscow Art Theatre repertoire and *Flight* went into rehearsal again on 10 March 1933.[51] In 1933 and 1934 Bulgakov revised the play, altering the finale.[52] The rehearsals were discontinued again on 15 October 1933, as the ideological liberty perceived after the disbanding of RAPP proved to be illusory. In 1937, however, Bulgakov returned to *Flight* and wrote a new 'final text', which is the text published in all editions of his plays to date (1962, 1965, 1986). This 1937 version was a thorough revision of the 1928 text, the dialogue of which was tightened by many minor deletions throughout but which retained its original finale: the émigrés Serafima, Golubkov and Khludov all return from Constantinople to Russia: Serafima and Golubkov to 'see the snow'; Khludov to atone for the crimes he has committed in the name of the White cause during the Civil War. In the 1933 and 1934 variants of the finale, Serafima and Golubkov do not return to Russia but go instead into permanent emigration in Paris. Khludov does not return to Russia either. He hears the music from the Constantinople fairground, the ballad of the 'Twelve Robbers' with its tale of how the fierce robber leader Kudeyar experienced a sudden awakening of conscience and retired to a monastery to atone for the innocent blood he had shed. Khludov, driven demented by this insistent moral reminder, fires his revolver in the direction of the music in order to silence it, and then uses the last bullet to shoot himself in the mouth. The Soviet scholar Violetta Gudkova has argued that there is another text, which has to be dated 1937, in which Golubkov and Serafima return to Russia but the 'suicide' finale is retained for Khludov. In Gudkova's view, this variant represents Bulgakov's preferred choice of ending. As evidence she cites the diary of the playwright's wife, Yelena Sergeyevna, which on 30 September 1937 records the following with reference to the revision of *Flight*: 'In the evening I tried to convince Misha that the first variant – without Khludov's suicide – is better. (But M. A. does not agree).'[53] However, by 1 October, when the revision was finished, Bulgakov had clearly been persuaded, for there is a 1937 text that follows Yelena Sergeyevna's preference for the original 1928 ending 'without the suicide of Khludov'.

The revision of *Flight* in 1937 was prompted by a request for a copy of the play from an official organ, the Theatrical Department of the Committee for the Arts. The purges that were mowing down whole sectors of Soviet society in 1937 were taking their toll of erstwhile members of RAPP, the zealots responsible for the destruction of Bulgakov's status as a dramatist in 1929 and there may well have been a sudden, paradoxical hope that some kind of 'justice' might yet be snatched from this monstrous parody of Judgement Day, opening up a path for the production of *Flight*.[54] In this context, the conversation of 30 September in the Bulgakov household concerning *Flight* reflected a very specific moment and were guesses at which finale might be 'better' for the purpose of seeing the play through to production, a matter quite distinct from considerations of a purely artistic nature and on which Bulgakov was prepared to compromise. Compromise had, after all, saved the production of *The Days of the Turbins*. Molière had compromised too in such circumstances, and as Bulgakov observed in his own biography of the French dramatist, *The Life of M. de Molière* ('Zhizn' gospodina de Mol'era'), which was written in 1932–3: 'Every lizard knows that it is better to live without a tail than to keep the tail at the expense of life itself.'[55] Nor was Yelena Sergeyevna one to argue for 'pure art' and posterity: what she wanted was recognition for her husband in his lifetime. These discussions about 'better' endings, therefore, had a very practical orientation on both sides. But in September 1937 Bulgakov was about to embark upon the third major draft of the novel *The Master and Margarita* ('Master i Margarita').[56] The motif of 'atonement' in the novel exercises a powerful gravitational force, the more so because the novel had been conceived in 1928, the year in which *Flight* had first been completed. In the 1933 and 1934 variants of the play's finale, Khludov rejects the possibility of atonement, thereby destroying himself in the process. In one of the 1937 variants, however, he embraces that possibility, so that the play nestles back into the contours of the great novel that takes the theme of guilt through to the last, necessary phase, where guilt and atonement yield to the state of forgiveness.

The publication of the variants for *Flight* in the four-volume edition of Bulgakov's drama will again allow directors to make their own choice. It has to be said, however, that Khludov's rejection of atonement in the 'suicide' variants does not imply the rejection of a moral universe. The moral universe triumphs as it kills him. There is nothing 'absurd' about *Flight*, which is constructed on a dual perception of the world: there is a universe ruled by ethical absolutes, and there is a world that acts as its buffoon double, ruled by money and chance. The play's fulcrum is in the intersection of these two concepts of the world and the single mode required to operate in both simultaneously. Even the 'flight' of the title is a mistranslation of the Russian *beg*, which simply means the act of running and, as the last line of the epigraph to the play implies, what is being run is the race of life itself: 'Rest, he who his race has run' (*Pokoysya, kto svoy konchil beg*). The 'race' here is that referred to in I Corinthians 9:24: 'Know ye not that they which run in a race run all, but one receiveth the prize? Even so run, that ye may attain' (*Ne znayete li, chto begushchiye na ristalishche begut vse, no odin poluchayet nagradu? Tak begite, chtoby poluchit'*). Sadly, the Russian Synod edition of the Bible does not retain that other 'race' metaphor in Hebrews 12:1: 'Let us run with patience the race that is set before us' (*S terpeniyem budem prokhodit' predlezhashcheye nam poprishche*). Both of these biblical quotations, however, would provide an English-speaking audience and director with the moral framework implicit in that single untranslatable title *Beg* with its concealed exhortation upon which the epigraph to the play insists.

Variants in the texts of the play *Molière* are not substantial, as long as production is based not upon the 1962 Moscow edition (*P'esy*) but upon the 1965 Moscow edition (*Dramy i komedii*), which restored various 'mystic' (religious and diabolical) details omitted by the editors of the earlier volume. (They were, after all, introducing to the public of an officially atheist state a dramatist whose status was by no means well-established, and too much mysticism might have alienated too many people at the outset.) By 1965 a successful Czech production had conferred upon the play some dramatic authority and at this point the 'mystic' details were restored. It appears, however, that the last line of the play is still missing: Lagrange, recording in his 'Register' the reason for Molière's death, concludes that it was caused by 'fate' (*Prichinoy etogo yavilas' sud'ba*).[57] There is, perhaps, room for the restoration of this last line with its statement of the predestiny of the artist. By the very nature of his talent he offends against the ruling ideologies of his time. Such was the bleakly contemplative conclusion of the dramatist who in 1930 surveyed the career that lay in ruins around him.

The play written in the rubble, so to speak, was *Adam and Eve*

('Adam i Yeva'), commissioned by the Red (or Krasny) Theatre in Leningrad by a contract of 5 July 1931 and by the Vakhtangov Theatre in Moscow by a contract of 8 July 1931 as a 'play about a future war'. It was completed by 22 August 1931.[58] First published in Paris in 1973, *Adam and Eve* was released in the Soviet Union in the middle of 1987.[59] Here again there are two variants of the finale, but this time the existence of two versions does not appear to relate to the exigencies of production. One of the two texts is set in an unnamed city and the nightmare events occur in what turns out to be a dream. In the other texts, the city is Leningrad and the near-destruction of the world happens in reality. Of the two versions, it is the 'reality' text rather than the 'dream' one which appears to be chronologically the later.[60] The play was written in what was for Bulgakov a curious period of suspension. He contracted it 'sight unseen' to two theatres that did not (unlike the Moscow Art Theatre!) require an author to return an advance on a play in the event of that play being subsequently banned.[61] It is almost as if *Adam and Eve* was written solely for the sake of the advance from the two theatres, without any concern for production. Rehearsals of *Flight* had stopped; *Molière* was banned. What future had any play by Bulgakov in the Soviet Union? *Adam and Eve* betrays the exhausted freedom of a man past bothering with the unguessable mind-set of the theatrical censor.

In the play the brilliant scientist Yefrosimov has invented an antidote to poison gas. His invention has a military application. Urged to place it at the service of the Soviet government, he replies that, in his opinion, such a discovery should be made available to all countries simultaneously. There is sufficient evidence to suggest that, even in the 1980s, such an action by a scientist would warrant trial for treason in any country of the world. Given the conditions of political life in the Soviet Union in 1931 Bulgakov's Utopian vision was a sublime refusal to engage with practical possibilities. The theatres knew instantly that they could not produce the play; the author showed neither distress nor surprise at this reaction.[62]

*Adam and Eve* is an abstract study in ideas, which predicts as an absolute certainty a military collision between two hostile ideologies, because each is recklessly fomenting hatred of the other. The play's abstraction combines, however, with an unexpectedly strong comic line to give it an 'absent-minded professorial' element, which echoes the character of Yefrosimov himself, who combines complete ethical integrity and creative concentration with dotty social behaviour. In that sense, the version of the ending which locates the catastrophe in the dream of a mind close to Yefrosimov's is aesthetically satisfactory. In the 'reality' version, the characters on stage have learned from disaster to abjure their international hatreds. In the 'dream' version no one has learned anything from the individual nightmare, and the factors which have bred it remain in full force at the end of the play: scientific invention and military application harnessed to two ideologies screeching slogans of hate at each other as they hurtle towards the ultimate war, a universal *'lutte finale'*. The end of the play circles back to a point near the start, the reality preceding the dream, and thus creates a cycle of recurrence for the nightmare, leaving the question: when is it going to happen and what must be done to prevent it? This question is just as effective as the 'reality' variant's representation of the disaster as having actually taken place.

Bulgakov's next two plays, *Bliss* ('Blazhenstvo') and *Ivan Vasil'evich* also utilise the dream framework. The comedy *Bliss*, apparently conceived in 1929, but written in 1933–4, bears the sub-title 'The Dream of Engineer Reyn'.[63] Engineer Reyn flies into the future in a time machine of his invention and in this dream of the future, Moscow in the year 2222, finds a totally unreconstructed mankind ready to act out life's perennial comedies in a setting that is aggressively pre-revolutionary: men wear dinner jackets, declare their love for women in time-honoured phrases, bring them flowers and suffer from their infidelity; women flirt, fall for handsome strangers and long for adventure. The Satire Theatre in Moscow could do nothing with such a play in 1934. Bulgakov then adapted it by turning the dial of the inventor's time machine to the past, taking him into the reign of Ivan the Terrible, the result being the play *Ivan Vasil'evich*, written in 1934–5. Here the possibility of a 'dream variant' is hinted at in one version, and is fully developed in another, which bears the note: 'Corrections as required [by the theatre – L.M.] with the added-on dream.'[64] Thus the 'play about a future war', *Adam and Eve*, with its two variants – 'dream' and 'reality' – set a pattern for two of the plays written by Bulgakov in the next four years. *Adam and Eve* was never even rehearsed in a theatre in its author's lifetime, nor was *Bliss*, so there was no pressure on the dramatist to vary his devices. Audiences cannot identify as repetition something they have never seen.

The play *Ivan Vasil'evich* was rehearsed, right up to its dress rehearsal in the Satire Theatre on 13 May 1936, after which the production was cancelled.[65] The reasons lay not in the play or the production but in the year 1936. *Molière* had opened on 15 February at the Moscow Art Theatre but had been taken off after only seven performances following an attack in *Pravda*.[66] Bulgakov's next play, *Pushkin* ('Posledniye dni. Pushkin'), written in 1934–5, had offered theatres a text with which to commemorate the Pushkin anniversary in 1937. In Moscow both the Art Theatre and the Vakhtangov Theatre were vying for the production rights and enquiries were coming in from theatres in Leningrad and the Ukraine, but, after *Molière*, discussions of the *Pushkin* production were quietly dropped everywhere. Another casualty was a project that had been taking shape in late 1935 and early 1936 involving Shostakovich and Prokofiev, who had been discussing with Bulgakov the idea of an opera based on *Pushkin*. For Bulgakov himself – a great opera-lover – this would have been something of an apotheosis and it might well have supplied Slavists world-wide with a *point d'appui* for that impossible explanation to those who speak no Russian of the significance of Pushkin in Russian culture. In January and February 1936 Shostakovich was the target of a press campaign attacking his opera *Katerina Izmaylova* as a 'muddle instead of music' and his ballet music for *The Bright Brook* ('Svetlyy ruchey') as 'balletic falsehood'.[67] 1936 was not a year in which to undertake anything artistically adventurous and the Pushkin celebrations in 1937 passed without any commemorative creative work of world stature. In Bulgakov's literary biography 1936–7 was a repeat of the pattern established in 1929–30. A series of plays – running and in rehearsal – was terminated. His stage adaptation of Cervantes's *Don Quixote* was written two years later and is suffused with an all-too-keen awareness of the quixoticism of his own career.

It cannot be too often reiterated that when theatre managements in the late 1920s and throughout the 1930s chose not to stage Bulgakov's plays, these decisions had nothing to do with the box-office. This was a criterion by which Bulgakov would have longed to be judged, as is clear from his biography of Molière, where the box-office is the barometer of his hero's success. But the circumstances in which Bulgakov was working reversed this criterion. In fact, a box-office success such as that enjoyed by *The Days of the Turbins* and *Zoyka's Apartment* was positively suspect from an ideological point of view. It was interpreted as meaning that the theatres were filling up with bourgeois elements and NEP profiteers. Walter Benjamin regarded with disapproval the audience at a performance of *The Days of the Turbins* in the Art Theatre: 'It was as if there were not a single communist present, not a black or blue tunic in sight.'[68] A survey conducted in 1927 on the theatrical preferences of the 'masses' revealed, however, that first and foremost they demanded artistry in new plays, that they protested against the stereotypes of 'positive' and 'negative' characters and that *The Days of the Turbins* shared first place with Konstantin Trenev's *Lyubov' Yarovaya* at the Maly Theatre as the best new production of the season.[69] But such evidence was merely taken as proof that vigilance in the class war had to be increased, and box-office success became a doubly cogent argument for the removal of a play from the repertoire: the production of *The Days of the Turbins* had cost 21 400 roubles and by February 1929 the box-office takings had amounted to 797 301 roubles – therefore the theatre could sustain the removal of the production. By the same token, *Crimson Island* at the Kamerny, having cost 9000 roubles and having attracted receipts of 49 011 roubles, could also be removed.[70] When box-office success becomes a financial argument against a play, what can the professional dramatist do?

In the theoretical model the fate of Bulgakov's plays would have been as follows. They would have enjoyed a course of simultaneous and sequential production throughout the Soviet Union in the 1920s and 1930s. They would have been published in texts verified by the author. These texts would have been translated and performed abroad. New theatrical developments would have found expression in their revival. They would have become part of the canon of reference, part of theatrical culture. The establishment of such status requires time.

Bulgakov set great store by historical models, especially those of his two great predecessors, Pushkin and Molière. Also strongly present in his works is the tradition of Griboyedov – witness, *Crimson Island*, the biography of Molière, and *The Master and Margarita* with its 'Griboyedov House'. The fate of Griboyedov's masterpiece *Woe from Wit* ('Gore ot uma') provides an alternative – and historically real – model for understanding the reception of Bulgakov as a dramatist. Completed in 1824, *Woe from Wit* was banned by the censor. Fragments of the text were played in amateur productions in 1827. Griboyedov, who was killed in Teheran in early 1829, never saw his comedy played on the professional stage. The first full professional production in 1831 was based on a text distorted by the censor. The first edition of the play, published in

1833, was also a censored version. This was the text performed by the great actors of the time, Shchepkin and Mochalov, who always took the play on tour as it was banned for production by provincial theatres until 1863. Only in 1875 was the full text of the play first published.[71] This, with a shift of approximately one hundred years, is the pattern to which Bulgakov's reception as a dramatist is conforming. Sorting out the texts in the late 1980s could be the point of departure into the next century and classic status.

## Notes

1. M. Chudakova, 'Zhizneopisaniye Mikhaila Bulgakova', *Moskva* (1987), no. 8, p. 68.
2. A. Smelyanskiy, *Mikhail Bulgakov v khudozhestvennom teatre* (Moscow, 1986) pp. 60, 264.
3. M. Bulgakov, 'Zoykina kvartira', *Sovremennaya dramaturgiya* (1982) no. 2, p. 192. It played in Leningrad, Baku, Rostov-on-Don, Saratov, Simferopol' and other towns.
4. Both plays ran until the end of the season in June, according to *Programmy komu kuda*, a free supplement to the theatre journals *Sovremennyy teatr* and *Novyy zritel'* for 1928 and 1929.
5. Rehearsal diary, Moscow Art Theatre Museum.
6. K. Rudnitsky, *Russian and Soviet Theatre. Tradition and the Avant-Garde* (London, 1988) p. 188.
7. A. C. Wright, *Mikhail Bulgakov, Life and Interpretations* (Toronto, 1978) pp. 192–3.
8. Paper presented by Violetta Gudkova at the 'Bulgakovskiye chteniya', Leningrad, 11–14 May 1988.
9. *Zoyka's Apartment* was published in *Sovremennaya dramaturgiya* (1982) no. 2, pp. 169–95; *Crimson Island* in *Druzhba narodov* (1987) no. 8, pp. 140–89.
10. L. Milne, 'M. A. Bulgakov and *Dead Souls*', *Slavonic and East European Review*, vol. LII (1974) p. 425; S. Yermolinskiy, 'O Mikhaile Bulgakove', *Teatr* (1966) no. 9, p. 90.
11. See the account of the period in P. Markov, *Noveyshiye teatral'nyye techeniya* (Moscow, 1924) pp. 12, 36, 44–5, 65.
12. A. Nove, *An Economic History of the USSR* (Harmondsworth, Middx, 1972) p. 136; J. P. Nettl, *The Soviet Achievement* (London, 1967) p. 109.
13. N. N. Aseyev, 'Liricheskoye otstupleniye', *Stikhotvoreniya i poemy* (Leningrad, 1967) p. 465.
14. M. Bulgakov, 'Sorok sorokov', in E. Proffer (ed.), *Sobraniye sochineniy*, vol. I (Ann Arbor, Mich., 1982) p. 298.
15. 'Zoykina kvartira M. Bulgakova (iz besedy s avtorom)', *Novyy zritel'*, 5 October 1926.
16. Bulgakov, 'Zoykina', p. 193; D. I. Zolotnitskiy, 'Komedii M. A.

Bulgakova na stsene 20-kh godov', in A. Ya. Al'tshuller *et al.* (eds), *Problemy teatral'nogo naslediya M. A. Bulgakova* (Leningrad, 1987) pp. 61–3, 67.

17. N. Shmelev, 'Avansy i dolgi', *Novyy mir* (1987) no. 6, pp. 142–58.
18. Wright, *Bulgakov*, pp. 107–8; E. Proffer, *Bulgakov. Life and Work* (Ann Arbor, Mich., 1984) p. 610.
19. M. Bulgakov, *P'esy* (Paris, 1971) pp. 193–252; M. Bulgakov, *P'esy* (Moscow, 1986) pp. 333–78.
20. M. Bulgakov, *P'esy 1920-kh godov. Teatral'noye naslediye* (Leningrad, 1989); *P'esy 1930-kh godov. Teatral'noye naslediye*, 2 vols (Leningrad, forthcoming: 1991); *Dramaticheskiye perelozheniya. Kinotsenarii. Opernyye libretto. Teatral'noye naslediye* (Leningrad, forthcoming: 1993); *Teatral'naya proza. Teatral'noye naslediye* (Leningrad, forthcoming: 1994). Each book will be published as a separate entity and will not be numbered in sequence, but cumulatively the enterprise will represent a scholarly collection approaching the status of an academic edition. (Information supplied by A. A. Ninov, general editor of the series.)
21. Smelyanskiy, pp. 109–28.
22. A. Popov, 'Vospominaniya', *Teatr* (1960) no. 5, p. 118.
23. Ye. Polyakova, *Teatr i dramaturg* (Moscow, 1959) pp. 34–70; Ya. Lur'e and I. Serman, 'Ot *Beloy gvardii* k *Dnyam Turbinykh*', *Russkaya literatura* (1965) no. 2; pp. 194–203; L. Milne, 'Mikhail Bulgakov and *Dni Turbinykh*: a case of censorship', in W. Harrison and A. Pyman (eds), *Poetry, Prose and Public Opinion: Aspects of Russia, 1850–1970* (Letchworth, Herts., 1984) pp. 214–40. Sources for information on textual alterations can be found in the last-named article, which forms the basis for the information supplied here.
24. H. Bergson, 'Laughter', in W. Sypher (ed.), *Comedy* (New York, 1956) p. 148.
25. M. Bulgakov, *Belaja gvardija, P'esa v četyrech dejstvijach. Vtoraja redakcija p'esy 'Dni Turbinych'*, ed. L. Milne (Munich, 1983) p. 103. Referred to hereafter as Bulgakov, *Belaya gvardiya*.
26. Quoted in the translation of the play's final text by Michael Glenny: M. Bulgakov, *The White Guard* (London, 1979) p. 2.
27. Bulgakov, *Belaya gvardiya*, p. 104.
28. Milne, 'Bulgakov and *Dni*', pp. 221–2, 226–30.
29. Chudakova, pp. 78–9.
30. Bulgakov, 'Bagrovyy ostrov', pp. 186–7.
31. E. Proffer (ed.), *Neizdannyy Bulgakov: teksty i materialy* (Ann Arbor, Mich., 1977) p. 77.
32. Bulgakov, *The White Guard*, p. 86.
33. Chudakova, p. 48.
34. Published in *Znamya*, 1987 (no. 6) pp. 76–135. Adapted for the stage by various theatres. Première in June 1987 at the Theatre of the Young Spectator, Moscow, in an adaptation by A. Chervinsky.
35. A. V. Lunacharskiy, *Sobraniye sochineniy*, vol. VII (Moscow, 1967) p. 505.
36. M. Chudakova, 'Master i voploshcheniye', *Literaturnaya gazeta*, 19 June 1985, p. 8.

37. Smelyanskiy, pp. 98–9.
38. A. A. Ninov, 'O teatral'nom nasledii M. Bulgakova', in Al'tshuller *et al.* (eds), p. 12.
39. Ya. S. Lur'e, 'M. Bulgakov v rabote nad tekstom *Dney Turbinykh*', in ibid., pp. 31–2, 37–8.
40. 'V zashchitu imeni i avtorstva Mikhaila Bulgakova. Pis'mo v redaktsiyu', *Sovetskaya Rossiya*, 6 Sept. 1987, p. 2.
41. M. Slonim, *Soviet Russian Literature* (New York, 1967) p. 56.
42. Chudakova, 'Zhizneopisaniye', p. 67; G. Lenhoff, 'Chronological Error and Irony in Bulgakov's *Days of the Turbins*', in K. N. Brostrom (ed.), *Russian Literature and American Critics* (Ann Arbor, Mich., 1984) pp. 155–6.
43. W. Benjamin, *Moscow Diary* (Cambridge, Mass., and London, 1986) p. 25.
44. *Neizdannyy Bulgakov* p. 76.
45. I. V. Stalin, *Sobraniye sochineniy*, vol. xi (Moscow, 1949) pp. 326–8.
46. Milne, 'Bulgakov and *Dni*'; Bulgakov, *Belaya gvardiya*, Introduction.
47. Lur'e, 'Bulgakov v rabote', pp. 37–8.
48. Letter from V. I. Vershilov to Ye. S. Bulgakova, 5 March 1956, Moscow Art Theatre Museum, no. 5787.
49. Bulgakov, *Belaya gvardiya*, p. 99.
50. Lur'e, 'Bulgakov v rabote', pp. 24–5, 38. Only the German translation was published: M. Bulgakow, *Die Tage der Geschwister Turbin. Die Weisse Garde* (Berlin–Charlottenburg, 1927).
51. Rehearsal diary, Moscow Art Theatre.
52. V. V. Gudkova, 'Sud'ba p'esy *Beg*', in Al'tshuller *et al.* (eds), pp. 46, 57–8.
53. Ibid., p. 57.
54. M. Chudakova, 'Bulgakov: god 1937-y', *Sovetskaya muzyka* (1988) no. 2, pp. 62–6.
55. M. Bulgakov, *Izbrannaya proza* (Moscow, 1966) p. 423.
56. M. Chudakova, 'Arkhiv M. A. Bulgakova', *Zapiski otdela rukopisey Vsesoynuzoy biblioteki SSSR im. V. I. Lenina*, vol. xxxvii (1976) pp. 124, 128.
57. Ibid., p. 92.
58. Ibid., pp. 98, 100.
59. *Oktyabr'* (1987) no. 6, pp. 138–73; *Sovremennaya dramaturgiya*, 1987, no. 3, pp. 190–225.
60. *Oktyabr'* (1987) no. 6, p. 173.
61. Letter from Bulgakov to Stanislavsky, 30 August 1931, Moscow Art Theatre Museum no. 7415.
62. Chudakova, 'Arkhiv', p. 100.
63. Ibid., pp. 112–13.
64. Ibid., pp. 119–20.
65. Ibid., p. 121.
66. Wright, pp. 191–2.
67. Chudakova, 'Arkhiv', p. 121; Chudakova, 'Pervaya i poslednyaya popytka', p. 209.
68. Benjamin, p. 25.

69. 'Chto skazal zritel'', *Novyy zritel'*, no. 25, 21 June 1927.
70. 'Polozhit' konets *Dnyam Turbinykh*', *Izvestiya*, 16 Feb. 1929.
71. P. Markov (ed.), *Teatral'naya entsiklopediya*, vol. II (Moscow, 1963) pp. 143–50.

# Index